THE CONNECTICUT CRIMINAL TRIAL HANDBOOK

By Attorney Jay Ruane

THE CONNECTICUT CRIMINAL TRIAL HANDBOOK

By Attorney Jay Ruane

With

Attorney Jim Ruane
State's Attorney David Applegate
Attorney Willie Dow
Attorney Ioannis Kaloidis
Attorney Kevin Smith
Attorney Timothy Greene
Attorney David Villa

First printing 2025

ISBN: 979-8-9889578-4-3

Different Middle Initial 1 Enterprise Drive, Suite 305 Shelton, CT 06484

Printed in the United States of America

DEDICATION

To all those brave enough to choose the profession of Criminal Trial Law, and who make sure the Constitution is enforced every day.

INTRODUCTION

Lawyers tend to love books. Page after page of prose, with long citations and footnotes to obscure dicta that may or may not impact an infinitesimally small number of factual scenarios but need to be included for the sake of "completeness." And these books have their place in law. Sometimes you need to dive deeply into a subject and understand every single nuance on a subject matter so you can effectively (and zealously) advocate for your client.

But then there are situations where you just need to know how to offer a complex piece of evidence and get it in so you can move on. Or you need to know which motions to file and when. Law books generally don't seem to cover that.

Until now.

This book is conceived as an antidote to the traditional legal treatise. While you will find some pages about theory here, they are included merely for context to the subject matter, and they are purposely limited.

What we have found over the years is that when you are in the stages of a legal battle, you don't need to know how the Magna Carta was drafted RIGHT NOW, you need the proper weapons for the assignment. The assignment is a TRIAL, not a debate in a classroom or pleasure reading in a library (if you can call most legal writing "pleasure reading"). And this book strives to give you those tools in abundance.

Each chapter focuses on a different segment of the criminal trial process in Connecticut - from motions through verdict. We broke it down this way so that if you are struggling with offering evidence, or how to frame a voir dire question or come upon a situation that needs an answer (especially a case right on point) and the ability to move on, you can turn to this resource in the throes of the battle. Then get back to the trial quickly, efficiently, and move on.

By tapping chapter contributors who are tops at their trade in each chapter, you get the best advice from someone who actually does the job. Not some academic espousing the theory - these authors are living the practice of trial law daily.

Like any book, this cannot and should not be your only tool or be considered the complete resource. In fact, trial law often gets more from inside the creative brain of a trial lawyer than any book can offer. But we can give you a guidebook that can help you identify, address, and conquer common issues in criminal trials in Connecticut, and that has always been the goal of this book. This guidebook doesn't contain a magical closing theme or even standardized motions. You are a lawyer, that is YOUR job to do.

And for the prosecutors who will purchase this book - we ask that you join us in fighting for fair trials with equal justice. I strived to eliminate many of the pro-defense and seemingly "anti-prosecution" quips in this book, but I am sure some slipped by my editors. I have tried many cases in this state over the years and have never encountered a prosecutor who wanted anything less than a fair trial with an honest verdict, which we can all hope for in this career we have chosen. Yes, we may be on opposite sides of the courtroom, but justice is what we both seek. I hope this makes your job easier too.

We hope it is a well used book in your library, it joins you on counsel table, and you see copies on the bench and opposing counsel table as well. When everyone knows the rules of the game AND knows how to play, a trial can be a beautiful thing to watch or participate in as a lawyer - and we all love the art of trial work. Use this as a foundation and head into that courtroom ready to do your best, as a Connecticut Criminal Trial Lawyer.

HOW TO USE THIS HANDBOOK

Purpose and Organization

The Connecticut Criminal Trial Handbook is designed to be your trusted companion in the courtroom—a practical resource you can quickly reference during trial preparation or even in the midst of proceedings. Unlike traditional legal treatises that explore exhaustive theory, this handbook focuses on actionable guidance for real-world trial scenarios. Each chapter is organized to provide immediate access to the procedural and tactical information you need.

How to Navigate This Book During Trial

This handbook is designed to be used in three distinct ways:

1. Pre-Trial Preparation

Before trial, review entire chapters to develop your comprehensive strategy. Pay special attention to the "Strategic Approaches" sections, which outline possible alternatives based on your case specifics.

2. Overnight Trial Preparation

During trial, use the handbook to prepare for the next day's proceedings. The sample questions and tactical guidance provide templates you can adapt to your specific witnesses and evidence.

3. Real-Time Trial Reference

In the courtroom, when faced with unexpected issues, the quick reference sections and case citations provide immediate guidance for objections, examination techniques, and procedural matters.

Keeping Current

Law evolves continuously, and effective trial practice requires current knowledge. Use this handbook as your foundation, but supplement it with:

1. Recent appellate decisions affecting criminal practice
2. Updates to the Connecticut Practice Book

3. Developments in scientific evidence standards

4. Changes in judicial policies within your courthouse

This handbook is meant to be a living document that serves as your starting point for effective advocacy. Make it your own by adding notes, case references, and insights from your personal experience in Connecticut courts.

Jay Ruane

TABLE OF CONTENTS

CHAPTER 1

MOTIONS

For many criminal lawyers in Connecticut, the lack of meaningful motion practice is an unfortunate reality we must acknowledge and accept. The fact that 99% of motions are "reserved until the time of trial" means that cases languish on dockets for years before dispositive motions are heard. This directly prejudices the defendant, and in turn, the state as a whole. Once you are in the "system," the lack of motions practice immediately turns defendants sour on the entire judicial process, and you can believe that they are not silent about this to their friends and family. We all know of a case or three that had a young client sit in jail for 2 years or more before it is dropped after a motion hearing. This isn't justice. This taints everyone involved in the future in the criminal justice process in our state, and even can impact venirepersons attitudes towards service.

While the courts may avoid a motion practice, it is incumbent on the parties to actually file and preserve the record for these issues to be addressed down the line or as a tool to defend their client *nunc pro tunc*. Too often (read: every. single. day.) cases are placed on the trial list merely as a storage shed because one side or the other is being unreasonable in their plea bargaining or a lawyer (on either side) isn't willing to have the tough conversations with a client to allow them to understand the legal scenario and how long a trial may take to come and the value in the current offer. They warehouse cases on the trial list, then scramble at an impending 24 hour notice call to file some boilerplate motions to cover themselves.

But you cannot effectively represent your client and counsel them about a trial list placement without giving some thought to your theory of the case, and that includes the motions you will file. You cannot place a case on a trial list without quickly identifying and filing appropriate motions on their behalf. To do otherwise would be to both violate the practice book and your commitment to your clients and to justice as a whole. Just because others seem to fly by the seat of their pants and survive this doesn't mean it is the right way. A good trial lawyer evaluates her case and decides which motions to file so that when it is time to address them - be it next week or years from now, they are well plead, protect the client, and help your case. You can't do that while also conducting jury selection AND prepping your cross examinations, and also running down the investigation or evidence again to get "ready."

Motions do matter, to your client most of all, and it is your job to get them filed for your client timely. In my experience, you can address your motions in stages.

There are 2 types of motions. Motions to combat constitutional issues, like a motion to dismiss or a motion to suppress; and *motions in limine* which deal with evidentiary issues which generally do not rise to the level of constitutional challenge, but still need to be litigated as to admissibility at trial.

For an easy way to approach motions in a criminal case, we recommend approaching your motions in stages, not moving to the next stage until all the motions have been done in the stage before. This way you can focus on building your motion theory as well as your defense theory.

First Stage of Pretrial Motions

Motion for Bill of Particulars:

A bill of particulars is a written document in which a party has to explain the allegations in his/her complaint, or petition, in more detail. A longform is the information that will be presented to the jury, where they read the crime and the elements of the crime that will be the subject of the prosecution. Judges and prosecutors may try to tell you that the longform is enough, especially if you file a Motion for a Bill of Particulars. If this occurs, you have to decide if they are giving enough information in the longform. For example, in a case where timing is an essential element, a longform may not give you enough information. A Bill of Particulars will give you critical information such as the exact timeframe the alleged incident occurred. This information could be critical for your case, such as for crafting an alibi defense, or in cases like a DUI which can be alleged as being committed in different ways, it locks the state into a type of DUI. *Don't settle for longform information, get a ruling on your motion for a bill of particulars.*

Motion to Dismiss

A motion to dismiss is an attempt to get the court to dismiss some or all of the charges on constitutional, jurisdictional or other reasons. For example, if the information fails to state a crime, statute of limitations has passed, or is unconstitutionally vague, you should file a motion to dismiss.[1]

Has the statute of limitations time passed? Remember, according to State v. Daren Y, 350 Conn, 393 (2024), a Motion to Dismiss is *an affirmative defense* in the criminal context. Be prepared to draft a motion, file it and argue it. Connecticut Practice Book 10-30 states that "a motion to dismiss shall be used to assert [one of the following:]" 1. lack of jurisdiction over the subject matter; 2. lack of jurisdiction over the person; 3. insufficiency of process; and 4. insufficiency of service of process. If a defendant wishes to contest the court's jurisdiction, the defendant must file a motion to dismiss within thirty days of the filing of an appearance. The motion shall be filed with a supporting memorandum of law and, where appropriate, with supporting affidavits as to facts not apparent on the record.

Motion to Compel Discovery

The Connecticut Practice Book states that you cannot start a trial until 45 days after a certification, on the record, that discovery is complete[2]. Specifically, the *judge* must certify that discovery is complete. This can be a tool against those who are hoping for a quick process and guilty plea by your client. From the time that the judge certifies that discovery is complete, you have 6 weeks to prepare for a trial. If you ensure to make sure that your Motion to Compel Discovery is solid, curated, and defensible, then until the judge

[1] CPB Secs.41-8,9,10,11,12, and Sec. 61-6
[2] CPB Sec. 44-15(b)

certifies that discovery is complete, you have time to prepare for trial to create the best defense for your client. This discovery is not what is currently in the state's file. The fallacy of an "open file" policy does not abrogate the state's obligation to turn over materials that they can obtain if they are defense related, such as expert reports and medical reports, statements of witnesses including any statements of the defendant, access (not merely photographs) of the actual physical evidence, and criminal records of witnesses. **But unless you file this motion for discovery**, and then follow up with a Motion to Compel, courts will look to defense counsel as failing to do what is necessary.

Obligations of Defense Counsel

As defense counsel, it is essential to understand the obligations surrounding notice and disclosure of defenses. There are several aspects to consider in this process. Regarding notice of defenses, it is crucial to determine if such notice is required. Additionally, it may be necessary to provide notice of an alibi[3] or a plea of not guilty by reason of insanity.[4]

You must also address whether the prosecutor is entitled to any information or evidence from the defense. To begin, one should verify if the prosecutor has made a proper request for such materials.[5] If so, there are several items that might fall within the scope of the request:[6]

- Witness statements intended for use during the trial.

---

[3] CPB Secs. 40-21,22,23,24,25

[4] CPB Sec.40-18,19,20

[5] CPB Secs. 41-5.13

[6] CPB Secs. 40-13(b), 26

- Physical evidence that is intended to be presented at the trial.
- Photos, documents, or other exhibits that will be utilized as evidence during the trial.
- Demonstrative exhibits planned for use in court.

However, it's important to assess whether there are any legal grounds to withhold a requested item. In certain situations, there might be a valid objection to the state's request for discovery, which must be considered thoroughly. You must consider a possible objection to the state's request for discovery.[7]

Being aware of these factors will ensure proper notice and disclosure while protecting your client's rights and interests.

Counts/Charges

The Connecticut Practice Book states that you can sever counts against your client if you have inconsistent defenses[8]. For example, you may have a defense of intoxication connected to an act *and* a DUI, so it may be necessary to sever the two charges. For the first charge, you need to prove that the person was intoxicated when they responded to something on the scene. For the second charge, there's a pending DUI because he left the scene in a car. You will want to request the charges be severed since you are putting into evidence that he was intoxicated to negate one element in the first count, but then

[7] CPB Sec. 40-8
[8] CPB Sec. 41-18

have to convince the jury not to convict them of a DUI on the second count.

Are there multiple counts? Consider filing a motion to sever counts. There is a presumption against joinder of multiple charges from different docket numbers, different dates, or different crimes as established in State v. Payne, 303 Conn. 538, 34 A.3d 370 (2012). This can be especially important if trying the counts together would prejudice your client.

Second Stage of Pretrial Motions

Now that the basics are done, you can focus on the second stage of motions. This stage focuses you more clearly on the issues that could hurt your client - the evidence that may be offered. You already dealt with the legal issues in Stage One. Now you focus on the factual and evidentiary issues.

Motions in Limine

A Motion in Limine is different from a Motion to Suppress or Motion to Dismiss because those deal with constitutional challenges, and a Motion in Limine deals with evidentiary issues that may not rise to a constitutional challenge. In order to effectively file Motions in Limine, you need to try the case in your head, from start to finish, and look for every issue that may arise and how you should deal with it. Nobody said being a criminal trial lawyer was easy. So find a quiet space, sit down, and mentally walk through the entire trial with a notepad in hand to write down all the issues which could arise.

Motion to Disclose Uncharged Misconduct

Identify the things that can be admitted against your client. Identify if this is a sex case or a non-sex case. If it's a sex case almost anything can be admitted, so you will have to get in front of it. You'll want to ask the prosecutor what's coming in so you can advise your client and address it. This will allow your client to prepare for what the prosecutor will bring, when and if they have to take the stand.

If it's a non-sex crime, prior wrongs or acts may be used to prove motive, opportunity, intent, preparation, plan, knowledge, identity, absence of mistake, or lack of accident.[9] You'll need to think about these things in the context of your case, and the context of your defense.

Evaluate whether a motion in limine to exclude uncharged misconduct is necessary if your client has previous bad behavior that the State might attempt to introduce. The admissibility standard differs significantly between sex and non-sex charges. Prior misconduct is admissible in sex cases even if simply to show propensity. However, propensity evidence is generally inadmissible in non-sex cases, unless used to prove intent, identity, malice, motive, a system of criminal activity, the elements of a crime, to corroborate crucial prosecution testimony, or to complete the story of the crime. Always analyze whether the probative value is outweighed by the prejudicial impact.

Knowing & Preparing for Your Opponents

As a trial lawyer, your first opponent will be **opposing counsel**. Sometimes, prosecutors or defense counsel have a reputation for doing things they shouldn't. Things such as vouching for witness credibility and police officer reliability, or speaking objections that get information to their witness. If you are trying a case against an attorney who you have not tried a case against before, seek out people who have to see what they are like. Read their transcripts and get a

---

[9] USCS Fed Rules Evid R 404(b)

sense for their style. Habeas attorneys are a great resource for this because they have amassed thousands of pages of transcripts. Doing this will give you a sense of who you are going up against in the courtroom. If a prosecutor is bringing in an expert, read some transcripts where they brought in that expert before. Get a sense of the flow, see how and where the defense objected and see if it was sustained or overruled. This will help you plan your objections carefully.

Consider filing a motion in limine if you're concerned that your opponent has a reputation for crossing ethical or procedural lines. Watch for prosecutors who personalize arguments with "I" statements, engage in name-calling of the defendant or defense counsel, vouch for witnesses by stating personal belief in their credibility, attempt to introduce irrelevant or inadmissible evidence that damages the defendant, argue facts not in evidence, or use speaking objections as a vehicle to argue their case to the jury.

What is the second kind of opponent you will encounter? **The police**. To help prepare when the police are expected to testify, use the Freedom of Information Act liberally. If there is a police officer in your case, get their records via FOIA, google their names, see if they're on Pacer for unnecessary roughness, get their Internal Affairs records. See if they have a propensity to lie in their affidavits, on the stand, or on their police records, like, for example faking hundreds of infractions over years like some State Troopers have done. All of this is available to you in motion form, which will frustrate the prosecutor. Not only is this good defensive lawyering for your case, but this will build the record for a possible appeal of the trial if you win the chance to appeal (read: Lose). For example, if there are two police officer witnesses in your case, you can file a motion to sequester the officers early in the case. That way, down the road if you get their records and find out they've been paired in a squad car the last 6 months, you can go to the judge and say that they've violated the order to sequester.

A motion in limine may be appropriate if police officer testimony needs to be controlled. Officers may attempt to offer unfounded expert opinions such as statements beginning with "Drug dealers always do..." They might try to reference your client's prior record or misconduct with statements like "I recognized him from when I arrested him before." Officers may also attempt to give legal conclusions, such as characterizing an arrest as "valid," which invades the province of the court.

The third kind of opponent is **experts**. When the prosecution offers experts, they are paid to be there and they are paid to hurt your case. They love to express their opinion on the ultimate issue, such as whether the client is guilty, whether they failed a test or whether your client was at fault. Experts love to pontificate on the stand. We can get ahead of that with a motion in limine.

Consider a motion in limine if an expert witness has a history of exceeding proper boundaries. Expert witnesses sometimes attempt to opine on the ultimate issue in the case, testify with insufficient supporting data, or inappropriately testify regarding the client's guilt or fault. These types of testimony can be highly prejudicial and may warrant exclusion before trial begins.

Read transcripts of testimony in similar cases. Identify when another lawyer objected during their testimony. Use that as a foundation for filing your motions.

Emotion

Read your case file, read your facts and find areas where emotions may come into play. Is this a child sex assault case? Is this a domestic assault case? Are you defending someone who has been accused of animal cruelty and the jury is going to see pictures of puppies who have been massacred and mistreated? Photos of blood with no context? Identify the things they will try to pile onto your client to paint them in a bad light. You want to be out in front of it, by filing a *motion in limine* saying that when this stuff comes up, you'll be objecting.

Third Stage of Pretrial Motions

Now that you have covered the Legal Challenges and the Evidentiary challenges - now you need to focus on making the state do their job. Being a defense lawyer means you are the last line in the defense of our constitution. If they don't get forced to do their job, it makes it easier for the police to understand they can cut corners.

The following are basic overviews on the subjects of science, sex and suppression. More in-depth discussions on these subjects will follow in the niche area chapters. Filing a motion on these topics, at a bare minimum, preserves the issue and makes a record that you flagged this issue before the case wound up in the hands of a trial judge. This way, when the case is called in and you have filed your motion, nobody can say BOO to you when a hearing on the scientific evidence impacts the Presiding judge's desire to control the schedule and move things faster. Justice is not a sport in that respect. **It takes as long as it takes**. There are no arbitrary clocks that say you only get 1 hour or 1 day for certain things - it takes as long as it takes. But these motions require preparation by counsel, because you can't effectively litigate the motion without studying up on the caselaw and facts and theory.

Science

Porter[10] deals with the admissibility of scientific evidence in Connecticut. In modern trial practice, science is more important than

---

[10] State v. Porter, 241 Conn. 57 (1997)

before. Whether it's DNA, breath test, chemical testing, finger prints, science is coming into almost every case in some way, shape, or form. Porter states that the burden shifts to the prosecution, they have to bring in the evidence and bring in the expert. The expert has to speak to the judge who is the gatekeeper and has to make findings. This benefits the defense, because judges don't like making findings because they can be reversed upon appeal.

Sex

Sex cases are some of the most contested litigated criminal cases and appear to be the majority of trial work in the coming years. Face it, nobody wants to plead guilty to being a sex offender, and some of the defendants refuse to consider good offers that come with such a requirement. If you're handling a child sex case you need to know the framework of sex caselaw. One such case is Jarzbek.[11] Jarzbek deals with the question of whether a child may testify outside of the presence of the court. The prosecution has to prove the victim is of tender years, but also a compelling need. The need must be compelling, not just "Oh we don't want this 7-year-old to testify because it's uncomfortable." It must be a *compelling* reason. Other cases which can turn into motions you might file deal with Bruno or Esposito motions. If those cases and their holdings don't immediately spring to mind as you read this chapter, you should read them and be familiar with them and what they say (or don't say).

---

[11] State v. Jarzbek, 204 Conn. 683, 704, 529 A.2d 1245, 1255 (1987)

Suppression

In every case, there will likely be evidence you want to keep out of the courtroom. Are there inculpatory statements? Is there evidence that does not fit in your case that could hurt you? File a motion to suppress. Even if you have no suppressible reason for the motion, for example maybe your client consented to a search, there are reasons to file a motion to suppress anyway. You want to be thorough when somebody's liberty is at stake. Additionally, it is an opportunity to go see the police officers before the trial, and get a feel for how they are going to approach the case, how they're going to act on the stand, and how they're going to react to your questioning.

Motion to Suppress Checklist

Was any physical evidence seized? Consider filing a motion to suppress. Carefully analyze the case using the 4th Amendment Flowchart and Connecticut Practice Book Sections 41-13 and 61-6. Physical evidence obtained through illegal searches or seizures may be excluded if proper procedures weren't followed or if constitutional rights were violated.

Did the defendant make any statements to law enforcement? Evaluate the need for a motion to suppress statements. Statements made without proper Miranda warnings, during illegal detention, or through coercive questioning may be inadmissible. Analyze the circumstances under which any statements were obtained to determine if grounds exist for suppression.

Was there any sort of identification procedure conducted, such as a lineup, show-up, or photo array? Consider a motion to suppress identification if the procedure was unduly suggestive or otherwise improper. Challenging identification procedures can be crucial, especially when eyewitness testimony forms a significant part of the state's case.

What kind of hearsay is present in the case? This requires a detailed analysis for a potential motion in limine. First, examine whether the state's witnesses will present hearsay testimony you want to exclude. For each instance, determine if it meets a recognized hearsay exception by carefully analyzing the elements of each applicable exception. Similarly, assess whether defense witnesses have hearsay testimony you want to introduce. For this favorable hearsay, identify which exceptions might apply and be prepared to argue the specific elements of those exceptions. This thorough hearsay analysis can significantly impact what evidence reaches the jury.

Fourth Stage of Motions

Now some of these motions may not always be necessary, and some are ALWAYS necessary, so be aware and take action.

Interstate Subpoenas

Read the statute on interstate subpoena[12], because it has to happen well in advance. First, you have to have a hearing in your court, then you have to send it to a court in jurisdiction where they live, they have to have a hearing, get an order from a judge and serve it to the witness that you want in that state, and then that order has to return back to you to show that they were subpoenaed. This is a lengthy process and you must adhere to it if you need to subpoena someone out of state. You cannot get an out of state subpoena done if you are in the process of picking the jury. There just isn't enough time.

Motions for Judgment of Acquittal

You will win one, maybe two of these in your career as a defense lawyer. Be ready to argue at the close of the state's case. At the close of the defense case, have a written stock motion that you created, with the law that you're going to argue, with cites that you know because they're from the cases you've read. Be ready to go with your bullet points that state what the elements of the crime are, and how the evidence did or didn't meet the criteria of certain elements. Make it a

---

[12] CPB Sec. 52-657

form so you can file it out so that when you go up you can read it off verbatim.

In a worst case scenario where you are completely unprepared, flip to this page and read the following into the record as the basis for your motion for Judgment of Acquittal

"That the evidence was insufficient to support the findings of guilty beyond a reasonable doubt made by the jury, and the finding entered by the court.

That the cumulative effect of the evidence was insufficient to justify the verdicts of guilty beyond a reasonable doubt. State vs. Williams, 202 Conn. 349 (1987). That the Defendant was denied his fundamental right protected by the due process clauses of the Federal and Connecticut Constitution, to be proven guilty of each element of the charged offenses beyond a reasonable doubt. State vs. Hill, 201 Conn. 505 (1986)." While marginally sufficient, at least you would have made a record for appeal.

Fifth Stage of Motions

It ain't over when it's over. After the trial, you need to file a motion for a new trial, a petition for a new trial, motion to vacate the judgment or a motion for extension of time on appeal. When the verdict comes in, your job is not done, you must keep fighting for your client's rights. You may have just taken lumps, but you need to take the 24 hours you get to mourn, then get back at it, or your client might lose even more.

Other Possible Motions

Consider filing a motion in limine if your opponent has a reputation for crossing ethical boundaries during trial. This preemptive measure can prevent prosecutorial misconduct such as personalizing arguments with inappropriate "I" statements, engaging in name-calling directed at the defendant or defense counsel, or vouching for witnesses by expressing personal belief in their credibility. The motion can also address tendencies to introduce irrelevant or inadmissible evidence that damages the defendant, argue facts not in evidence, or use speaking objections as a vehicle to make arguments to the jury outside proper channels.

When your client has previous misconduct in their background, evaluate the need for a motion in limine to exclude uncharged misconduct evidence. The admissibility standards differ significantly between case types. Prior misconduct is admissible in sex cases even if only to show propensity. However, propensity evidence is generally inadmissible in non-sex cases, with limited exceptions when used to prove intent, identity, malice, motive, a system of criminal activity, elements of a crime, to corroborate crucial prosecution testimony, or to complete the story of the crime. Always analyze whether the probative value is outweighed by the prejudicial impact before determining your approach.

For physical evidence, statements, or identifications, consider appropriate motions to suppress. When physical evidence was seized, review the case under the 4th Amendment framework and Connecticut Practice Book Sections 41-13 and 61-6 to determine if a motion to suppress is warranted. Similarly, evaluate whether the defendant made any statements that might be suppressible, or if identification procedures were conducted that could be challenged as unduly suggestive or otherwise improper.

Analyze what hearsay might be presented in the case and prepare appropriate motions. Carefully examine whether state witnesses will present hearsay you want excluded, determining if such testimony meets recognized exceptions by looking at the specific elements of each potential exception. Conversely, assess whether defense witnesses have hearsay testimony you want to introduce and identify which exceptions might apply to ensure admission of favorable evidence.

If the defendant has a criminal record, consider filing a motion to compel discovery or a motion in limine regarding the admissibility of prior convictions or arrests. Analyze whether priors are admissible in the state's case-in-chief, as substantive evidence, or only for credibility purposes. This strategic evaluation can significantly impact how the jury perceives your client.

For cases involving inflammatory facts, prepare appropriate motions in limine or motions regarding jury selection procedures when your case involves disturbing elements such as graphic injuries, intimidating weapons, or emotionally charged victim evidence like stolen sentimental items or damaged family mementos. These motions can help manage the emotional impact of potentially prejudicial evidence.

In cases with co-defendants, consider special discovery motions such as requests to disclose plea agreements or to produce statements related to co-defendants. Evaluate whether a motion to sever defendants or an objection to joinder is appropriate, particularly if a co-defendant made statements implicating your client. These procedural mechanisms can be crucial in cases where the interests of multiple defendants conflict or where evidence admissible against one defendant would unfairly prejudice another.

Maybe you don't need to file a motion in limine, you need to file a Motion to Dismiss!

Connecticut courts have consistently held that "a trial court, in determining whether the defendant had been deprived of his rights under either the federal or state constitutions, to weigh several factors. These factors included 'the materiality of the missing evidence, the likelihood of mistaken interpretation of it by witnesses or the jury, the reason for its nonavailability to the defense and the prejudice to the defendant caused by the unavailability of the evidence.' State v. Asherman, 193 Conn. 695, 724, 478 A.2d 227 (1984), cert. denied, 470 U.S. 1050, 105 S. Ct. 1749, 84 L. Ed. 2d 814 (1985) (federal due process clause)." State v. Morales, 232 Conn. 707, 719-20, 657 A.2d 585 (1995).

In sum, there are four factors in determining whether a defendant had been deprived of their rights under the state or federal constitutions. These four factors are:

1. the materiality of the missing evidence,
2. the likelihood of mistaken interpretation of it by witnesses or the jury,
3. the reason for its nonavailability to the defense, and
4. the prejudice to the defendant caused by the unavailability of the evidence

Regard the first factor, the materiality of the missing evidence, our courts have had occasion to consider the failure to preserve video evidence of DUI arrests, and in two cases where the booking video was not preserved, each court independently found that while booking video may not be especially probative, the roadside and pre-arrest footage would have been more significant. See State v. Gonzalez, Docket No. H12MMV150434597S, 2016 Conn. Super. LEXIS 2521, at *8 (Super. Sep. 29, 2016):

> *[T]he more temporally significant evidence relative to these charges would be evidence of the pre-stop operation of the defendant's motor vehicle, his mental, physical or nervous*

processes at or immediately after the stop, the arresting trooper's observations and the roadside/cruiser video.

See also State v. Schmidt, Docket No. MV13429920S, 2014 Conn. Super. LEXIS 2916, at *7 (Super. Nov. 25, 2014):

> *The more temporally significant evidence as to the defendant's condition at the time of operation will be provided by the arresting officer's testimony and that presented by the roadside video. Evidence of the defendant's pre-stop operation of her motor vehicle, her mental, physical or nervous processes at or immediately after the stop and the defendant's performance of roadside sobriety tests, as revealed by the trooper's observations and the roadside/cruiser video, are of more significant materiality to an evaluation of her condition at the time of the operation of the vehicle than any evidence demonstrating her condition at some later time during booking.*

Regarding the second Asherman factor requires this court to consider "the likelihood of mistaken interpretation of [the missing evidence] by witnesses or the jury." While it is tautological that video which is unavailable cannot be misinterpreted by a jury that cannot view it, that video would have contained concrete evidence that either supports the police report or discredits it, either in whole or in part.

"The third Asherman factor addresses the reasons for the unavailability of the evidence and requires an examination of the motive underlying the loss of the evidence. State v. Morales, supra, 90 Conn. App. 91. 'In examining the motives . . . our courts have considered such factors as whether the destruction was deliberate and intentional rather than negligent . . . or done in bad faith or with malice

. . . or with reckless disregard . . . or calculated to hinder the defendant's defense, out of other animus or improper motive, or in reckless disregard of the defendant's rights.' Id." State v. Polanco, 126 Conn. App. 323, 334-35, 11 A.3d 188 (2011). Here, you must determine a reason for the unavailability of evidence. In a case handled by Ruane Attorneys at Law, a motion to preserve evidence was filed in a timely manner with the court prior to the destruction of the bodycam arrest and booking videos. In this case, the police department destroyed the videos 2 months after the arrest and never produced them to defense counsel.

The fourth and final Asherman factor involves consideration of the prejudice caused to the defendant as a result of the unavailability of the video. The prejudice caused to the Defendant by the unavailability of the pre-and-post-arrest videos in this case cannot be understated. If you are missing pre or post arrest videos, the preservation of the video would have been useful in many ways. Some examples are:

1. Demonstrating that, in contrast to the police report, the arresting officer may have lacked reasonable suspicion to initiate an investigatory stop.

2. Demonstrating that, in contrast to the police report, the Defendant's conduct and performance on the Standardized Field Sobriety Tests did not give sufficient probable cause to arrest the Defendant.

3. Providing context with regard to the breath testing procedure to enable the Defendant and a jury to better evaluate whether proper procedures were followed and results were likely to be accurate.

4. Providing defense counsel with a more concrete basis to cross-examine the arresting officer on his observations and procedures were the matter to proceed to trial. It should be noted that the first two of these, if established, would give rise to their own grounds for a motion to dismiss. The fourth factor, therefore, weighs towards a violation of Defendant's due process rights.

If you are missing pre or post arrest footage, you may request dismissal as a remedy because the list of things that the Defendant is deprived of the meaningful ability to do, based on the unavailability of the missing evidence, is significant and includes options that might have led to independent bases for dismissal on other grounds.

EMERGENCY MOTIONS DURING TRIAL

This section provides templates and procedural guidance for time-sensitive motions that may become necessary during the course of trial. Each template includes the legal standard under Connecticut law, procedural requirements, strategic considerations, and sample language.

MOTION FOR MISTRIAL

Legal Standard in Connecticut

Connecticut courts recognize that a mistrial is an extraordinary remedy that should be granted only when it is apparent that some occurrence during trial has so prejudiced a party that they can no longer receive a fair trial. The decision to grant a mistrial lies within the sound discretion of the trial court. *State v. Ortiz*, 280 Conn. 686, 702 (2006).

A mistrial is appropriate only when:

The occurrence was of such a nature that it cannot effectively be cured by other means, and the occurrence was so prejudicial that it deprives the defendant of a fair trial. *State v. Nash*, 278 Conn. 620, 659 (2006).

A court will consider the following factors:

- Whether the prejudicial event was the result of the state's actions
- The frequency of the conduct
- The severity of the prejudice
- The strength of the state's case
- The efficacy of curative measures adopted

Procedural Requirements

1. Make the motion immediately upon the occurrence of the prejudicial event

2. If necessary, request that the jury be excused during argument on the motion
3. Clearly articulate the specific grounds for the motion
4. Request that the argument and decision be placed on the record
5. If denied, consider requesting specific curative instructions
6. Renew the motion before the conclusion of trial to preserve the issue for appeal

COMMON GROUNDS FOR MISTRIAL IN CONNECTICUT PRACTICE

1. Prosecutorial Impropriety

Connecticut courts evaluate prosecutorial impropriety using a two-step analysis:

- First, determine whether impropriety occurred
- Second, if impropriety occurred, apply the six factors from State v. Williams, 204 Conn. 523, 540 (1987):
    1. Extent to which the misconduct was invited by defense conduct
    2. Severity of the misconduct
    3. Frequency of the misconduct
    4. Centrality of the misconduct to the critical issues in the case
    5. Strength of the curative measures adopted
    6. Strength of the state's case

2. Prejudicial Testimony or Evidence

A mistrial may be warranted when inadmissible and prejudicial testimony or evidence reaches the jury despite prior rulings excluding it or where the prejudicial effect is so severe that no curative instruction could remedy it. See *State v. Asherman*, 193 Conn. 695, 736 (1984).

3. Jury Misconduct or Improper External Influence

When there are allegations of jury misconduct or improper external influences on the jury, a mistrial may be warranted if the misconduct deprives the defendant of a fair trial. *State v. Brown*, 235 Conn. 502, 524 (1995).

4. Discovery Violations

When the state fails to disclose exculpatory evidence or otherwise violates discovery obligations, a mistrial may be appropriate, particularly when the violation is discovered mid-trial. *State v. Ortiz*, 280 Conn. 686, 703-04 (2006).

Strategic Considerations for Mistrial Motions

1. **Timing**: Make the motion immediately after the prejudicial event occurs. Waiting too long may suggest the prejudice was not severe.
2. **Specificity**: Clearly identify the specific prejudicial conduct and its impact on your client's right to a fair trial.

3. **Record Development**: Ensure that the prejudicial event and all arguments regarding the mistrial motion are thoroughly reflected in the record for potential appeal.

4. **Alternative Remedies**: Consider whether lesser remedies (such as striking testimony or curative instructions) might be sufficient, but be prepared to argue why they are inadequate.

5. **Consider Double Jeopardy**: If prosecutorial misconduct deliberately provoked a mistrial motion, consider arguing that double jeopardy should bar retrial. See *Oregon v. Kennedy*, 456 U.S. 667 (1982).

6. **Renewal**: If the motion is denied, consider renewing it at the close of evidence to preserve the issue for appeal.

MOTION FOR JUDGMENT OF ACQUITTAL

Legal Standard in Connecticut

In Connecticut, a motion for judgment of acquittal challenges the sufficiency of the evidence. The standard is whether "there is a reasonable view of the evidence that would support a guilty verdict." *State v. Capasso 203 Conn. App. 333* (2021).

When ruling on a motion for judgment of acquittal, the court:

1. Construes the evidence in the light most favorable to sustaining the verdict

2. Determines whether, from the evidence and all reasonable inferences, a rational trier of fact could have concluded that the defendant was guilty beyond a reasonable doubt

Practice Book § 42-40 provides that this motion may be made at the close of the prosecution's case and at the close of all evidence.

Procedural Requirements

1. Make the motion outside the presence of the jury
2. Make the motion at the close of the state's case-in-chief
3. Renew the motion at the close of all evidence (if denied initially)
4. Specify each count for which you seek acquittal
5. Articulate which specific elements of each count the state has failed to prove
6. If denied, file a written motion for judgment of acquittal notwithstanding the verdict after trial

Strategic Considerations for Judgment of Acquittal Motions

1. **Specificity**: Identify with precision which elements of each count lack sufficient evidence, rather than making a general claim of insufficient evidence.
2. **Legal Elements**: Frame your argument around the legal elements of the offense as defined by statute and case law, not just factual disputes.

3. **Standard of Review**: Remember that the evidence will be viewed in the light most favorable to the state, so focus on complete absence of evidence or logical impossibilities rather than credibility issues.
4. **Preservation**: Even if you believe the motion is unlikely to be granted, making a detailed motion preserves issues for appeal.
5. **Partial Acquittal**: Consider seeking acquittal on specific counts or lesser included offenses even if the evidence appears sufficient on other counts.
6. **Renewal**: If initially denied, renew the motion at the close of all evidence, particularly if the defense case has highlighted additional weaknesses in the state's case.

MOTION TO STRIKE TESTIMONY

Legal Standard in Connecticut

A motion to strike testimony is appropriate when:

1. A witness provides testimony that is inadmissible (hearsay, irrelevant, prejudicial, etc.)
2. A witness is non-responsive to the question asked
3. A witness provides testimony contrary to a prior ruling on a motion in limine
4. A witness provides testimony for which proper foundation has not been laid

Procedural Requirements

1. Make the motion immediately following the objectionable testimony
2. State the specific ground for striking the testimony
3. Request that the jury be instructed to disregard the stricken testimony
4. If the testimony is particularly prejudicial, consider requesting a sidebar to argue for a more detailed curative instruction

SAMPLE CURATIVE INSTRUCTIONS

General Curative Instruction

"Ladies and gentlemen of the jury, I am instructing you to disregard the last statement made by the witness. That statement has been stricken from the record and should not be considered by you in your deliberations. You must decide this case solely on the evidence that I have admitted."

SPECIFIC CURATIVE INSTRUCTIONS FOR COMMON SITUATIONS

Hearsay

"Ladies and gentlemen, the witness just testified about what someone else allegedly said. This is what we call hearsay, and it is not admissible evidence in this case. You must disregard that testimony and not consider it in any way during your deliberations."

Prior Ruling Violation

"Ladies and gentlemen, the witness's testimony regarding [SUBJECT MATTER] violates a previous ruling of this Court. That testimony is stricken from the record, and you must disregard it entirely. It is not evidence in this case and should play no part in your deliberations."

Improper Character Evidence

"Ladies and gentlemen, the witness's testimony regarding the defendant's alleged [PRIOR ACT/CHARACTER TRAIT] is not admissible for the purpose of suggesting that the defendant has a propensity to commit the crime charged. You must disregard this testimony and not consider it for any purpose in your deliberations."

Non-Responsive Answer

"Ladies and gentlemen, the witness's answer went beyond the scope of the question that was asked. The portion of the answer that stated [SPECIFY] is stricken from the record. You must disregard that statement and not consider it during your deliberations."

Strategic Considerations for Motions to Strike

1. Balancing Act: Consider whether moving to strike will draw more attention to the testimony than simply letting it pass. Sometimes an objection and motion to strike can highlight prejudicial testimony.

2. Immediacy: Move to strike immediately after the objectionable testimony to prevent it from being considered by the jury.
3. Specific Request: Request a specific curative instruction tailored to the particular testimony rather than a general instruction.
4. Repeated Violations: If a witness repeatedly provides inadmissible testimony despite instructions to avoid certain topics, consider requesting a sidebar to address the issue outside the jury's presence.
5. Record Development: Ensure that both the objectionable testimony and the Court's ruling are clearly reflected in the record for potential appeal.
6. Follow-Up: If particularly prejudicial testimony has been stricken, consider requesting that the Court remind the jury of the instruction during final jury instructions.

MOTIONS FOR IMMEDIATE EVIDENTIARY HEARING

When unexpected issues arise during trial that require factual development outside the presence of the jury, you may need to request an immediate evidentiary hearing.

Common Situations Requiring Mid-Trial Evidentiary Hearings

1. Newly Discovered Brady Material: When evidence potentially favorable to the defense is disclosed mid-trial.
2. Witness Tampering or Intimidation: When allegations arise that a witness has been improperly influenced.
3. Batson Challenges: When claiming discriminatory use of peremptory challenges during ongoing jury selection.
4. Violation of Sequestration Order: When witnesses may have discussed testimony in violation of a sequestration order.
5. Chain of Custody Issues: When questions arise about the handling of physical evidence.

Strategic Considerations for Mid-Trial Evidentiary Hearings

1. Timing: Request the hearing at the earliest possible moment after becoming aware of the issue.
2. Specificity: Clearly articulate what evidence needs to be developed and why it cannot be addressed through other means.
3. Constitutional Dimensions: Frame the issue in terms of constitutional rights whenever possible, as courts are more likely to grant hearings when constitutional rights are at stake.

4. Preparation: Even though the hearing may be unexpected, prepare an outline of questions and identify specific evidence you seek to develop.

5. Record Development: Ensure that the hearing is on the record and that all evidence and testimony are clearly documented for potential appeal.

6. Remedies: Be prepared to articulate what remedy you seek based on the results of the hearing (e.g., mistrial, striking testimony, limiting instructions, etc.).

ORAL MOTION FOR RECONSIDERATION OF EVIDENTIARY RULING

During trial, circumstances may arise that warrant reconsideration of a previous evidentiary ruling.

Grounds for Reconsideration

1. **Changed Circumstances**: New evidence or testimony has emerged that changes the context of the previously excluded/admitted evidence.

2. **Opening the Door**: The opposing party has introduced evidence or made arguments that "open the door" to previously excluded evidence.

3. **Plain Error**: A previous ruling was clearly erroneous and causes manifest injustice.

4. **Clarification Needed**: The scope or application of a previous ruling requires clarification in light of trial developments.

Strategic Considerations for Reconsideration Motions

1. **Timing**: Make the motion as soon as the grounds for reconsideration become apparent.
2. **Specificity**: Clearly identify what has changed since the original ruling.
3. **New Arguments**: Avoid simply rehashing arguments already rejected by the court; focus on new developments or perspectives.
4. **Limited Scope**: Consider seeking partial reconsideration if appropriate, rather than wholesale reversal of the previous ruling.
5. **Alternative Proposals**: Offer alternative approaches that might address the court's concerns from the original ruling.
6. **Record Development**: Ensure that all grounds for reconsideration are clearly stated on the record for potential appeal.

CHAPTER 2

VOIR DIRE

Introduction by Willie Dow

"In all criminal prosecutions, the accused shall enjoy a right to a speedy and public trial, by an impartial jury…"

Federal Constitution, 6th Amendment

"In all criminal prosecutions, the accused shall have a right to be heard by himself and by counsel; to demand the nature and cause of the accusation; to be confronted by the witnesses against him; to have compulsory process to obtain witnesses in his favour; and in all prosecutions by indictment or information, a speedy public trial by an impartial jury.

State Constitution, Article I, Section 9

"...no state in the union, nor any court in the federal system, is more liberal in the conduct of a voir dire than this state."

State v. Marsh, 168 Conn. 520, 528 (1975)

INTRODUCTION BY WILLIE DOW

It is probably easier to describe the taste of a Pepe's Pizza to someone who has never been to Wooster Street than to adequately describe all the ingredients of a good criminal voir dire. Conducting criminal voir dire is an intuitive and interpretive process. The goal is to listen to information from people who will sit and pass judgment on our clients in order to determine if they are favorably disposed to the theme of the defense, and to commit those people favorably disposed to act on that disposition. While many feel the questioning process is a boring exercise and mindless, folks who are paid to study such matters strongly disagree. I am in their camp.

We are told that trials are mosaics of many parts. Each part is important because it contributes to the whole picture. Voir dire is especially important, for as the t-shirt slogan goes, "You never get a second chance to make a good first impression." Let's face it, trial lawyers are in the sales and promotion business and good sales are based on trust. Rather than them waiting in sales rooms for customers, however, we can select our target audiences. We choose which people will be inclined to purchase our product with all of its pluses and minuses. We select those who can be accepting of our shortcomings and supportive of our strengths, those who either want to assure that justice is done or to prevent an injustice from occurring. Connecticut's voir dire is without equal, for it allows us to examine the thought processes of the people who decide our cases.

Millions have passed judgments on trial lawyers by watching the endless coverage of high profile trials on TV. In doing so, they've learned of the criminal process, become familiar with the courts words', if not the concept of reasonable doubt, watched police officers lie, observed courtroom theatrics by bickering lawyers, learned to distrust witnesses sworn to testify truthfully, and formed countless other impressions of criminal trials. These cases and jurors' reactions to it provide a goldmine of information about the common themes of almost all criminal trials. More about that later. Offered here is an approach to conducting a criminal voir dire. The customary mandated disclaimer requires that I state that my observations are neither unique, nor necessarily correct. Mine is only one perspective.

The nature of each case dictates the manner, style, and conduct of the voir dire. The big picture defines the shapes of the individual pieces to the overall process. What the jury will see at trial dictates what approach and, more articulately, what questions are asked on voir dire. The crime alleged, the type of defense, the substance and style of prosecution and defense witnesses, as well as the defendant, all work into the mix. A criminal defense lawyer asks first whether the prosecution can prove his claims beyond a reasonable doubt. And if so, "How will it go about doing so? What will the case look like when it's presented to a jury."

Next, the lawyer asks, "What defense will be mounted to defeat or undermine the allegations? Will the defendant testify? Will prosecution witnesses support the defense's position? Can the state, in its case, fall on its sword? And if so, will it be through a cross-examination or by contradictory evidence from the defense? What will the judge instruct the jury at the end of the case?" A criminal lawyer asks these basic questions to design a trial strategy. The strategy then becomes the theme of the case. In addition, the theme provides a description of the type of jurors receptive to that theme. The voir dire identifies the receptive jurors.

Cynicism is a wonderful thing. We question everything. Above all, we question anyone's ability to be a fair juror in a criminal case. I have come to employ certain operating assumptions in selecting criminal jurors. A more politically correct description of this attitude would label these as "operating presumptions subject to rebuttal." Whatever the appropriate sobriquet, they are, most jurors don't want to be there.

Think of your uncle, your mother, your neighbor. How do they react when they open the mailing from the Judicial Department summoning them to jury service? Is it too far-fetched to presume that each one of them said, "Shit, how do I get out of this? I don't want to sit. Who do I know that can help get me out of this? What should I say when they question me so that I can be sure to get out of this?" That attitude comes with the jurors to the courthouse.

Next: jurors do not trust lawyers. This is, I submit, an irrebuttable presumption. Anyone who doesn't feel that anti-lawyer acrimony and distrust have increased in recent years have severely overdosed on "12 Angry Men" and "To Kill a Mockingbird."

Also, jurors hate crime. God, mother, apple pie, hate crime, they're all the same. This, incidentally, is true only so long as the juror has neither a friend or relative who has been unjustly accused, a relatively rare event.

Finally, a person arrested is probably guilty. For those with at least some grey hairs, this is what our parents taught us. It is safe to presume that is what many people think.

Don't forget, if the defendant is a minority, he or she is definitely guilty. Sad, but true. A rebuttable presumption, perhaps, but one worth seriously entertaining. All of us, despite our positations, have those darker sides we hesitate to acknowledge that nevertheless, somehow, enter our thought process. We live in an age where Jesse

Jackson states that he experiences fear when he walks down a city street and is confronted by a young African American male. All of us are troubled by race. It can and does affect our thought process.

Remember, jurors are afraid of defendants. Wouldn't you be afraid of someone accused of murder, selling drugs, or some other type of violence? Will the defendant find out where a juror lives or works? Will his friends try to get revenge or influence the decision?

While rebuttable, these presumptions or assumptions are a guide to areas for exploration in voir dire. The voir dire process is an acknowledgement that we are all shaped by our individual experiences and that we bring those experiences into the courtroom. We all carry emotional baggage we have acquired in our homes, our schools, and in social settings. Acknowledging the existence of this baggage is not a value judgment. It simply recognizes reality and the frailty of the human condition. Life experiences are a prism through which a juror views what happens in the courtroom. Voir dire is the opportunity to explore that prism. One purpose of voir dire then is to analyze these presumptions as they affect each case. If jurors can acknowledge areas of possible bias or prejudice, they may at best be able to exclude those influences from their thought processes or, worse, acknowledge an inability to do so.

Willie Dow

July 2025

Qualification of Jurors

Below is a list of reasons an individual may be disqualified from serving on the jury in Connecticut[13]:

1. Seventy-five years of age or older and chooses not to perform juror service.
2. Convicted of a felony within the past three years.
3. Defendant in a pending felony case, or is incarcerated.
4. Unable to speak or understand English.
5. Is incapable due to mental or physical ability.
6. Not a U.S. citizen.
7. The governor, Lieutenant Governor, Secretary of State, Treasurer, Comptroller or Attorney General.
8. Member of the General Assembly, while in session.
9. Judge of the Probate Court, Superior Court, Appellate Court or Supreme Court.
10. State Referee, family support magistrate or federal court judge.
11. Registrar of voters, or deputy registrar of voters of a municipality, while 21 days before the date of a federal, state or municipal election, primary or referendum, inclusive.

[13] Conn. Gen. Stat. § 51-217

12. Found by the judge of the superior court to exhibit any quality which will impair the capacity for jury service. (Except due to deafness).

Peremptory Challenges[14]

As a trial lawyer, you have the chance to peremptorily challenge any possible jurors without reason. There are limitations on how many jurors you may challenge. In Connecticut, the accused may challenge:

a. **25 jurors** for any offense punishable by life imprisonment without the possibility of release

b. **15 jurors** for any offense punishable by life imprisonment

c. **6 jurors** for any offense punishable by more than one year in prison and less than life

d. **3 jurors** for any other offense

Just as you have the chance to "challenge" any possible juror, you have a chance to challenge any possible alternate juror. Such alternate jurors shall have the same qualifications and be selected and subject to examination and challenge in the same manner and to the same extent as the jurors constituting the regular panel, provided, in any case when the court directs the selection of alternate jurors, the number of peremptory challenges allowed shall be as follows:[15]

---

[14] Conn. Gen. Stat. § 54-82g

[15] Conn. Gen. Stat. § 54-82h

a. **<u>30 jurors</u>** for any offense punishable by life imprisonment without the possibility of release

b. **<u>18 jurors</u>** for any offense punishable by life imprisonment

c. **<u>8 jurors</u>** for any offense punishable by more than one year in prison and less than life

d. **<u>4 jurors</u>** for any other offense

<u>Requesting Additional Peremptory Challenges</u>

In any criminal trial in which the defendant is charged with more than one count, the number of challenges is determined by the count carrying the highest maximum punishment.

You may request additional peremptory challenges if you exhaust your allotted challenges. If you are denied your request and believe the denial created a reversible error at trial, you must prove that:

1. if you had an additional peremptory challenge, you would have used it to remove an identifiable juror, and

2. because you were unable to do so, that juror ultimately sat on the jury.[16]

When selecting jurors it is important, especially in the GA courts, to inquire if you can use your peremptory challenges altogether with your main panel challenges or if the court will restrict your challenges to the panel and alternates as set forth. Many judges will allow you to use all your challenges as you see fit, but you must get acquiescence

---

[16] State v. Ross, 269 Conn. 213, 232, 849 A.2d 648, 670 (2004)

from the court in advance or you may run out of main panel preemptory challenges before you fashion your panel if you don't clearly know if you can use your alternate challenges in your main panel voir dire.

Exhaustion Requirement

In order to assign error in jury selection, the appellant must exhaust all peremptory challenges.

State v. Vitale, 190 Conn. 219, 225 (1983)

State v. Mercer, 208 Conn. 52, 61-62 (1988).

Premature Jury Deliberation

Jury cannot discuss the case prior to its submission by court.

State v. Castonguay, 194 Conn. 416, 433-34 (1984)

State v. Washington, 182 Conn. 419, 429 (1980)

Economics of Jury Service

If employed full time, the employer pays regular wages for the first 5 days.

If employed part-time or unemployed, the state pays out-of-pocket expenses not less than $20 nor more than $50 per day of service.

For trials lasting more than 5 days, the state pays $50.00 per day for the 6th day and each day thereafter.

Presence of Judge

"The rationale of voir dire also mandates that the trial judge be present in the courtroom at all times during voir dire in a criminal action."

State v. Patterson, 31 Conn. App. 278, 287 (1993)

Absence of Judge from the courtroom is per se reversible error.

Patterson, at 303.

Time Limits Imposed by Court

"Because a party has a right to examine individual jurors on the voir dire he must be allowed a reasonable amount of time to exercise that right."

State v. Haskins, 188 Conn. 432, 447 (1982)

State v. Anthony, 172 Conn. 172, 176-77 (1976)

Level of Proof for Challenge

"Party has the burden of raising his claim of actual bias from the realm of speculation to the realm of fact."

State v. Cubano, 203 Conn. 81, 90-91 (1987)

State v. Bowen, 167 Conn. 526, 537 (1975)

"Juror's mind must be fixed and settled, and not a mere impression."

State v. Ziel, 197 Conn. 60, 66 (1985)

"A mere impression of the case when no fixed opinion has been drawn is an insufficient grounds to excuse a juror for cause."

State v. Potter, 18 Conn. 166, 174-75 (1846)

"It is sufficient if a juror can lay aside his impression and render a verdict based on the evidence presented in court."

Irvin v. Dowd, 366 U.S. 717, 723 (1961)

"A Court is invested with wide discretion in determining the competency of jurors to serve."

Ziel, at 65.

"Individual" Voir Dire

Court places 14 venirepersons in jury box and permits counsel to question venirepersons directly while in the box. Venirepersons given opportunity to answer any question by counsel in absence of other venirepersons. Such a procedure is permissible in absence of prejudice due to the presence of other venirepersons.

Childs v. Blesso, 158 Conn. 389, 394 (1969)

State v. Burns, 173 Conn. 317, 321-22 (1977)

Shackled Defendant

"Court should make every reasonable effort to present the defendant before the jury in a manner that does not suggest, directly or impliedly, that he or she is a dangerous character whose guilt is a foregone conclusion. The negative connotations of restraints are without significance, unless the fact of the restraints comes to the attention of the jury."

State v. Tweedy, 219 Conn. 489, 508 (1991)

State v. Haskins, 188 Conn. 432, 455 (1982)

<u>Duty to Object</u>

"...defendant failed to object to the [voir dire] questions and comments that he now claims constituted prosecutorial misconduct..."

State v. Brown, 256 Con. 291, 301 (2001)

<u>How to Successfully Vet Jurors</u>

Jury selection is the art of understanding potential jurors, engaging them in meaningful conversations, and making informed decisions. Here are 15 key tips:

1. Ask open-ended questions to encourage jurors to share their thoughts.
2. Listen attentively to every word they say.
3. Embrace uncomfortable answers for better decision-making.
4. If you get a 'bad' answer, seek clarification and validate their response.
5. Use their words, not yours, when discussing their answers.

6. Balance open and closed-ended questions for a comprehensive view.
7. Consider rehabilitation to turn unfavorable jurors into assets.
8. Speak in everyday language, not legal jargon.
9. Be flexible with your questions, deviating from the script when necessary.
10. Tailor questions to your case's specifics.
11. Explore personal experiences to understand their viewpoints.
12. Let jurors explain their understanding of the law.
13. Ensure every question has a purpose.
14. Take your time; don't rush the process.
15. Collaborate with colleagues for different perspectives.

Jury selection is an art that requires strategic questioning, active listening, and understanding human nature—a crucial part of the pursuit of justice.

QUESTIONS YOU CANNOT ASK

a. Hypothetical questions or questions of law related to the case

"Hypothetical questions and questions of law which call for prejudgment of any supposed case on the facts are not permissible in voir dire examination."

State v. Ross, 269 Conn. 213, 221, 849 A.2d 648, 663 (2004)

b. Verdict returned in a prior case

"Standing alone, the fact that a jury returns a guilty verdict is not probative of the personal views of the individual jurors. The trial court did not abuse it's discretion in sustaining the State's objection to the defendant's question." (The question was whether the prior verdict was guilty or not guilty).

State v. Couture, 218 Conn. 309, 318-19 (1991)

c. Assumptions built into questions

"Do you believe that blacks have equal rights in the society with whites?"

State v. Edwards, 201 Conn. 128, 161 (1986)

d. Juror's knowledge of the law

"Jurors' knowledge or ignorance with respect to questions of law is not a proper subject of inquiry on voir dire."

State v. Anthony, 172 conn. 172, 176 (1976)

"Questions addressed to veniremen involving assumptions or hypotheses concerning evidence which may be offered at the trial or instructions which may be given by the court should be discouraged."

State v. Mendill, 141 Conn. 360, 362 (1954)

State v. Van Volkenburg, 160 Conn. 171, 173 (1970)

BUT... "because the purpose of voir dire is to elicit information on which the Court and parties can fairly evaluate a venire member's ability to serve as a juror, it is customary for counsel to inquire of venire members whether they are inclined to adhere to and apply the legal principles that generally will apply to the matter before them."

State v. Holley, 90 Conn. App. 350, 355 (2005)

e. **Questions concerning "coming out of the closet," or how a venireperson knew a man was struggling with his sexual orientation**

"The trial court did not prohibit [the] defendant from asking venirepersons general questions regarding their attitudes toward homosexuality, either before or after, sustaining the prosecutor's objection to questions pertaining to "coming out of the closet" and how a venireperson knew that a man was struggling with his sexual orientation. **[BUT]** It had stated that questions about the latter would be permitted if [the] defendant could show that this was an issue."

State v. Thornton, 112 Conn. App. 694, 695, 963 A.2d 1099, 1101 (2009)

QUESTIONS YOU CAN ASK

a. More Weight to Police Testimony

A trial court's refusal to allow defense counsel to inquire whether the jurors would be inclined to give more weight to police officers' testimony because of his status constitutes reversible error.

State v. Rogers, 197 Conn. 314 (1985)

State v. Hill, 196 Conn. 667 (1985)

State v. Dolphin, 203 Conn. 506, 513 (1987)

"Would you believe a statement solely because it is made by a police officer?"

State v. Faust, 237 Conn. 454, 458 f.n. 5 (1996)

b. Juror's Assurance of "Fairness"

Juror's assurance that he or she is equal to the task is not dispositive.

State v. Cubano, 203 Conn. 81, 92 (1987)

State v. Tucker, 226 Conn. 618, 644 (1993)

c. Living Close to the Crime Scene

"Would you have an interest in this case because it occurred near where you live?"

State v. Esposito, 223 Conn. 299, 307 (1992)

d. Knowing Friend / Acquaintance of Defendant

Defense must raise issue and prove bias or premature opinion.

Cubano, at 90-91

State v. Alston, 272 Conn. 432, 453 f.n. 13 (2004)

e. Incarcerated Client / Presumption of Guilt

"Do you believe the defendant must have committed the crimes charges solely because he is incarcerated?"

State v. Faust, 237 Conn. 454, 458 f.n. 5 (1996)

f. Identification

"Questions regarding [juror's] thoughts on the ability of the witness to make an accurate identification, and whether the witness, even an extremely confident one, could make a mistaken identification are admissible."

State v. Rios, 74 Conn. App. 110, 118 (2002)

"Would you automatically believe every witness who testified?"

"Do you think a person who takes an oath can be honestly mistaken about what they're testifying about?"

"If the Judge told you that one of the things the State had to prove beyond a reasonable doubt was the identity or identification and if he gave you instructions on that subject matter, would you follow his instructions?"

State v. Pollitt, 205 Conn. 61, 74 (1981)

Pretrial Publicity

Juror read part of one article concerning the defendant. Juror stated he "still had an open mind... and could judge this case squarely on the facts of this case." Juror excused.

State v. Marra, 195 Conn. 421, 435 (1985)

Sympathy for Complainant

The defendant has a right to inquire as to whether a juror has an unusual level of sympathy for the complaining party.

Lamb v. Burns, 202 Conn. 158, 165 (1987)

Alibi

"If the judge were to tell you... [a]libi is recognized as a proper defense and you should consider this, that, and the other, would you follow what the Judge told you?"

Pollitt, at 74.

Race

"Would it require any less evidence for you to find a Negro person guilty of such a crime than it would to find a white person?

State v. Higgs, 143 Conn. 138, 140 (1956)

"Would you be less inclined to believe a Negro witness than a white witness simply because of the former's color?"

Higgs, at 141.

"Would you have any reluctance in following any instruction the Court may give you as to the weight which may be given to the fact that the defendant or any witness in this case is a Negro?"

Higgs, at 140.

"Would you have any prejudice against the defendant because of his color?"

Id.

"Discrimination on the basis of race is a subject which is the examination of jurors the Court must allow if requested by a party."

State v. Marsh, 168 Conn. 520, 522 (1975)

"How would you feel if a relative of yours, a son or a daughter, brother or sister… expressed an intent to you that he wanted to marry a black person?

"The question on interracial marriage is relevant in that it might reveal subconscious racism on the party of a prospective juror."

State v. Smith, 222 conn. 1, 7 (1992)

"Are African-Americans more inclined to commit crimes than white people?"

State v. Faust, 237 Conn. 454, 458 f.n. 5 (1996)

Gangs

Defendant permitted to question jurors about gangs in a general way, not as to a specific gang.

State v. Lugo, 266 Conn. 673 (2003)

TIPS FOR DEFENDING AGAINST A CHALLENGE FOR CAUSE

Your opponent has elicited juror testimony that he/she will use to challenge a juror you like for cause. You want to remove these grounds.

a. Shut the door with close-ended questions

"Even though you feel that way, you can put those feelings aside and follow the law that the judge gives you, isn't that true?"

"You want to do your civic duty as a juror, right?"

"Your answer suggests that you might be biased, but you want to be fair to both sides, don't you?"

"Even with these feelings, if the proof, in your mind, reaches the level of "beyond a reasonable doubt," you can follow the flaw as the Judge explains it, isn't that right?"

b. Argue the constitutional and statutory right to a fair trial and fair-cross section of society

<u>Tips for Maintaining Cause When Opponent has Attempted Rehabilitation</u>

Inquire if anything the Opponent has said has caused venireperson to want to change any of the answers to your questions. Then quote back their original answers and confirm them to the court and venireperson.

Race/Gender Challenges

Race: Batson v. Kentucky, 476 U.S. 79 (1986)

Gender: J.E.B. v. Alabama ex. rel. T.B., 511 U.S. 127 (1994)

Steps in Making a Claim

1. Movant makes a claim of excusal due to race or gender.
2. Opponent advances a neutral explanation of basis for challenge.
3. Movant argues that explanation is pretextual or insufficient.
4. The Trial Court decides if purposeful discrimination is established.

State v. Peeler, 267Bc Conn. 611, 620-22 (2004)

State v. Monroe, 98 Conn. App. 588 (2006)

Note: Under State v. Holloway, 209 Conn. 636, 645-46 (1989), movant **does not** need to make a prima facie case of discrimination prior to the opponent advancing a neutral explanation.

Grounds Recognized for Sustaining Challenge

1. Reasons given are not related to the trial of the case.
2. Challenging party did not question venireperson or did so only perfunctorily.
3. Venireperson of one race/gender was asked a question to elicit a response that was not asked of other venireperson.

4. Venireperson with the same characteristics as, but of a different race/gender than the challenged venireperson was not challenged.
5. Challenger advanced an explanation based on group bias where the group trait does not apply specifically to the challenged venireperson.
6. Disproportionate number of strikes were used to exclude one race or gender.

State v. Mukhtaar, 253 Conn. 280, 284-85 (2000)

State v. Hinton, 227 Conn. 301, 325 (1993)

<u>Race-Neutral Reasons</u>

Prospective juror has a close relative who has been prosecuted. (That juror may resent prosecutors in general).

State v. Hodge, 248 Conn. 207, 321 (1999)

The prosecutor distrusts prospective juror or thinks his/her answers are not credible can be sufficiently race-neutral reason to use peremptory challenge

Hinton, at 326-27

Prospective juror's great familiarity with industry that victims work in may affect his/her perception of victims.

Hodge, at 234.

Prospective juror's acquaintance with employees of public defender's office.

Id.

Prospective juror's familiarity with the crime scene.

Id.

Prospective juror's eagerness to serve as a juror.

Id.

Prospective juror's inability to understand evidence and appropriate legal standards.

Hodge, at 236.

Prospective juror's prior arrest record is permissible ground to use peremptory challenge.

Hodge, at 248-49.

Prosecutor can strike a prospective juror because he/she appeared inattentive or hostile to the government.

State v. Robinson, 237 Conn. 238, 254 f.n. 15 (1996)

Reasonable to strike prospective jurors because of "perceived lack of a demonstrated ability to make decisions."

Hodge, at 254-55.

<u>Notable Points in Decided Cases</u>

Not all grounds of excusal need to be considered if at least one reason is race/gender neutral.

State v. Smith, 222 conn. 1, 14 f.n. 8 (1992)

But see: **Hodge, at 223-24**

When a claim of pretext is asserted, movant must prove the same by a preponderance of evidence.

State v. Morales, 71 Conn. App. 790, 814 (2002)

Failure to oppose a proffer of a race/gender neutral reason is acquiescence in the validity of the reason.

Morales, at 804.

State v. Beltran, 246 Conn. 268, 280 (1998)

The movant does not have to be of the same race/gender as venireman to make the claim.

State v. Rigual, 256 Conn. 1, 10 f.n. 10 (2001)

Powers v. Ohio, 499 U.S. 400 (1991)

An impression of the conduct and demeanor of a prospective juror during voir dire may provide a legitimate basis for the exercise of the challenge.

State v. Robinson, 237 Conn. 238 (1996)

"Dual motivation" is not a challenge based on impermissible discriminatory reasons and valid nondiscriminatory reasons.

State v. Hodge, 248 Conn. 207, 226 (1999)

Youth is not a cognizable group for <u>Batson</u> purposes.

State v. McDougal, 241 Conn. 502, 515 (1997)

It is impermissible to challenge based on venireman's religion but religious beliefs interfering with the obligations of a juror is a valid challenge. (For example, a venireman whose religious belief prohibits him/her from judging anyone).

Hodge, at 245 f.n. 44

Batson challenges must be made before the jury is sworn.

Robinson, at 243, 250.

Sample General Voir Dire Questions

- Have you ever served on a jury before? If yes, can you briefly share your experience but not your verdict?
- Do you have any personal biases or prejudices that you think might affect your ability to be fair and impartial in this case?
- Are you familiar with the parties involved in this case, such as the plaintiff, defendant, or any witnesses?
- Have you ever been a victim of a similar crime or involved in a similar incident to the one being discussed in this case?
- Do you have any professional or personal experience that might influence your perspective on the issues raised in this case?
- Are you comfortable making a decision based solely on the evidence presented in court and following the judge's instructions on the law?

- How do you feel about the presumption of innocence, and can you apply it in this case?
- Are you a member of any organizations or groups that have a particular interest in the outcome of this case?
- Have you formed any opinions about the case/criminal cases based on media coverage or other sources of information?
- Do you have any personal, religious, or moral beliefs that could impact your ability to make a fair and unbiased decision in this case?
- Can you commit to giving equal weight to the testimony of all witnesses, regardless of their background or occupation?
- Are you comfortable evaluating witness credibility and determining the reliability of their testimony?
- Are you capable of deliberating with other jurors and reaching a decision based on the evidence presented in court?
- Is there any reason why you believe you should be excused from serving as a juror in this case?

CHAPTER 3

DIRECT EXAMINATION

Introduction by State's Attorney David Applegate

"If the lawyer does well in her role as a teacher, she will seem to disappear during direct examination as the jury becomes locked in on what the witnesses are saying."

McElhaney, James W., "The Case is Falling Apart… And Continuity is the Glue that Keeps Things Together," A.B.A.J. 74 (1998)

An attorney's role at trial is complicated. A trial is an opportunity for attorneys to showcase all of their talents in front of an audience. Arguing motions and objections, guiding experts through complex analyses, and, of course, confronting witnesses on key points during cross-examination, are all commonplace. The entire proceeding, from selecting a jury to calling witnesses and entering exhibits, builds up to a closing argument where the lawyers invariably become the center of attention. It is a great disservice to the parties and the case, however, for the attorneys to make this process about themselves. This is especially true when it comes to direct examination. It is the witness who must shine when telling his or her story. Although this requires skillful guidance and encouragement from counsel, it should be the witness who receives all of the jury's attention. The sole objective of an attorney conducting a direct examination must be to bring out all of the relevant information possessed by the witness in a way that highlights the witness's credibility.

The success of any direct examination is determined by how well it fits into the larger web of facts, evidence, and arguments presented at trial. It is not simply about asking each person the right questions.

The testimony of each witness should comprise a cohesive theme that supports what a party is trying to prove, or disprove. Although particular witnesses will stand out, and their testimony will be more memorable to a jury during deliberations, each witness should serve a tangible purpose. Calling a witness simply because her name appeared in a report signifies a lack of preparation, and a failure to understand one's case. As discussed below, deciding which witnesses to call, and in what order to put them on the stand, is far more complicated than merely knowing what questions to ask. Trials require a discerning grasp of every detail of a case, along with thoughtful and systematic planning.

During the earliest stages of a case, attorneys should be considering what the story is they wish to tell the judge or jury, and carefully planning how to tell that story. The first step to accomplishing this is to thoroughly read and understand every report, statement, and other document contained in the file, and to watch or listen to any digital media, such as taped interviews, surveillance footage, or body-worn camera recordings. By attentively and meticulously watching a video or reading a report multiple times, one will invariably recognize useful facts that were not apparent upon an initial review of the file. A complete review of all the materials will shape and guide the direction taken when outlining or writing out questions to ask during direct examination. Throughout this methodical process, the attorney should be mindful of how all of the facts and details, no matter how seemingly minor, fit into the larger picture the attorney wishes to present at trial, and how those facts ultimately allow the attorney to advance a powerful, convergent closing argument.

Careful planning also means understanding the evidence that has already been collected, and determining whether there are additional items that could be obtained and presented at trial. Records may exist that corroborate the statement of an important witness. Telephone records, which often include historical cell site data, may show which witnesses were communicating with each other, as well as where they were or were not located. Social media records may provide insight into relationships, motives, and the credibility of witnesses. Depending upon the type of case, other records, such as banking records or medical records, might explain a great deal. All of these materials provide background that will assist in knowing what areas to cover with a witness, and to anticipate what the other side will ask during cross-examination. Being able to foresee problematic issues that may arise with a witness allows counsel to prepare the witness for what may come. A witness who has been blindsided with a line of questioning may not respond well. Also, when potentially harmful facts are known in advance of trial, a tactical decision can be made whether to get into that area during direct examination, thereby softening whatever blows the other side might take.

Attorneys must also know what forensic testing or examination was conducted and understand the results. They must consider whether additional procedures could be performed, which might better allow them tell their story to the factfinder. This is not just important for dealing with expert witnesses, such as doctors, chemists or DNA analysts, it directly affects the testimony of fact witnesses, as well. Seemingly insignificant observations made by a witness often become critically important when they are corroborated by the subsequent testimony of an expert witness. For example, many items collected from a crime scene are not initially tested or examined by a forensic analyst. This is because someone along the chain of custody determined the results would be inconsequential. If the defendant's presence at the crime scene is not in dispute, and the item was not used as a weapon, it is often true that there would be no value to testing the item; but if a witness were to mention seeing the assailant touch such an item, testing of that item might reveal the presence of the defendant's DNA. The fact that the witness accurately recalled specifically what the defendant touched would demonstrate the witness's attention to detail and might serve to reinforce the witness's credibility. Direct examination is an opportunity to present facts that mesh together within a witness's testimony, and that corroborate and coincide with points and observations made by other witnesses. This is how the cumulative effect of minor details becomes powerful. Each item of evidence and source of information can be a building block upon which an effective trial attorney crafts and assembles a creative and compelling argument that will steer the course of the trial.

Truly understanding a file enables an attorney to prepare a compelling direct examination. At the core of such an understanding is the ability to identify the case's strengths and weaknesses. This is a challenge to even the most seasoned attorneys. The culture of litigation demands that an attorney be able to read a file and evaluate it quickly and decisively. Every day, prosecutors make plea offers based upon police incident reports, and criminal defense attorneys advise their clients whether those offers are reasonable based upon those same documents. Similarly, civil attorneys decide whether to put time and money into a case based upon accident reports, medical records, or witness statements, among other materials. Settlement negotiations often occur before a single deposition takes place. Make no mistake, there is a tremendous amount of skill, generally borne from experience, that goes into this process, but trials are comprised of a human element that cannot be divined so easily. A case never looks the same at trial as it did on paper. Accurately gauging the strength of a case demands more than just reading a statement. It requires actually meeting and getting to know a witness. How will this person respond to being pressed or challenged? This is equally true for fact witnesses and expert witnesses. It is a mistake to assume that someone whose expert opinion has been sought will automatically make a strong witness. Many capable experts are proficient in their trade, but either lose confidence or become unlikeable when their conclusions are called into question.

Realistically estimating how witnesses will fare at trial is just one component of knowing a case's strengths and weaknesses. Every time an attorney considers what to offer as evidence, there should be an equal consideration as to how it will be used by the other side at trial. Talented trial lawyers see the arguments opposing counsel should raise and find a way to use those arguments to their advantage. Ineffective lawyers fail to see the potential problems in their own cases. They often refuse to listen during pre-trial negotiations when opposing counsel lays out those problems, foreshadowing what will be presented and argued at trial.

Understanding a case's weaknesses should shape decisions regarding which witnesses to call, and how they must be questioned. As discussed in earlier chapters, this type of careful planning often guides how jury selection is approached. Questions for potential jurors can be crafted to align with the evidence expected to be presented at trial, and can be used to combat positions the other side is expected to take. If, for example, the trial hinges upon the strength of a single witness, it is important to raise that issue during jury selection. Jurors may be more receptive to the argument that a single witness's testimony can be just as persuasive as the testimony of numerous witnesses if those jurors had an opportunity to discuss that area of the law before trial started.

The preparation outlined above should begin during the earliest stages of litigation and continue throughout the discovery process. It is a mistake to shelve a file when it is placed on a trial list. Conversely, it should be seen as an opportunity to scrutinize what is lacking and work to make the case stronger. As trial draws near, however, preparation naturally shifts to putting the exhibits in order, and getting the witnesses ready to testify. This will often be the first time the trial attorney meets with witnesses. It is common for eyewitnesses to be reluctant to testify, particularly in criminal cases. Thus, it is crucial to establish trust from the outset. Attorneys should explain to witnesses how their testimony fits into the case, and why it is an important piece of the story. It is equally important to listen to the witnesses' concerns and to let them know that the issues they raise are being taken seriously, and that their time is respected.

Witnesses should be brought into the office within a few weeks of the trial. They should be given an opportunity to review any prior statements they provided. If there is an audio or video recording of a statement, it should be played for the witness in its entirety, preferably more than once, in a room with no distractions. While prior statements provide a framework for a witness's testimony, witnesses should be regularly reminded that the most important aspect of their testimony is to tell the truth.

Witnesses must be made to understand that telling the truth means not holding back details. It also means never sanitizing facts that the witness finds troubling or embarrassing. For example, a police officer who is forced to wrestle with a suspect should not downplay the altercation. Jurors are perceptive, and they will likely sense that the officer is being insincere. Furthermore, proof may be submitted later that the defendant sustained physical injuries, calling into question the officer's credibility.

When meeting with a witness for a preparation session an attorney should have a detailed outline ready to go over every point that is likely to come up at trial. The goal is not to have the witness memorize answers to questions, but rather to make sure the witness is ready to discuss all of the issues that may arise. The attorney must know how the witness is expected to respond on the witness stand to successfully map out the course of the trial. The witness should also look over every exhibit that might be shown to her at trial. On the stand, witnesses are all too often shown photographs or maps for the first time, and the result can be disastrous. In the courtroom, with all eyes fixed on her, a witness may get confused or disoriented and find herself unable to locate or identify a location that should be well known to her. This is not the fault of the witness; it is a failure of the attorney to properly prepare for trial. Thorough preparation means there should be no surprises for the attorney, but also for the witness.

A preparation session can be an indicator of how a witness will testify in court. Strong witnesses are good listeners who are careful in their responses. They know when to concede a point, and when to stand their ground. If a witness struggles with providing responsive answers to questions prior to trial, scheduling additional preparation sessions sometimes helps. If after meeting with someone extensively it is clear that the individual will make a poor witness, it is important for an attorney to be able to pivot and devise a solution. Counsel should consider whether this witness is essential to the case, or whether a different person could be called to provide the same testimony. If this is the only person who can testify to an important fact, then the witness's testimony must be tailored to avoid the pitfalls that are likely to occur at trial. Although a shorter, narrowly focused direct examination might be less impactful upon a jury, it would prevent losing focus and giving opposing counsel an opening to confuse the issues.

During the preparation phase immediately leading up to trial, counsel should be paring down the original list of potential witnesses. This is often a very fluid process that can change at any time, even during trial. Anyone who has tried a case knows how important it is to be flexible, because events often occur that are beyond anyone's control. As mentioned earlier, it is not necessary to call every person whose name is mentioned in a report. Calling multiple witnesses to testify to the same facts should only occur with respect to the most important aspects of the case. Deciding which witnesses to call should be based upon what each person can offer to further the story being told to the jury. Attorneys should consider the argument they wish to make and be sure to have a witness ready to address every fact contained within that argument.

Additionally, the order in which witnesses testify matters. It is important to call witnesses early on who can set the stage for the more important witnesses. It will take time for the jury to understand what the case is about, and calling an important witness too soon will not be as impactful. Starting out by spending hours on minutiae, however, risks losing the jury's interest and attention. Part of the art of telling a complicated story is knowing in what sequence to describe the events. There should be order to it, even if it seems chaotic at first.

No matter how much preparation takes place, many witnesses will be visibly nervous when the time comes to provide testimony. Sometimes this can even interfere with their ability to answer questions. When that occurs, it is up to counsel to calm a witness down and stay on track. Introductory questions are often a helpful way to simultaneously make a witness feel at ease and endear that witness to the factfinder. Spending a few extra minutes delving into the witness's work history, living arrangements, or educational background often leads to a seamless transition to questions about the actual cause of action.

There is no single correct way to conduct a direct examination. Lawyers should always strive to develop their own style in the courtroom. One goal is to make the direct as conversational as possible. This is in line with telling an interesting and compelling story to the jury. Conversations, however, have a tendency to meander. Sticking to an outline or set of questions is a way to maintain focus, but it can also be very rigid and less likely to capture the attention of jurors. One way to strike a balance is to have a detailed outline of the areas that need to be covered by each witness, but to create a dialog within each of those specific topics. The biggest mistake an attorney can make during a direct examination is to not listen to the witness's answers. Sticking to a script of questions can lead to repetitive testimony, because the witness already answered the question as part of an earlier response. Instead of running through questions like a checklist, an attorney should be carefully listening to the witness's answers and asking meaningful follow up questions. When a topic has been exhausted, the attorney can refer back to the outline so as not to forget to cover an area of importance.

In sum, the foundation to conducting an effective direct examination is careful planning. The ability to present one's case to a jury in an engaging and creative way hinges upon a thorough understanding of what, exactly, each witness contributes to the case, and how that testimony fits into the broader picture.

When fashioning your direct, you should work to have your questions answer a question in the juror's mind. The following chart identifies the main topic areas that you might consider for your direct examinations:

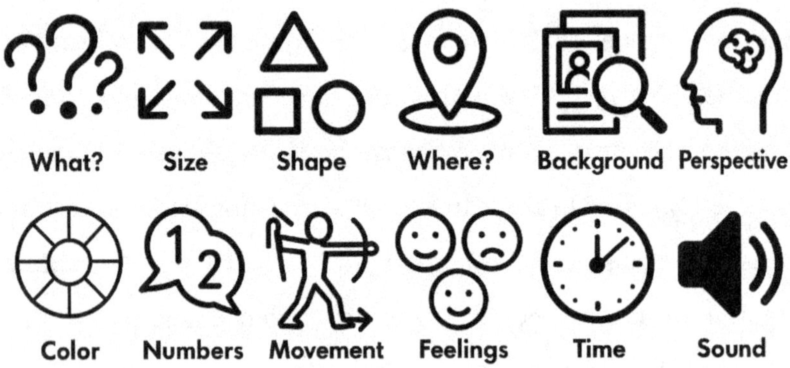

David Applegate July 2025

INTRODUCTION TO WITNESS PREPARATION

The effectiveness of direct examination hinges not only on the attorney's skill in questioning but on thorough witness preparation. An unprepared witness can unravel even the strongest case, while a well-prepared witness can overcome challenges in the evidence. This section provides a comprehensive framework for preparing witnesses for direct examination in criminal trials.

ETHICAL BOUNDARIES OF WITNESS PREPARATION

Permissible Preparation vs. Improper Coaching

The line between proper preparation and improper coaching must be clearly understood:

- **Permissible preparation** includes familiarizing witnesses with courtroom procedures, reviewing prior statements, discussing testimony organization, and practicing responses to anticipated questions.
- **Improper coaching** involves suggesting false testimony, instructing witnesses to feign memory lapses, or creating scripted responses that do not reflect the witness's actual recollection.

Connecticut Rules of Professional Conduct 3.4(b) prohibits attorneys from counseling or assisting a witness to testify falsely. However, assisting witnesses to testify truthfully and effectively is not only permitted but constitutes effective representation.

Documentation of Preparation Sessions

Maintain detailed notes of witness preparation sessions, including:

- Dates and duration of meetings
- Topics discussed
- Materials reviewed
- Persons present

These records protect against allegations of improper coaching and provide reference points for follow-up sessions.

INITIAL WITNESS ASSESSMENT

Evaluating Witness Capabilities

Before substantive preparation begins, assess each witness's:

- **Cognitive abilities**: Memory capacity, ability to understand complex questions, language proficiency
- **Emotional stability**: Stress tolerance, emotional reactions to difficult topics
- **Communication style**: Verbal clarity, nonverbal cues, tendency toward narrative or brief responses
- **Demeanor characteristics**: Eye contact, posture, fidgeting, voice modulation
- **Credibility vulnerabilities**: Prior inconsistent statements, biases, criminal history

Determining Preparation Intensity

Based on initial assessment, classify witnesses into preparation categories:

- **Minimal preparation**: Professional witnesses with extensive testimony experience (e.g., veteran police officers)
- **Moderate preparation**: Witnesses with some familiarity with legal proceedings but limited testimony experience

- **Intensive preparation**: First-time witnesses, vulnerable witnesses (children, elderly, those with cognitive limitations), and witnesses with significant credibility challenges

FOUNDATIONAL PREPARATION ELEMENTS

Courtroom Orientation

All witnesses benefit from understanding the physical and procedural environment:

- **Physical layout**: Provide diagrams or photographs of the courtroom, identifying the witness stand, judge's bench, jury box, and counsel tables
- **Role introductions**: Explain the roles of the judge, jury, prosecutor, defense counsel, and court personnel
- **Procedural steps**: Detail the oath administration, direct examination, cross-examination, redirect, and rules for entering/exiting the courtroom
- **Courtroom visit**: When possible, arrange for witnesses to visit an empty courtroom before testimony

Testimony Mechanics

Instruct witnesses on fundamental testimony techniques:

- **Listening fully**: Wait until the question is completely asked before answering

- **Answering precisely**: Answer only the question asked, without volunteering additional information
- **Admitting uncertainty**: Say "I don't know" or "I don't recall" when accurate
- **Speaking clearly**: Use a moderate pace and adequate volume
- **Avoiding jargon**: Explain technical terms when necessary
- **Managing exhibits**: Practice handling and referring to documents or physical evidence
- **Addressing the jury**: Maintain appropriate eye contact with jurors during substantive answers

SUBSTANTIVE TESTIMONY PREPARATION

Document Review

Review all relevant documents with the witness, including:

- **Prior statements**: Police reports, grand jury testimony, preliminary hearing testimony, depositions
- **Physical evidence**: Photographs, diagrams, weapons, clothing, or other objects
- **Expert reports**: Technical findings relevant to the witness's testimony
- **Other witness statements**: When legally and ethically appropriate

When reviewing documents, focus on consistency between documents and the witness's current recollection. Address inconsistencies directly, exploring reasons for the discrepancy (elapsed time, stress during initial statement, misunderstanding of questions, etc.).

Testimony Organization

Develop a logical structure for testimony that follows one of these effective patterns:

- **Chronological narrative**: Organizing testimony in time sequence
- **Topical framework**: Addressing distinct subject areas sequentially
- **Spatial progression**: Describing events based on physical locations
- **Problem-solution format**: Presenting issues and their resolutions

Question Anticipation and Response Practice

Prepare witnesses for the types of questions they will face:

- **Open-ended narrative questions**: "What happened next?"
- **Specific fact questions**: "What time did you arrive?"
- **Perception questions**: "What could you see from your position?"

- **Identification questions**: "Do you see that person in the courtroom today?"
- **Sensory questions**: "What did you hear/smell/feel?"

Practice responses using actual questions planned for direct examination, focusing on clarity, completeness, and brevity.

SPECIALIZED WITNESS PREPARATION

Expert Witness Preparation

Expert witnesses require specialized preparation:

- **Qualification development**: Create a comprehensive presentation of credentials
- **Opinion foundation**: Establish clear basis for expert conclusions
- **Methodology explanation**: Prepare accessible explanations of technical processes
- **Visual aids**: Develop demonstrative exhibits that simplify complex concepts
- **Terminology translation**: Practice explaining technical concepts in layperson's terms
- **Anticipatory critique**: Prepare for challenges to methodology, bias, and alternative explanations

Vulnerable Witness Preparation

Witnesses with special needs require tailored approaches:

- **Child witnesses**: Use age-appropriate language, consider comfort objects, prepare for developmental limitations
- **Elderly witnesses**: Account for fatigue, potential hearing issues, and memory challenges
- **Witnesses with disabilities**: Address accommodation needs and communication adaptations
- **Traumatized witnesses**: Implement trauma-informed approaches, develop coping strategies for emotional responses

Character Witnesses

Character witnesses require specific guidance:

- **Concrete examples**: Prepare specific instances that illustrate character traits
- **Relationship foundation**: Establish depth and duration of relationship with defendant
- **Opinion limitations**: Clarify permissible scope of character opinions
- **Avoiding exaggeration**: Emphasize realistic assessment over hyperbole

CREDIBILITY ENHANCEMENT STRATEGIES

Addressing Witness Vulnerabilities

Prepare witnesses to handle credibility challenges by:

- **Acknowledging inconsistencies**: Practice straightforward acknowledgment of prior inconsistent statements with explanations
- **Addressing bias**: Develop honest responses about relationships or interests that might suggest bias
- **Criminal history**: Prepare for questions about prior convictions with forthright, brief responses
- **Memory limitations**: Practice articulating the basis for remembering certain details while forgetting others

Demeanor Coaching

Help witnesses project credibility through:

- **Eye contact**: Maintain appropriate eye contact with the questioner and jury
- **Posture**: Sit upright but relaxed, leaning slightly forward when appropriate
- **Voice modulation**: Vary tone to emphasize key points without appearing rehearsed
- **Emotional management**: Express genuine emotion when appropriate while maintaining composure

TRIAL SIMULATION

Mock Direct Examination

Conduct full mock examinations that:

- Use actual planned questions

- Take place in a setting resembling a courtroom
- Include interruptions for objections
- Are recorded for review when appropriate

Feedback and Refinement

Provide constructive feedback focused on:

- Answer clarity and brevity
- Nonverbal communication
- Technical accuracy
- Emotional appropriateness
- Narrative coherence

DAY-OF-TESTIMONY PREPARATION

Final Review Session

Conduct a brief final preparation session:

- Review key testimony points
- Refresh on important dates, times, and sequences
- Address last-minute concerns
- Reinforce confidence

Logistics Preparation

Ensure witnesses are prepared for practical matters:

- Arrival time and location
- Security procedures
- Waiting procedures
- Dress code recommendations

- Personal comfort (water, medication, etc.)

Thorough witness preparation strengthens direct examination by ensuring witnesses can effectively communicate their testimony while maintaining credibility. The investment of time in preparation pays dividends in the quality and impact of testimony presented to the factfinder.

Remember that the goal of witness preparation is not to script testimony but to empower witnesses to tell their truthful accounts effectively within the constraints of the courtroom environment. A well-prepared witness appears confident and credible without seeming rehearsed—striking the delicate balance that maximizes testimonial impact.

The Mechanics of Offering an Item as an Exhibit

1. Have the item marked for identification
2. Show the item to opposing counsel
3. Ask Court's permission to approach the witness
4. Show the exhibit to the witness
5. Lay the foundation for the exhibit
6. Offer the exhibit into evidence
7. Have clerk mark the exhibit as full
8. Publish the exhibit to the jury if appropriate or have witness testify with exhibit as an aid

Exhibits, Foundations and Predicate Questions

HANDLING EXHIBITS

The effective presentation of exhibits can make the difference between a confusing collection of evidence and a compelling narrative that persuades the factfinder. This section covers the practical aspects of marking, introducing, and publishing exhibits in Connecticut courts.

Marking Exhibits

Exhibit marking establishes the foundation for all subsequent references to physical evidence. In Connecticut courts, each exhibit receives a unique identifier that distinguishes it throughout the proceedings. The court clerk typically assigns numbers to prosecution/plaintiff exhibits and letters to defense exhibits, though practices may vary by courthouse. Some judges prefer that all potential exhibits be marked before trial during the pretrial conference, while others allow marking as the trial progresses.

When requesting an exhibit be marked, use precise language: "Your Honor, may I have this document marked as State's Exhibit 1?" Avoid unnecessarily verbose language such as "previously marked" – if an item is marked, it has necessarily been marked previously. Such redundant language appears pretentious and wastes the court's time.

Always maintain a detailed exhibit list that includes the exhibit number/letter, a brief description, the witness through whom it was identified, and its status (marked for identification, admitted as full exhibit, or denied admission). This running list proves invaluable during closing arguments and for preserving the record on appeal.

Laying Foundation and Introduction

Before an exhibit can be admitted into evidence, you must establish its foundation through witness testimony. The specific foundational requirements vary depending on the type of evidence (see Chapter 3 for detailed foundation requirements for different evidence types), but the general procedure remains consistent.

Begin by approaching the witness with the marked exhibit: "Your Honor, may I approach the witness?" Then show the exhibit to opposing counsel before handing it to the witness. This common courtesy prevents objections and allows counsel to review what the witness will see.

After handing the exhibit to the witness, establish foundation through a series of questions designed to meet the authentication requirements for that type of evidence. For example, with a photograph:

"Ms. Jones, I'm showing you what has been marked as State's Exhibit 2. Do you recognize what this depicts?"

"Yes, it shows the intersection of Main and Elm Streets."

"Are you familiar with that location?"

"Yes, I pass through it daily on my way to work."

"Was this how the intersection appeared on March 15, 2024, the date of the incident?"

"Yes, it looks just as it did that day."

"Does this photograph fairly and accurately represent the intersection as it appeared on that date?"

"Yes, it does."

Once foundation is established, move for admission: "Your Honor, I offer State's Exhibit 2 as a full exhibit." This phrasing signals to the court that you are requesting the exhibit be admitted into evidence, not merely marked for identification.

If opposing counsel objects, be prepared to articulate the legal basis for admissibility, citing the relevant section of the Connecticut Code of Evidence. If the court admits the exhibit, the clerk will mark it as a "full exhibit," changing its status from identification to evidence.

Publishing Exhibits

Once an exhibit is admitted as a full exhibit, you may request permission to publish it to the jury: "Your Honor, I request permission to publish State's Exhibit 2 to the jury." Publishing means allowing the jurors to view the exhibit, either by passing the physical item among them or by displaying it through courtroom technology.

Modern Connecticut courtrooms increasingly feature digital display systems that allow simultaneous viewing of exhibits on monitors positioned throughout the courtroom. When available, these systems dramatically enhance juror engagement with the evidence. When using digital display systems, familiarize yourself with the equipment before trial begins. Nothing undermines your credibility faster than fumbling with technology while the jury waits.

For physical exhibits that will be handed to jurors, establish ground rules with the court beforehand. Some judges prefer that jurors not discuss exhibits while reviewing them, while others allow quiet consultation. Follow the court's protocol for handling sensitive or dangerous exhibits—the clerk or court officer may need to maintain control of certain items.

When publishing exhibits during witness testimony, incorporate the exhibit into your questioning to maximize its impact:

"Ms. Jones, looking at State's Exhibit 2 now before the jury, could you please point out where your vehicle was located at the time of impact?"

Use the exhibit to guide the witness's testimony, helping the jury understand complex facts or spatial relationships that might otherwise be difficult to visualize. When finished with an exhibit, explicitly state that you have no further questions about it, which signals to the court and jury that you are moving to a new topic.

Effective Exhibit Management Techniques

Preparation is paramount in exhibit management. Create an exhibit notebook with tabs for each anticipated exhibit, including copies of the exhibits and notes about the witnesses through whom each will be introduced. Prepare exhibit labels in advance to streamline the marking process.

Consider the order of introduction carefully. Strategic sequencing of exhibits can build a narrative that enhances comprehension and retention. When presenting multiple related exhibits, establish a complete foundation for each rather than attempting to introduce them as a group.

For large or complex document exhibits, consider using excerpts or summaries with the court's permission under Connecticut Code of Evidence § 10-5. This approach helps focus the jury's attention on relevant portions without overwhelming them with extraneous material.

When handling physical evidence, maintain the chain of custody meticulously. Each transfer of possession should be documented, and witnesses should be prepared to testify about their handling of the item. Use gloves when appropriate to preserve fingerprints or other trace evidence.

Digital and Demonstrative Exhibits

Digital evidence presents unique challenges and opportunities. Electronic records, social media content, text messages, and similar material must be authenticated like any other evidence, but may require technical expertise to establish foundation properly. Work closely with your expert witnesses to develop clear, accessible explanations of digital evidence collection and preservation.

Demonstrative aids that are not themselves evidence (such as charts summarizing admitted evidence or illustrations clarifying testimony) need not be formally admitted but still require court approval before presentation. The opposing party has the right to review such aids before they are shown to the jury.

When creating demonstrative exhibits, prioritize clarity over complexity. Use consistent color schemes, clear labels, and appropriate scale. Text should be large enough to read from the jury box, and visual elements should be simple enough to comprehend quickly.

Handling Objections to Exhibits

Anticipate potential objections to each exhibit and prepare responses grounded in the Connecticut Code of Evidence. Common objections include relevance (§ 4-1), authentication (§ 9-1), hearsay (§ 8-1), best evidence (§ 10-1), and prejudice outweighing probative value (§ 4-3).

If opposing counsel objects to an exhibit, listen carefully to the specific basis of the objection. Respond directly to that basis rather than offering a generalized argument for admissibility. If the court sustains the objection, consider whether you can cure the defect through additional foundation questions or by limiting the scope of the exhibit.

For exhibits excluded from evidence, make an offer of proof to preserve the issue for appeal. Request permission to approach the bench or ask for the jury to be excused, then state for the record what the exhibit would have shown and why it is relevant and admissible.

Final Considerations

At the conclusion of your case, confirm with the clerk which exhibits have been admitted as full exhibits and which remain marked for identification only. This verification ensures that only properly admitted exhibits go to the jury room during deliberations.

Remember that effective exhibit management is both a science and an art. The technical requirements of authentication and admission must be met, but the true value of exhibits lies in how they enhance the jury's understanding of your case theory. Used skillfully, exhibits transform abstract testimony into concrete reality, creating lasting impressions that can determine the outcome of your case.

The following are the necessary foundations for the admission of certain types of exhibits. The foundation rules are governed by the Connecticut Rules of Evidence.

General Foundations - be able to address each one of these issues for anything you wish to admit

Relevance: Ensure that the exhibit is directly relevant to the issues at hand in the case. It should provide information or visual evidence that is material to the facts in dispute or supports your legal arguments.

Authenticity: Establish the authenticity and integrity of the exhibit. You may need to prove its origin, chain of custody, and that it has not been tampered with or altered. This can be achieved through witness testimony, documentation, or expert analysis, depending on the nature of the exhibit.

Admissibility: Understand the rules of evidence in the specific court where your case is being heard. Determine if there are any specific requirements for admitting exhibits, such as hearsay exceptions or authentication standards. Ensure that your exhibit meets these requirements to be considered admissible.

Legal Basis: Clearly articulate the legal basis for introducing the exhibit. Explain how it relates to the applicable laws, regulations, or legal precedents. Provide a persuasive argument for why the exhibit should be considered in the court's decision-making process.

Organization: Present the exhibit in a well-organized manner. Use appropriate labeling, numbering, or tagging to make it easy for the court, opposing counsel, and witnesses to follow and refer to the exhibit during proceedings. Prepare a summary or index if necessary.

Clarity and Readability: Make sure the exhibit is clear, legible, and easily understandable. If it contains text, ensure that it is readable from a reasonable distance. Consider using appropriate fonts, font sizes, colors, or enlargements if needed. Graphs, charts, or diagrams should be clear and well-labeled.

Demonstrative Aids: Consider using demonstrative aids to enhance the presentation of your exhibit. This may include enlargements, slideshows, video presentations, or interactive displays. Visual aids can help simplify complex information and make it more accessible to the court and the jury, if applicable.

Presentation Technique: Develop an effective presentation strategy for your exhibit. Consider how you will introduce it, explain its relevance, and guide the court through the content. Prepare any necessary verbal explanations or arguments to accompany the exhibit and enhance its impact.

Pretrial Preparation: Be well-prepared before presenting the exhibit in court. Familiarize yourself with its content, anticipate potential challenges or objections, and practice your presentation. This will help you confidently navigate through the exhibit during the proceedings.

Adapting to Court Procedures: Understand the specific procedures and protocols of the court where your case is being heard. Be prepared to follow the court's rules regarding the timing, manner of presentation, and any additional requirements for exhibits. Respect the court's instructions and seek clarification if needed.

Tangible Objects

1. Exhibit is relevant
2. Exhibit can be identified visibly or through other senses
3. Witness recognizes the exhibit
4. Witness knows what the exhibit looked like on the relevant date
5. Exhibit is in the same or substantially the same condition now as it was when the witness saw it on the relevant date

Tangible Objects (Chain of Custody)

When an object cannot be uniquely identified through the senses, a chain of custody must be established to demonstrate it is the same object that was previously found.

There are 2 methods to show a chain of custody:

1. Show that the exhibit has been in one or more persons' continuous and exclusive and secure care, custody or control at all times
2. Show that the exhibit was in a uniquely marked, sealed, tamper-proof container at all times

Cell Phone (and the data inside the cell phone)

1. The cell phone and/or data is relevant to your case.
2. Cell phone is in its original state OR the data that has been obtained is in its original state.
3. Establish the authenticity of the cell phone.
4. Chain of custody for the cell phone is clean.
5. Be prepared to provide instructions to access specific information or files on the phone, if necessary.

Social Media Post

1. The social media post is relevant.
2. Note the date and time the social media post was created.
3. Preserve the digital evidence in its original form.
4. Authenticate the social media post to establish its genuineness. There are a few methods to consider:

a. Gather information about the user who posted the content.

b. If possible, collect metadata associated with the social media post.

c. A witness who can testify to the authenticity of the social media post.

5. Be aware of potential hearsay issues related to social media posts.
6. Anticipate potential objections from the opposing party regarding the authenticity, relevance, or hearsay nature of the social media post.

Photographs

1. Image is relevant.
2. Witness is familiar with the scene portrayed in the image.
3. Witness was familiar with the scene at the relevant date and time.
4. Image is a "fair and accurate" representation of the scene.

Diagrams, Models or Maps

1. Diagram is relevant.
2. Witness is familiar with the scene at the relevant time.
3. Drawing is useful in helping the witness explain his or her testimony.
4. Drawing is reasonably accurate.

Drawings by Witnesses

1. Drawing is relevant.
2. Witness is familiar with the scene at the relevant time.
3. Drawing is useful in helping the witness explain his or her testimony.
4. Drawing is reasonably accurate.

General Videotapes

1. Recording is relevant.
2. Recording machine was in proper working order.
3. Recording machine can accurately record and reproduce video/audio.
4. Officer does/does not have control of the recording mechanism.
5. Officer was trained or otherwise knowledgeable in the use of the recording device and the method to preserve recording.
6. Officer saw/heard what was being said.
7. Officer reviewed the recording to confirm it was accurate.
8. Medium was then sealed and labeled, or placed in a secure place to guard against tampering.
9. Officer recognizes the persons, things, or voices on the medium and can identify them.

Bodycam Footage

1. Recording is relevant.
2. Provide authentication via recording officer.

3. Confirm recording accurately represents a true and unaltered record of the events.
4. Confirm that the presented body camera footage is the complete and unedited recording of the incident.
    a. If necessary, explain any redactions or edits made to the video and their purpose.
5. Ensure there were no unauthorized access or alterations to the footage.
6. Remember: research whether the recording officer followed all applicable laws, departmental policies, and regulations regarding the use of body cameras and the handling of recorded footage.

Computer Generated Graphics

1. Exhibit is relevant.
2. The data used in the creation of the exhibit is accurate.
3. The data was accurately transferred into the computer.
4. The computer program used to create the graphic is based on valid and accepted scientific methodology.
5. The graphic accurately reflects the witness' opinion of how the event happened.
6. The graphic will help the jury understand the witness' testimony.

Signed Documents

There are a variety of ways to prove that a signature on a document was made by the person by whose signature it purports to be. There are 4 methods:

1. Call a witness who saw the person sign the document.
2. Call a witness who is familiar with the signature of the signer to authenticate.
3. Call the signer to authenticate.
4. Call a handwriting expert who can testify as an expert that the signatures match.

Business Records[17]

1. The record is relevant.
2. The record is a memorandum, report or record.
3. The witness is the custodian of the records or the creator of the record.
4. The record was made by a person with knowledge of the facts or was made with information transmitted from a person with knowledge of the facts.
5. The record was made at or near the time of the acts, events, condition, opinions, or diagnosis appearing in it.
6. The record was made in the regular practice of that business activity.
7. The record was kept in the normal course of business.

---

[17] Connecticut Rule of Evidence, 8-3(7)

Recorded Recollections

1. Exhibit is relevant.
2. The witness has no full or accurate present recollection of the facts or statements contained in the document.
3. The witness had firsthand knowledge of the facts at the time they occurred.
4. The witness made a record of the facts at the time or near the time the facts occurred.
5. The record was accurate and complete when made.
6. The record is in the same condition now as when made.

Certified Copies

Certified copies of public records are self-authenticating. They need only be marked and offered into evidence.

FOUNDATION QUESTIONS FOR DIFFERENT WITNESS TYPES

LAW ENFORCEMENT WITNESSES

Foundation for Patrol Officer

- What is your name and current occupation?
- How long have you been employed as a police officer?
- What training did you receive to become a police officer?
- What specialized training have you received since becoming a police officer?
- Were you on duty on [relevant date]?
- What shift were you working that day?
- Were you dispatched to or did you respond to [relevant location]?
- What time did you arrive at the scene?
- What did you observe upon arrival?
- Did you document your observations? How?
- Were you wearing a body camera? Was it functioning properly?
- Did you prepare a police report related to this incident?
- When did you prepare this report?
- Did you rely on anything to refresh your recollection while preparing the report?

Foundation for Detective

- What is your name and current occupation?

- How long have you been a detective?
- Did you serve as a patrol officer before becoming a detective?
- What specialized training have you received as a detective?
- Were you assigned to investigate the case involving [defendant/incident]?
- When were you assigned to this case?
- What investigative steps did you take during your investigation?
- Did you personally visit the crime scene? When?
- Did you review evidence collected by other officers?
- Did you interview any witnesses? If so, whom did you interview?
- Did you interview the defendant? When and where?
- Did you prepare reports documenting your investigation?
- When did you prepare these reports?

MEDICAL WITNESSES

Foundation for Treating Physician

- What is your name and occupation?
- Where are you currently employed?
- What is your educational background?
- Are you licensed to practice medicine in Connecticut?
- What board certifications do you hold, if any?
- How long have you been practicing medicine?

- Do you have any particular areas of specialization or expertise?
- Did you provide medical treatment to [victim/witness] on [date]?
- Where did this treatment take place?
- What was the purpose of your examination/treatment?
- Did you create medical records documenting your examination and treatment?
- Were these records created in the ordinary course of your medical practice?
- Were these records created at or near the time of your examination and treatment?

Foundation for Medical Examiner

- What is your name and occupation?
- How long have you been a medical examiner?
- What education, training, and experience do you have in forensic pathology?
- Are you licensed to practice medicine in Connecticut?
- Are you board certified in forensic pathology?
- Approximately how many autopsies have you performed in your career?
- Did you perform an autopsy on [victim] on [date]?
- Where did you perform this autopsy?
- What was the purpose of conducting this autopsy?
- Did you prepare a report documenting your findings?
- When did you prepare this report?

- Did you determine a cause of death?
- Did you determine a manner of death?

LAY WITNESSES

Foundation for Eyewitness

- What is your name?
- Where do you live? (general area only if appropriate)
- What is your occupation?
- Were you present at [location] on [date]?
- Why were you at that location?
- What time did you arrive?
- How long were you there?
- Did anything unusual happen while you were there?
- Did you observe [relevant event/incident]?
- From where were you observing?
- What was the lighting like?
- Were there any obstructions to your view?
- How far away were you from what you observed?
- Had you consumed any alcohol or drugs that day?
- Do you wear corrective lenses? Were you wearing them at that time?
- Did you know any of the people involved prior to this incident?

Foundation for Character Witness

- What is your name?

- What is your occupation?
- Do you know [defendant/witness]?
- How long have you known him/her?
- What is the nature of your relationship?
- How frequently do you see or interact with him/her?
- In what settings or contexts do you typically interact?
- Are you familiar with [defendant/witness]'s reputation in the community?
- How have you become aware of his/her reputation?
- Are you aware of his/her reputation for [truthfulness/peacefulness/relevant trait]?

TECHNOLOGY/DIGITAL EVIDENCE WITNESSES

Foundation for Digital Forensic Examiner

- What is your name and occupation?
- What is your educational background?
- What specialized training have you received in digital forensics?
- What certifications do you hold in digital forensics?
- How long have you worked in digital forensics?
- Approximately how many digital forensic examinations have you conducted?
- Were you asked to examine [digital device] in this case?
- When did you receive this device?
- What condition was the device in when you received it?
- What steps did you take to preserve the data on the device?

- What forensic tools did you use to examine the device?
- Did you document your examination process?
- Did you prepare a report of your findings?

Foundation for Surveillance Video/Photo Authentication

- What is your name and occupation?
- Were you responsible for [obtaining/maintaining] the surveillance system at [location]?
- How long have you worked with this surveillance system?
- Was the surveillance system functioning properly on [relevant date]?
- How do you know it was functioning properly?
- Does the surveillance system record date and time information?
- Is the date and time information accurate? How do you know?
- Did you retrieve video footage from [date, time, location]?
- How did you retrieve this footage?
- Has the footage been altered or edited in any way?
- How was the footage preserved after retrieval?

HANDLING HOSTILE WITNESSES ON DIRECT EXAMINATION

Identifying a Potentially Hostile Witness

A hostile witness is one who demonstrates antagonism or unwillingness to cooperate with the examining party. These witnesses may be crucial to your case despite their hostility. Indicators include:

1. Witness has a relationship with the opposing party
2. Witness has previously made inconsistent statements
3. Witness has expressed reluctance to testify
4. Witness has failed to appear for pre-trial interviews
5. Witness has changed their story after speaking with opposing counsel

Pre-Trial Preparation for Potentially Hostile Witnesses

Before examining a potentially hostile witness, consider these preparatory steps:

1. **Document prior statements** - Obtain all written statements, recordings, or reports containing the witness's prior statements
2. **Prepare impeachment materials** - Have readily available any documents you may need to refresh recollection or impeach
3. **Consider declaration as hostile** - Determine whether you will request the court declare the witness hostile at the outset or wait until hostility manifests

4. **Plan limited questioning** - Prepare concise, specific questions focused on essential information
5. **Anticipate evasion** - Develop follow-up questions that address potential evasive responses

PROCEDURAL STEPS FOR HANDLING A HOSTILE WITNESS

Declaration of Hostility

When a witness demonstrates hostility on the stand, you may request the court to declare the witness hostile:

"Your Honor, may I approach the bench? [At sidebar] I request that [witness] be declared a hostile witness pursuant to Connecticut Rule of Evidence 6-8, as the witness is exhibiting clear antagonism toward the examination and has [specific behaviors demonstrating hostility]."

Techniques for Examining Hostile Witnesses

Once a witness is declared hostile, you may employ these techniques:

1. **Leading questions** - After the court declares the witness hostile, you may use leading questions to control the testimony
2. **Short, specific questions** - Limit each question to a single fact
3. **Document-based questioning** - Anchor questions in documented evidence

4. **Avoid argumentative tone** - Maintain professional demeanor regardless of the witness's attitude
5. **Lock in testimony** - Confirm important points before moving to new topics

STRATEGIC APPROACHES TO COMMON HOSTILE WITNESS BEHAVIORS

Memory Failures

When a witness claims not to remember facts they previously provided:

1. **Refresh recollection** - "Would reviewing [document] help refresh your recollection about [topic]?"
2. **Document timeline** - "You spoke to Detective Smith on [date], correct? That was [X] days after the incident, correct?"
3. **Context questions** - "Do you recall where you were when you gave this statement to the police?"

Contradictions to Prior Statements

When a witness contradicts their prior statements:

1. **Confirm current testimony** - "So your testimony today is [restate current testimony], is that correct?"
2. **Establish prior statement** - "Do you recall giving a statement to [person] on [date]?"
3. **Present the contradiction** - "I'm going to show you what has been marked as State's Exhibit #3. Is that your

signature on the bottom of the page? Please read the highlighted portion to yourself. Did you make that statement on [date]?"

Evasive Answers

When a witness provides non-responsive or evasive answers:

1. **Politely redirect** - "I appreciate that information, but my question was specifically about [restate question]."
2. **Request intervention** - "Your Honor, I ask that the witness be directed to answer the specific question asked."
3. **Simplify the question** - Break complex questions into simpler components.

Overtly Antagonistic Behavior

When a witness becomes openly hostile or argumentative:

1. **Maintain composure** - Never respond with matching hostility
2. **Document the behavior** - Let the record reflect the witness's demeanor
3. **Pivot to documented evidence** - Move away from opinion or recollection to documented facts
4. **Consider limiting questioning** - Focus only on essential points and move on

Completion of Testimony

After examining a hostile witness, consider these steps:

1. **Summarize key points** - Reiterate the important facts established during questioning
2. **Request to recall if needed** - If the witness's testimony raises new issues requiring further investigation, request the right to recall the witness
3. **Document preservation** - Ensure all documents used during the examination are properly marked and preserved for the record

Legal Framework for Hostile Witness Examination

Connecticut Rule of Evidence 6-8(b) provides: "Leading questions shall not be used on the direct or redirect examination of a witness, except that the court may permit leading questions, in its discretion, in circumstances such as, but not limited to, the following: (1) when a party calls a hostile witness or a witness identified with an adverse party..."

This rule gives the court discretion to allow leading questions when a witness is declared hostile. The determination of hostility is within the court's discretion, but generally requires a showing that the witness's interests are aligned with the opposing party or that the witness demonstrates clear antagonism toward the examining party.

Remember that examining a hostile witness effectively requires balancing the need to obtain crucial testimony against the risk of alienating the jury with aggressive questioning. Maintaining professional composure while methodically presenting the witness with documented facts is typically the most effective approach.

CHAPTER 4

CROSS EXAMINATION

Introduction by Jim Ruane

Natura inest in mentibus nortris insatiablibis quaedam cupiditas ver vivendi.

"Nature has planted in our minds an insatiable longing to see the truth."

M. Tullius Cicero 63 B.C.

Tusculan Disputations

"Cross examination is beyond any doubt the greatest legal engine ever invented for the discovery of truth."

5 J. Wigmore, Evidence (Chadbourn Rev. 1974)

Sec. 1367, p. 32

Each method or style of cross-examination has its strengths and weaknesses, and the choice of which to use will depend on the specific case, the witness, and the cross-examiner's personal style and preferences. Often, a combination of methods will be employed to create an effective cross-examination strategy. The ultimate goal is to challenge the witness's credibility and the reliability of their testimony in a manner that best serves the case and persuades the judge or jury.

Always remember: The purpose of cross examination is to do one of 4 things:

1. Expose favorable testimony
2. Repeat favorable testimony
3. Demonstrate bias, or

4. Impeach credibility

There are several methods or styles of cross-examination that attorneys may use depending on their goals, the specific case, and the witness. Some common methods and styles include:

The Chapter Method: As popularized by Larry Posner and Roger Dodd,[18] this method involves organizing questions into "chapters" or categories based on different aspects of the witness's testimony. It allows for a structured and coherent presentation, making it easier for the judge or jury to follow the line of questioning.

Key features of the Chapter method include:

- **Organization:** The cross-examiner plans and organizes questions in advance, dividing them into specific themes or topics. This approach helps to maintain a clear line of questioning and avoid confusion or repetition.
- **Coherence:** By addressing one topic at a time, the Chapter Method allows the cross-examiner to build a coherent narrative that highlights inconsistencies or weaknesses in the witness's testimony.
- **Flexibility:** Although the Chapter Method is structured, it allows the cross-examiner to adapt their line of questioning as new information emerges during the examination.

---

[18] Dodd, Roger and Pozner, Larry, "Cross-Examination: Science and Techniques," Lexis-Nexis (1993)

<u>The "Look Good" Method:</u> This method focuses on the cross-examiner's demeanor and appearance, aiming to create a favorable impression on the judge or jury. The cross-examiner maintains a confident and professional demeanor, controls the pace of questioning, and prepares thoroughly to avoid being caught off-guard. This model was created and perfected by renowned Criminal Trial Lawyer Terry MacCarthy, and when combined with the chapter method, is this author's preferred method of cross examination.

Key features of the <u>"Look Good"</u> method include:

- **Demeanor:** The cross-examiner maintains a professional and confident demeanor throughout the examination, using body language, tone of voice and facial expressions to convey authority and credibility. This helps establish rapport with the judge or jury and makes the cross-examiner appear more trustworthy.
- **Control:** The "Look Good" Method emphasizes the importance of maintaining control over the cross-examination process. This includes controlling the pace of questioning, the order of topics, and the manner in which questions are asked. By maintaining control, the cross-examiner can guide the examination in a way that best serves their case.
- **Preparation:** A key aspect of the "Look Good" Method is thorough preparation, which helps the cross-examiner anticipate potential issues and avoid being caught off-guard. This includes researching the witness's

background, reviewing their testimony, and preparing questions that address any inconsistencies or weaknesses.

<u>**The Socratic Method:**</u> This method involves asking a series of probing questions designed to reveal inconsistencies, contradictions, or weaknesses in the witness's testimony. The cross-examiner may use hypothetical scenarios, analogies, or comparisons to challenge the witness's statements.

Key features of the <u>Socratic</u> method include:

- **Open-ended questions:** The cross-examiner uses open-ended questions that require the witness to explain, clarify, or elaborate on their testimony. By asking questions that cannot be answered with a simple "yes" or "no," the cross-examiner encourages the witness to provide more information, which can be used to identify inconsistencies or contradictions.
- **Logical reasoning:** The Socratic Method relies on logical reasoning to challenge the witness's testimony. The cross-examiner may use hypothetical scenarios, analogies, or comparisons to test the validity of the witness's statements and expose flaws in their reasoning or understanding of the facts. By revealing gaps in the witness's logic, the cross-examiner can weaken the credibility of their testimony.
- **Incremental revelations:** The Socratic Method involves gradually leading the witness to reveal inconsistencies or

contradictions through a series of seemingly unrelated or innocuous questions. The cross-examiner skillfully guides the witness through a logical progression of questions, allowing the witness to recognize the flaws in their testimony. This approach can be particularly effective in undermining a witness's confidence, as they may not initially realize the purpose behind the line of questioning.

The Impeachment Method: This method seeks to undermine the credibility of a witness by exposing prior inconsistent statements, biases, or conflicts of interest. This can include presenting contradictory evidence, highlighting prior convictions, or demonstrating a witness's motive to lie.

The key features of the Impeachment method of cross-examination include:

- **Prior inconsistent statements:** The cross-examiner highlights any statements the witness has made in the past that contradict their current testimony. This can involve presenting documentary evidence, such as written statements, emails, or text messages, or referring to previous oral statements made during depositions or interviews. Demonstrating inconsistencies in the witness's account can cast doubt on the reliability of their testimony.
- **Bias or conflicts of interest:** The cross-examiner seeks to expose any biases or conflicts of interest that may impact the witness's credibility or motivation for testifying. This

can include personal or financial relationships with parties involved in the case, a history of animosity toward the defendant, or any other factors that may suggest the witness has a reason to be untruthful or biased in their testimony.

- **Prior convictions or misconduct:** The cross-examiner may introduce evidence of the witness's prior criminal convictions or misconduct to question their credibility and character. Depending on the jurisdiction, rules of evidence, and the nature of the prior convictions, this information can be used to suggest that the witness is less trustworthy or has a propensity for dishonesty.

The Confrontational Method: This aggressive style of cross-examination involves directly challenging the witness's testimony, often through the use of leading questions, sarcasm, or strong language. This method can be effective in rattling or intimidating a witness but may also backfire if it alienates the judge or jury. It is essential for the cross-examiner to strike the right balance and not appear overly aggressive or disrespectful.

The key features of the Confrontational method of cross-examination include:

- **Leading questions:** The cross-examiner uses leading questions that suggest the desired answer or contain the information they want the witness to confirm. This technique can be effective in guiding the witness towards a particular point, as well as in controlling the narrative and exposing inconsistencies or weaknesses in their testimony.

- **Aggressive demeanor:** The cross-examiner adopts an assertive and confrontational demeanor, using strong language, sarcasm, or even interruptions to challenge the witness's statements. This approach can unsettle the witness, making them more likely to make mistakes, reveal inconsistencies, or appear less credible to the judge or jury.
- **Rapid-fire questioning:** The cross-examiner may employ rapid-fire questioning, quickly moving from one topic to another or asking a series of short, pointed questions in rapid succession. This technique can be disorienting for the witness, making it more difficult for them to maintain their composure and provide consistent, coherent answers.

The Sympathetic Method: This method involves building rapport with the witness by adopting a more empathetic and understanding approach. The cross-examiner may use open-ended questions and a friendly demeanor to encourage the witness to open up and reveal more information, potentially leading to contradictions or admissions that weaken their testimony.

The key features of the Sympathetic method of cross-examination include:

- **Friendly demeanor:** The cross-examiner maintains a friendly and non-threatening demeanor, using a calm and respectful tone of voice, as well as open and inviting body language. This approach helps put the witness at ease and makes them more likely to share information or let their guard down during the questioning.
- **Open-ended questions:** The cross-examiner uses open-ended questions that encourage the witness to provide more detailed answers or elaborate on their testimony. By allowing the witness to speak freely, the cross-examiner may uncover inconsistencies, contradictions, or additional information that can be used to challenge the witness's testimony.
- **Establishing common ground:** The cross-examiner seeks to establish common ground with the witness, demonstrating empathy and understanding for their situation or experiences. This may involve acknowledging the witness's feelings, showing genuine interest in their perspective, or expressing shared values. By building rapport with the witness, the cross-examiner can create a sense of trust and connection, making the witness more likely to reveal critical information.

<u>The Looping Method:</u> In this method, the cross-examiner listens carefully to the witness's answers and "loops" back to key points by incorporating them into subsequent questions. This technique helps reinforce important facts, expose inconsistencies, and keep the witness focused on specific details.

The key features of the Looping Method of cross-examination include:

- **Active listening:** The cross-examiner listens carefully to the witness's answers, identifying key points, inconsistencies, or vulnerabilities that can be used to challenge their testimony. Active listening is essential for the Looping Method, as it enables the cross-examiner to craft questions that build on the witness's previous responses.
- **Reinforcing key points:** The cross-examiner "loops" back to important facts or statements by incorporating them into follow-up questions. This repetition serves to emphasize key points to the judge or jury, ensuring that they remember the most critical aspects of the witness's testimony. Looping can also help the cross-examiner establish a clear and coherent narrative that connects different parts of the witness's testimony.
- **Exposing inconsistencies:** By looping back to previous statements, the cross-examiner can highlight any inconsistencies or contradictions in the witness's testimony. If a witness provides conflicting information or changes their story, the cross-examiner can use the Looping Method to expose these inconsistencies and cast doubt on the witness's credibility.

TRANSITIONING BETWEEN CROSS-EXAMINATION TOPICS

Effective cross-examination requires not only well-crafted questions but also strategic transitions between different topic areas. Smooth transitions maintain the flow of examination, prevent witness recovery time, and create a coherent narrative for the jury. The following techniques will help you navigate between topics while maintaining control of your cross-examination.

THE IMPORTANCE OF TRANSITIONS

Transitions serve several critical functions during cross-examination:

1. **Maintaining narrative coherence** - Helps the jury follow your theory of the case
2. **Preventing witness preparation** - Reduces the witness's ability to anticipate your next line of questioning
3. **Controlling pace and emphasis** - Allows you to highlight important points and de-emphasize others
4. **Creating psychological momentum** - Builds pressure on difficult witnesses through controlled progression
5. **Preserving the record** - Creates clear topical separations for appellate review

TRANSITION TECHNIQUES

The Signpost Transition

The signpost explicitly signals to the judge, jury, and witness that you are changing topics. This approach works well when you want to emphasize a shift to an important new area.

Example: "Now, Officer Johnson, I'd like to turn to what happened after you arrived at the scene."

When to use:

- When moving to a critical topic that requires jury attention
- When transitioning to impeachment material
- When the record needs absolute clarity about topical shifts

The Bridge Transition

The bridge transition connects two topics through a logical relationship, creating continuity while shifting focus.

Example: "You've testified that you observed my client from 50 feet away. During this observation, what was the lighting like in the area?"

When to use:

- When topics are naturally related
- When building a cumulative case
- When you want the jury to connect disparate facts

The Loop-Back Transition

This technique references earlier testimony before moving to a new area, reinforcing key points while transitioning.

Example: "You've told us three times that you're certain about the identification. Let's talk about the lineup procedure that was used..."

When to use:

- When reinforcing contradictions
- When building on earlier admissions
- When emphasizing a witness's overconfidence

The Contrast Transition

The contrast transition highlights a discrepancy by immediately juxtaposing two contradictory topics.

Example: "So in your police report written that night, you described one suspect. But today, over a year later, you're describing two suspects?"

When to use:

- When exposing inconsistencies
- When the contradiction is striking
- When undermining witness credibility

Document Use in Transitions

Documents and exhibits can serve as natural transition points:

"You've testified about what you observed. I'd like to show you what has been marked as Defense Exhibit 3. Do you recognize this document?"

The Silent Transition

Sometimes the most effective transition is no verbal transition at all—simply pausing briefly and beginning a new line of questioning.

Example: [After completing questions about observation conditions, pause, consult notes briefly, then:] "What time did you call for backup?"

When to use:

- When you want to appear conversational
- When surprising the witness
- When you don't want to telegraph importance

STRATEGIC CONSIDERATIONS FOR TRANSITIONS

Topic Sequencing

The order of topics can significantly impact effectiveness. Consider these approaches:

1. **Chronological** - Following the timeline of events
2. **Importance-based** - Starting with or building toward the most critical topics
3. **Confidence-based** - Beginning with areas where the witness must agree with you

4. **Concession-gathering** - Organizing topics to build a pattern of admissions
5. **Scatter pattern** - Deliberately mixing topics to prevent witness preparation

Adjusting to Witness Responses

Be prepared to modify your transitions based on witness behavior:

- **For the cooperative witness** - Use smoother, less pronounced transitions
- **For the evasive witness** - Use more explicit signposting to maintain control
- **For the hostile witness** - Consider more abrupt transitions to prevent preparation
- **For the expert witness** - Use more formal, structured transitions to maintain decorum

COMMON TRANSITION PITFALLS

1. **Telegraphing** - Overly detailed transitions that allow the witness to prepare
2. **Lecture transitions** - Using transitions to argue rather than question
3. **Abrupt shifts** - Changing topics without any connection, confusing the jury
4. **Repetitive patterns** - Using the same transition technique repeatedly, creating predictability

5. **Losing the narrative** - Transitions that obscure rather than clarify your theory of the case

SPECIALIZED CROSS-EXAMINATION APPROACHES

The Funnel Approach

Start with broad, general questions that the witness must agree with, then gradually narrow to specific, damaging points.

The Looping Technique

Incorporate the witness's answers into subsequent questions to lock in key admissions and build upon them.

The Chapter Method with Built-In Transitions

When using the chapter method of cross-examination, integrate transition techniques within your chapter structure:

1. **Internal transitions** - Smooth movements between points within a chapter
2. **Chapter transitions** - More pronounced shifts between major topic areas
3. **Temporal signposts** - "Before we discuss what happened next..." or "Let's go back to when you first arrived..."

Remember that effective cross-examination sequences maintain control through question structure while building toward key points that support your theory of the case. The transition between topics should be deliberate and strategic, not merely an afterthought.

Scope of Cross Examination

"Cross examination… shall be limited to the subject matter of the preceding examination and matters affecting the credibility of the witness, except in the discretion of the court."

Conn. Code Evid. § 6-8(b)

Use of Leading Questions

A leading question is a question that suggests the answer desired by the examiner in accord with the examiner's view of the facts.

State v. McNally, 39 Conn. App. 419, 423 (1995)

"Leading questions shall not be used on the direct or redirect examination of a witness, except that the court may permit leading questions, in its discretion, in circumstances such as, but not limited to the following:

- when a party calls a hostile witness or a witness identified with an adverse party,
- when a witness testifies so as to work a surprise or deceit on the examiner,
- when necessary to develop the witness' testimony, or
- when necessary to establish preliminary matters."

Conn. Code Evid. § 6-8(b)

Impeachment of Your Witness

A party can impeach a witness he calls without showing surprise, hostility or adversity in the witness.

State v. Whelan, 200 Conn. 743 (1986)

QUESTIONS YOU CANNOT ASK IN CROSS EXAMINATION

Whether the testimony of a previous witness is a lie.

State v. Schleifer, 102 Conn. 708, 724 (1925)

The truth of the facts that the witness did not testify to and with which the witness disagrees.

State v. Rogers, 41 Conn. App. 204, 211 (1996)

Areas already covered, have been testified to, and are designed to re-emphasize such testimony.

State v. Gaynor, 182 Conn. 501-509-10 (1980)

Confidential non-privileged information unless the Court finds the information admissible for impeachment.

State v. Pierson, 201 Conn. 211, 225 (1986)

State v. Esposito, 192 Conn. 166, 177-80 (1984)

Questions calling for legal conclusions.

Turner's Appeal, 72 conn. 305, 316 (1899)

Taking or refusing a polygraph.

State v. Porter, 241 Conn. 57 (1997)

Questions that assume facts not in evidence.

State v. Isaacson, 114 Conn. 567, 574 (1932)

Cross-examination from a document not in evidence. General rule: witnesses may not be examined on the contents of a document not in evidence.

Shulman v. Shulman, 150 Conn. 651, 662 (1963)

Exceptions:

Witness has verified the signature on the letter, and examination is of the genuineness of the signature or letter - this constitutes a preliminary matter restricted to the genuineness of the letter, not an examination of its contents.

Shulman, at 658.

Witness has referred to the writing on his direct examination.

Shulman, at 660-61.

Witness has admitted making statements referred to in the document, so there is no need to introduce the document into evidence.

State v. Sullivan, 2 Conn. Cir. Ct. 412, 416 (1964)

Witness has disclaimed all knowledge of the document, and the examination is an attempt to get the witness to identify the document.

Scalora v. Shaughnessy, 151 Conn. 252, 258-59 (1963)

If Witness is an Expert:

Examining attorney has some room to argue for examination of contents of document not in evidence.

Conn. Code Evid. § 7-4

§ 7-4(a) requires disclosure of sufficient factual basis for expert's opinion.

If document or data is the type that an expert may regularly rely on when he forms an opinion, it is possible to argue that the questions are allowable as introducing facts to the expert at trial is permitted by § 7-4(b) without having to introduce entire documen

2 C. McCormick, Evidence (5th Ed. 1999) § 324.3, p. 356

Cross-examiner may frame the question with facts contained about the document not in evidence as a hypothetical question, which is permitted under § 7-4(c) to impeach and test the accuracy of the expert's opinion.

State v. Gaynor, 182 Conn. 501, 510 (1980)

Kirchner v. Yale University, 150 Conn. 623, 629 (1963)

Livingstone v. New Haven, 125 Conn. 123, 127-28 (1939)

Strategies to Avoid Objection Because Document is not in Evidence

Place the document on the counsel table and ask the witness if he/she made that statement. If they have no recollection, use it to refresh recollection.

If the witness admits the statement, the document is not admissible itself under **Conn. Code Evid. § 6-10(c).**

If the witness denies the statement, call the witness to the statement so as to avoid the entire contents of the statement coming in under the rule of completeness.

QUESTIONS YOU CAN ASK IN CROSS EXAMINATION

Bias as to a party

Conn. Code Evid. § 6-5

Implied bias due to relationship.

State v. Greene, 209 Conn. 458, 473 (1988)

State v. Aponte, 249 Conn. 735, 752 (1999)

State v. Oehman, 212 Conn. 325, 331 (1989)

Demeanor.

State v. McLaughlin, 126 Conn. 257, 264 (1939)

Defendant's prior conviction of crime, but only when the prejudicial effect does not "far outweigh" the relevance and materiality of the evidence.

State v. Geyer, 194 Conn. 1, 6-7 (1984)

Acts involving dishonesty not resulting in conviction to attack the witness's credibility, even if the evidence is irrelevant to issue in the case.

State v. Dolphin, 195 Conn. 444, 459 (1985)

Pending criminal charges.

State v. Pittman, 209 Conn. 596, 603 (1989)

State v. Arline, 223 Conn. 52, 60-63 (1992)

Belief in obligation of oath/affirmation.

State v. Jones, 205 Conn. 723, 739 (1988)

N B: Distinguish from religious beliefs that are not proper areas of cross except for during Voir Dire of venireperson.

Sexual misconduct.

Vogel v. Sharpe, 195 conn. 651, 658 (1985)

Income tax fraud to indicate lack of veracity.

State v. Sharpe, 195 Conn. 651, 658 (1985)

Mental competency.

a. Inability to recall/recollect.

   Conn. Code Evid. § 6-3(b)

b. Inability to narrate.

   State v. Boulay, 189 conn. 106, 108 (1983)

c. Incapable of understanding the duty to tell the truth.

   State v. Manning, 162 Conn. 112, 115 (1971)

d. Whether witness is undergoing psychiatric treatment

   Manning v. Michael, 188 Conn. 607, 610-11 (1982)

e. Past mental problems and psychiatric care.

   State v. Bruno, 1 Conn. App. 384, 391-92 (1984)

f. Mental condition must relate to ability to observe.

   State v. Cardinal, 194 Conn. 114, 118-19 (1984)

Experts.

a. Inadequate foundation for opinion.

Conn. Code Evid. § 7-4

b. Opinions in sources recognized by the witness as authoritative and are contrary to the opinion being given by the witness.

State v. Solek, 66 Conn. App. 72, 86-87 (2001), as to whether or not the sources should themselves be admitted into evidence.

c. Opinion on the mental state of the defendant.

Conn. Gen. Stat. § 54-86i prohibits the admissibility of an opinion on the ultimate issue of mental state.

Favors/gifts given to witnesses by the State's Attorney.

State v. Aponte, 249 Conn. 735, 752 (1999), where a child witness was given a doll.

Relationship with law enforcement is always relevant.

State v. Santiago, 224 Conn. 325, 332 (1992)

Threats to be charged with crime if testimony changes.

State v. Johnson, 21 Conn. App. 291, 295 (1990)

Questions regarding residence, employment, business relations or associates.

Spiro v. Nitkin, 72 Conn. 202, 205 (1899)

Thergood v. Tedford, 473 F.Supp. 339, 344 (1978)

Use of narcotics on night of crime.

State v. Ramirez, 16 Conn. App. 284, 290-91 (1988)

Relationship of witness with defendant and witness's brother.

State v. Cooper, 227 Conn. 417, 428-31 (1993)

Effect of alcohol on ability to recall.

State v. Henry, 3 Conn. App. 80, 84-85 (1984)

Persons to whom the witness spoke before testifying, to attack the credibility of the witness.

State v. Petrelli, 116 Conn. 144, 147 (1933)

Pendency of civil suit.

"As a general rule cross-examination of the prosecuting witness should be allowed to show the pendency, existence and state of civil action against the accused arising out of the same set of circumstances as those which served the basis of the criminal prosecution."

State v. Milum, 197 Conn. 602, 610 (1985)

Refusal to speak with defense. Stronger if coupled with willingness to cooperate with the opposing side.

State v. Haskins, 188 Conn. 432, 454-55 (1982)

Catch All

"The test of relevancy is not whether the answer sought will elucidate any of the main issues, but whether it will be useful extent aid the court of jury in apprising the credibility of the witness and assessing the probative value of the direct testimony...under these circumstances any plausible basis put forth for such cross examination satisfies the relevance requirement."

State v. Beliveau, 237 Conn. 576, 605 (Berdon, dissent).

Impeachment by Prior Inconsistent Statement

Inconsistency Defined

Inconsistency is not limited to diametrically opposed assertions.

State v. Whelan, 200 Conn. 743, 748 f.n. 4 (1986)

Can be established by omission, change of position, denial of recollection or evasive answers.

Failure to include a fact that would naturally be included in a prior written statement is an inconsistent statement.

State v. Chesney, 166 Conn. 630, 636 (1974)

State v. Esposito, 235 Conn. 802, 818 (1996)

Procedure if Statement is Written

Statement should be shown to the witness; if witness admits to the statement, then the evidence of the statement is inadmissible, except in the Court's discretion. If the witness denies the statement, independent evidence o f the statement is admissible.

Conn. Code Evid. § 6-10(c)

Procedure if Statement is NOT Written

Identify for the witness the date, time (if available), place and person to whom the statement was made. Quote the witness' statement precisely.

If the witness admits to making the inconsistent statement, independent evidence is not admissible, except in the Court's discretion.

Conn. Code Evid. § 6-10(c)

If the witness denies the statement, independent evidence of the statement is admissible as an exception to the hearsay rule. This evidence can take the form of a written document or witness to whom the statement was made. Note the teaching of State v. Quiles, 96 Conn. App. 354, 359 (2006), where the failure to call the pearson to whom inconsistent statement was made was final to the claim.

<u>Refreshed Recollection</u>

Anything can be used to refresh the recollection of a witness.

Conn. Code Evid. § 6-9(a)

State v. Rado, 172 Conn. 74, 79 (1976)

Neff v. Neff, 96 Conn. 273, 279-81 (1921)

<u>Past Recollection Recorded</u>

Witness must have no present recollection of the information.

Neff, at 278-79.

Witness must have personal knowledge of the information.

Pappas v. Aetna Insurance Co., 111 Conn. 415, 420 (1930)

Witness must swear that information contained in the memorandum was true at the time the memorandum was created.

State v. Vennard, 159 Conn. 385, 397 (1970)

Memorandum was created at the time the events that are recorded occurred.

Neff, at 278.

Conn. Code Evid. § 8-3(6)

CHAPTER 5

EXPERTS

Over the course of the last 3 decades, more and more criminal trials involve the use of subject matter experts who, presumably, are proffered to aid the jurors in making their factual determination. The use of expert witnesses has also increased due to the sheer amount of highly technical evidence that is being offered in even simple cases, a by product of the "CSI Effect" on trials (jurors come to expect scientific evidence and counsel rely on it to help show they have a complete case) or because of nuances of brain development and psychiatric or psychological explanations for the actions of victims or witnesses. If you haven't had an expert in one of your trials, you should expect one in your next.

Now, trial lawyers don't like to admit it, but many experts are seen as more trustworthy than lawyers in a courtroom, and the best experts assume a professorial demeanor that puts them in a role of teacher to the jury. Your experience may vary, but preparing to deal with an expert requires 2 critical approaches. First, you need to understand what exactly they will be called to testify upon. You must learn as much about this as possible in the time between disclosure and examination. Get transcripts. Ask other attorneys. Experts like to appear that they are objective, but rarely are they so. They are generally called by one side or another. They have prepared with materials provided to them by one side or the other, They may be paid by one side or the other. They are keyed into the theory of the case by one side or the other. They simply cannot be truly objective. Your role is to highlight this when it is the opposition's expert witness, and downplay it when it is yours.

There is an old southern adage to "never plow with another farmer's mule." You must decide if your case will become a battle of the experts or you will rely on your cross examination skills to try to turn your opponent's witness into one that supports your theory. In many cases, it is foolish ego that allows a trial lawyer to think they can effectively convert a witness into supporting their theory. At best you muddy the water, but you will not clearly and cleanly get your theory to the jury without utilizing an expert of your own.

PREPARING YOUR EXPERT WITNESS

Effective expert witness testimony begins with thorough preparation. Unlike fact witnesses who testify to personal observations, expert witnesses provide specialized knowledge requiring careful development and presentation.

Initial Selection and Vetting

The qualifications assessment process should examine more than formal credentials. Evaluate the relevance of the expert's education and training to the specific issues in your case. Previous testimony experience often reduces nervousness and improves presentation quality. Consider the expert's publications and research record, which strengthens credibility and demonstrates specialized knowledge. Assess their professional reputation, particularly whether they've faced criticism in previous cases. Teaching experience often correlates with an ability to explain complex concepts effectively to jurors.

Conduct an initial consultation to assess communication skills and ability to explain technical concepts. Evaluate the expert's temperament and ability to withstand challenging cross-examination. Determine their willingness to consider alternative perspectives and identify areas of potential vulnerability in their background or methodology. Screen for potential conflicts of interest that could undermine credibility.

Case-Specific Preparation

When providing information to your expert, limit materials to those relevant to prevent information overload. Ensure the expert understands the legal framework for their opinions. Clarify the specific questions the expert will address and define the scope precisely. Address weaknesses proactively rather than allowing them to emerge as surprises. Maintain detailed records of all materials provided to the expert.

During opinion development, allow the expert to form genuine independent opinions. Review preliminary findings to identify areas needing clarification. Test the strength of opinions through devil's advocate questioning. Ensure the expert can clearly explain their analytical approach. Prepare explanations for studies or opinions that differ from the expert's conclusions.

Testimony Preparation

For direct examination practice, develop clear language replacing technical jargon with accessible analogies. Create visual aids that clarify complex concepts. Organize testimony in a logical progression from foundations to conclusions. Work on verbal delivery including pace, volume, and emphasis of key points. Develop natural communication patterns with examining counsel.

In cross-examination preparation, anticipate opposing questions and develop expected lines of attack. Practice maintaining composure during aggressive or confrontational questioning. Determine what points can be conceded without undermining key opinions. Review prior testimony to address any inconsistencies with current opinions. Develop strategies for clarifying mischaracterized answers.

Day-of-Testimony Preparation

Conduct a condensed review of key opinions and supporting facts before testimony. Practice transitioning between topics smoothly. Review demonstrative exhibits and ensure proper courtroom setup. Confirm understanding of courtroom protocol and procedures. Discuss appropriate professional attire and presentation.

For emotional preparation, discuss anxiety management techniques. Remind the expert of their role as an educator to the jury. Emphasize the importance of neutrality and objectivity. Discourage defensive responses to challenging questions. Review strategies for requesting clarification when needed.

COMMON EXPERT WITNESS PITFALLS

Credibility Undermining Behaviors

Advocacy instead of objectivity manifests when experts use absolute language, become defensive, or refuse reasonable concessions. Prevent this by emphasizing that persuasiveness comes from balanced analysis, not advocacy. If it occurs, guide the witness back to neutral analytical language during redirect.

Testimony beyond expertise occurs when experts offer opinions on matters outside their field or provide legal conclusions. Define the scope of expertise clearly during preparation. If overstepping occurs, clarify proper boundaries of expertise during redirect examination.

Inconsistency with prior statements becomes problematic when experts contradict previous testimony, reports, publications, or deposition statements. Thoroughly review all prior statements and address discrepancies before trial. If inconsistencies emerge, provide an opportunity to explain apparent contradictions through context.

Technical Communication Failures

Excessive jargon appears when experts use field-specific terminology without explanation or overwhelm with technical detail. Practice translating complex concepts into accessible language during preparation. If jargon emerges during testimony, ask the expert to rephrase using simpler terms or analogies during redirect.

Failure to connect methodology to conclusions occurs when experts make conclusory statements without clear explanation of their analytical process. Develop a step-by-step explanation of methodology during preparation. If this connection is missing, return to fundamentals during redirect, walking through the reasoning process.

Overconfidence in scientific certainty manifests when experts fail to acknowledge limitations or margins of error. Discuss appropriate expression of scientific confidence levels during preparation. If necessary, explore the concept of reasonable scientific certainty during redirect.

Cross-Examination Vulnerabilities

Argumentative responses occur when experts engage in debates with cross-examining counsel or show irritation. Practice maintaining professional demeanor regardless of questioning style. Use redirect to allow experts to provide full, calm explanations if argumentative exchanges occur.

Failure to listen carefully to questions results in experts answering questions not asked or missing qualifiers in questions. Practice answering precisely what is asked, nothing more. Clarify misunderstood questions and answers during redirect.

Inability to explain fee arrangements creates problems when experts appear uncomfortable discussing compensation or evasive about payment. Prepare straightforward explanations of fee structures and relationships. Emphasize the standard nature of arrangements and independence of opinions if needed.

Presentation Issues

Poor courtroom demeanor appears when experts seem disinterested, arrogant, or nervous, or maintain poor eye contact. Practice testimony delivery with feedback on non-verbal communication. During testimony, options for correction are limited; address critical issues during breaks.

Ineffective use of visual aids manifests through confusing graphics, text-heavy slides, or poor integration with testimony. Develop and practice with simplified, clear demonstrative exhibits. If possible, modify or simplify exhibits during breaks.

Inconsistent level of detail occurs when experts over-explain simple concepts while under-explaining complex ones. Develop balanced presentation with appropriate detail for each concept. Use redirect to adjust detail level where needed.

COST-BENEFIT ANALYSIS OF EXPERT TESTIMONY

Financial Considerations

Direct costs include initial consultation fees, typically $500-1,500 depending on expertise. Report preparation often ranges from $2,000-10,000 depending on complexity. Deposition testimony generally costs $2,000-5,000 for preparation and attendance. Trial testimony usually costs $5,000-15,000 for preparation and court appearance. Ancillary costs such as travel, accommodations, and exhibit preparation often add $1,000-5,000.

Hidden costs include internal preparation time involving attorney and staff hours devoted to expert preparation. Risks of adverse rulings may result in potential for exclusion after significant investment. Discovery costs include expenses related to expert disclosure and discovery responses. Opportunity costs represent resources diverted from other case development activities. Expert coordination involves time spent managing schedules and logistics.

Strategic Value Assessment

Case enhancement factors include explanatory value when experts clarify complex technical or specialized information. Credibility reinforcement occurs when experts validate a client's account or theory of the case. Narrative development happens when experts connect evidence points into coherent explanations. Experts bridge evidentiary gaps through specialized knowledge. Jury education provided by experts creates a framework for understanding technical evidence.

Risk factors include expert vulnerability from potential weaknesses in qualifications or methodology. Jury skepticism may emerge from perception of "hired gun" testimony. Opposing expert neutralization presents the possibility that opposing experts will nullify impact. Judicial limitations may restrict the scope of testimony. Unnecessary complication can arise from overcomplicating straightforward issues.

Decision Framework

Necessity evaluation starts by determining whether expert testimony is required by law, as some claims require expert support. Consider whether the issue exceeds common knowledge beyond juror understanding. Evaluate if the testimony substantially advances your theory rather than being merely cumulative. Determine if it addresses a critical element of claim or defense, distinguishing essential from peripheral information. Consider whether the absence of expert testimony would create a significant gap in expected evidence.

Alternative approaches include establishing key facts through stipulation instead of expert testimony. Consider whether relevant facts are appropriate for judicial notice. Determine if fact witnesses with specialized knowledge can provide the necessary information. Examine whether demonstrative evidence can convey information without expert testimony. Evaluate the possibility of making points through cross-examination of opposing experts.

Cost optimization strategies begin with precisely defining and limiting the scope of expert engagement. Balance between established experts and newer professionals in experience-based selection. Provide organized, focused materials to minimize review time for preparation efficiency. Use remote preparation and video testimony where permitted for technology utilization. Develop ongoing relationships with experts for cost efficiency across multiple cases.

Expert Testimony ROI Calculation

Quantitative factors include impact on settlement value representing potential change in case valuation with expert testimony. Consider likelihood of admissibility, the probability of successful Daubert/Frye challenge. Evaluate cost relative to case value, measuring expert expenses as percentage of case worth. Assess trial outcome probability shift, the statistical change in win probability. Consider post-trial value, the potential value for appeals or related litigation.

Qualitative factors include educational value for clients, improving their understanding and engagement. Strategic positioning affects opposing counsel's case preparation. Judicial impression involves the court's perception of case preparation thoroughness. Practice development represents knowledge gained for future similar cases. Professional relationships provide value of developing expert connections.

Foundation for Qualifying a Witness as an Expert

To proffer testimony through a witness who you wish to be considered or recognized as an expert in Connecticut, A three-part test is used to determine whether these requirements are met.

- First, the expert must possess knowledge, skill, experience, training, education or some other source of learning directly applicable to a matter in issue?
- Second, the witness' skill or knowledge must not be common to the average person.
- Third, the testimony must be helpful to the fact finder in considering the issues.

Testimony by Experts, Conn. R. Evid. 7-2

INTRODUCTION QUESTIONS FOR EXPERT WITNESSES

Qualifications and Background:

- Could you please state your name, educational background, and current occupation?
- What degrees or certifications do you hold in your field of expertise?
- How many years of experience do you have in your area of expertise?
- Have you previously testified as an expert witness? If so, how many times?

Expertise and Specialization:

- What is your area of expertise and specialization?
- Can you briefly explain the nature of your work within your field?
- Have you conducted research or published any articles or papers related to your expertise?
- Are you a member of any professional organizations or associations relevant to your field?

Relevance to the Case:

- How does your expertise relate to the issues being discussed in this case?
- Were you specifically retained or consulted for this case? If so, by whom and why?
- What specific tasks or analysis did you perform in relation to this case?

Methodology and Opinions:

- Could you describe the methodologies or techniques you used in your analysis?
- What data or information did you rely on to form your opinions?
- What conclusions or opinions have you formed based on your analysis?
- How confident are you in the accuracy and reliability of your opinions?

Impartiality and Independence:

- Are you being compensated for your testimony in this case? If yes, how much?
- Have you ever been employed or retained by the opposing party in this case?
- Are you able to provide unbiased and independent opinions based solely on the evidence and your expertise?

FOUNDATION QUESTIONS FOR EXPERT WITNESSES

Expertise and Qualifications:

- Could you please state your area of expertise?
- What educational background and degrees do you have in your field of expertise?
- Have you received any specialized training or certifications relevant to your area of expertise?
- How many years of experience do you have working in your field?

Professional Experience:

- Could you provide an overview of your professional experience and positions held within your field?
- Have you ever worked as a consultant or expert witness in previous legal cases?
- Have you taught or conducted research in your field? If so, can you elaborate on those experiences?

Publications and Contributions:

- Have you authored or co-authored any books, articles, or papers related to your area of expertise?
- Have you presented at any conferences or seminars within your field?
- Are you a member of any professional organizations or associations? If yes, please specify.

Courtroom Experience:

- Have you previously testified as an expert witness in court? If yes, could you provide an estimate of how many times?
- In what types of cases have you previously provided expert testimony?
- Have you ever been subject to cross-examination during your testimony? If yes, please elaborate.

Opinion Formation:

- How do you typically go about forming your expert opinions?
- What sources of information or data do you rely on when forming your opinions?
- Do you follow any specific methodologies or guidelines within your field?

Continuing Education:

- How do you stay updated on the latest developments and advancements in your field?
- Do you regularly attend conferences, seminars, or workshops relevant to your area of expertise?
- Are you an active participant in any professional development activities?
- Are the sources of information relied upon in formulating the opinion of a type that are reasonably relied upon in this field?
- Is the form (opinion or otherwise) and the extent (if used for the ultimate issue) proper in the context of the case?[19]
- Is the relevance of the testimony outweighed by its prejudicial, confusing or misleading effect?

CROSS-EXAMINATION OF EXPERT WITNESS

General rule: witnesses may not be examined on the contents of a document not in evidence.

Shulman v. Shulman, 150 Conn. 651, 662 (1963)

- If Witness is an Expert:
  Examining attorney has some room to argue for examination of contents of document not in evidence.
  Conn. Code Evid. § 7-4

[19] For example, State v. Pjura, 68 Conn. App. 119 (2002)

§ 7-4(a) requires disclosure of sufficient factual basis for expert's opinion.

If document or data is the type that an expert may regularly rely on when he forms an opinion, it is possible to argue that the questions are allowable as introducing facts to the expert at trial is permitted by § 7-4(b) without having to introduce entire document.

- **2 C. McCormick, Evidence (5th Ed. 1999) § 324.3, p. 356**

  Cross-examiner may frame the question with facts contained about the document not in evidence as a hypothetical question, which is permitted under § 7-4(c) to impeach and test the accuracy of the expert's opinion.

- **State v. Gaynor, 182 Conn. 501, 510 (1980)**
- **Kirchner v. Yale University, 150 Conn. 623, 629 (1963)**
- **Livingstone v. New Haven, 125 Conn. 123, 127-28 (1939)**

<u>Questions you CAN ask an expert during cross-examination:</u>

a. Inadequate foundation for opinion.

   Conn. Code Evid. § 7-4

b. Opinions in sources recognized by the witness as authoritative and are contrary to the opinion being given by the witness.

State v. Solek, 66 Conn. App. 72, 86-87 (2001), as to whether or not the sources should themselves be admitted into evidence.

c. Opinion on the mental state of the defendant.

Conn. Gen. Stat. § 54-86i prohibits the admissibility of an opinion on the ultimate issue of mental state.

CHAPTER 6

OBJECTIONS

CONSTITUTIONAL OBJECTIONS

Constitutional objections represent the most powerful tools in a criminal defense attorney's arsenal. Unlike evidentiary objections, which may exclude particular items of evidence, successful constitutional objections can terminate prosecutions entirely, suppress critical evidence, or preserve powerful issues for appeal. Constitutional objections derive their authority from both the United States Constitution and the Connecticut Constitution. Connecticut's Constitution often provides greater protections than its federal counterpart in several crucial areas. Mastering constitutional objections requires understanding both the substantive constitutional rights at issue and the procedural mechanisms for asserting those rights effectively.

The timing of constitutional objections is critical. Some must be raised before trial through written motions, while others must be asserted contemporaneously during trial proceedings. Failure to raise constitutional objections at the appropriate time frequently results in waiver. This section provides a comprehensive framework for identifying, articulating, and preserving constitutional objections throughout criminal proceedings in Connecticut courts.

FOURTH AMENDMENT OBJECTIONS

Fourth Amendment objections target evidence obtained through unconstitutional searches and seizures. Connecticut courts have developed a rich body of Fourth Amendment jurisprudence that often provides greater protections than federal counterparts. When raising

Fourth Amendment objections, defense counsel should specify the precise constitutional violation and articulate why the evidence at issue constitutes "fruit of the poisonous tree."

The foundational Fourth Amendment objection involves challenging evidence obtained without a warrant when no exception to the warrant requirement applies. For such objections, counsel should state: "Objection, Your Honor. The evidence the State seeks to introduce was obtained through a warrantless search that does not fall within any recognized exception to the warrant requirement, violating my client's rights under the Fourth Amendment to the United States Constitution and Article First, Section 7 of the Connecticut Constitution." Specificity enhances preservation of the issue for appeal.

When challenging evidence obtained via warrant, focus objections on deficiencies in the warrant application, such as lack of probable cause, material misrepresentations, or failure to particularly describe the places to be searched or items to be seized. For example: "Objection, Your Honor. The warrant pursuant to which this evidence was seized failed to establish probable cause because the affidavit contained material misrepresentations without which probable cause could not be established, violating my client's rights under the Fourth Amendment to the United States Constitution and Article First, Section 7 of the Connecticut Constitution."

Traffic stop challenges require counsel to distinguish between reasonable suspicion for the initial stop and probable cause for any subsequent search. Connecticut courts recognize enhanced protections against pretextual stops under State v. Harrison, 228 Conn. 758 (1994). Articulate precisely which aspect of the stop or subsequent investigation violated constitutional standards: "Objection, Your Honor. The officer lacked reasonable, articulable suspicion to extend the traffic stop beyond its initial purpose, making the subsequent discovery of evidence the product of an unconstitutional seizure under Rodriguez v. United States and Article First, Sections 7 and 9 of the Connecticut Constitution."

When raising objections based on the automobile exception established in Carroll v. United States, emphasize the absence of probable cause or challenge the scope of the search: "Objection, Your Honor. While the automobile exception permits warrantless searches of vehicles based on probable cause, the officer's observations in this case failed to establish probable cause to believe the vehicle contained contraband or evidence of a crime."

Connecticut recognizes greater protections against canine sniffs under State v. Waz, 240 Conn. 365 (1997), which should be specifically invoked when relevant: "Objection, Your Honor. Under State v. Waz, a canine sniff constitutes a search under our state constitution, requiring reasonable suspicion, which was lacking in this case."

FIFTH AMENDMENT OBJECTIONS

Fifth Amendment objections encompass the privilege against self-incrimination, double jeopardy protections, due process rights, and grand jury guarantees. Connecticut practice demands precise articulation of which aspect of the Fifth Amendment is being invoked.

Miranda violations constitute the most common Fifth Amendment objection in criminal trials. When raising Miranda objections, specify the precise deficiency in the warnings or waiver: "Objection, Your Honor. The prosecution seeks to introduce statements obtained while my client was subjected to custodial interrogation without adequate Miranda warnings, violating the Fifth Amendment to the United States Constitution and Article First, Section 8 of the Connecticut Constitution."

Connecticut courts recognize enhanced protections against involuntary confessions under State v. Piorkowski, 243 Conn. 205 (1997). When challenging statements as involuntary, articulate the specific coercive factors: "Objection, Your Honor. The defendant's statements were involuntary due to the coercive interrogation techniques employed, including [specific techniques], rendering their admission a violation of due process under the Fifth Amendment and Article First, Section 8 of the Connecticut Constitution."

For violations of the right to remain silent, Connecticut follows Doyle v. Ohio, 426 U.S. 610 (1976), prohibiting the use of post-Miranda silence. Objections should highlight when the prosecution improperly comments on or elicits testimony about the defendant's silence: "Objection, Your Honor. The prosecutor's question improperly elicits testimony about my client's exercise of his constitutional right to remain silent after receiving Miranda warnings, in violation of Doyle v. Ohio and Article First, Section 8 of the Connecticut Constitution."

Double jeopardy objections require counsel to specify which aspect of double jeopardy protection is at issue – successive prosecution or multiple punishment: "Objection, Your Honor. This prosecution violates the double jeopardy clause of the Fifth Amendment and Article First, Section 9 of the Connecticut Constitution because the defendant has already been prosecuted for this same offense as defined under the Blockburger test."

Due process objections under the Fifth Amendment should identify the specific aspect of fundamental fairness being violated: "Objection, Your Honor. The prosecution's late disclosure of this exculpatory evidence violates my client's due process rights under Brady v. Maryland and Article First, Section 8 of the Connecticut Constitution."

SIXTH AMENDMENT OBJECTIONS

Sixth Amendment objections protect the right to counsel, confrontation, compulsory process, speedy trial, public trial, and impartial jury. Connecticut jurisprudence has developed distinctive applications of these rights that defense counsel must incorporate into objections.

Confrontation Clause objections have gained renewed importance following Crawford v. Washington, 541 U.S. 36 (2004). When objecting to testimonial hearsay, specify why the statement is testimonial and why the declarant is unavailable: "Objection, Your

Honor. The statement the prosecution seeks to introduce is testimonial hearsay offered against my client without prior opportunity for cross-examination, violating the Confrontation Clause of the Sixth Amendment and Article First, Section 8 of the Connecticut Constitution as interpreted by Crawford v. Washington and State v. Kirby."

For violations of the right to counsel, Connecticut recognizes greater protections under State v. Stoddard, 206 Conn. 157 (1988), which requires police to inform suspects when attorneys are attempting to contact them. Incorporate this precedent when appropriate: "Objection, Your Honor. Under State v. Stoddard, my client's right to counsel under Article First, Section 8 of the Connecticut Constitution was violated when police failed to inform him that counsel was attempting to reach him during interrogation."

Speedy trial objections in Connecticut must reference both constitutional and statutory grounds under C.G.S. § 54-82m: "Objection, Your Honor. This prosecution violates my client's right to a speedy trial under the Sixth Amendment, Article First, Section 8 of the Connecticut Constitution, and Connecticut General Statutes § 54-82m, as 18 months have elapsed since arrest without justifiable delay."

Impartial jury objections should identify the specific factor undermining impartiality: "Objection, Your Honor. The extensive prejudicial pretrial publicity in this case has tainted the jury pool, making it impossible to seat an impartial jury as required by the Sixth

Amendment and Article First, Section 8 of the Connecticut Constitution. We request a change of venue under State v. Reynolds."

Public trial objections must be raised immediately when courtroom closure is proposed: "Objection, Your Honor. The proposed courtroom closure violates my client's right to a public trial under the Sixth Amendment and Article First, Section 8 of the Connecticut Constitution. Under Waller v. Georgia, the court must consider alternatives to closure and make specific findings supporting any restriction of public access."

EIGHTH AMENDMENT OBJECTIONS

Eighth Amendment objections primarily arise during sentencing but may be relevant earlier in proceedings when pretrial detention or bail conditions are at issue. Connecticut's Constitution provides parallel protections under Article First, Section 8.

Excessive bail objections should specify why the bail amount is disproportionate: "Objection, Your Honor. The proposed bail amount of $1,000,000 is excessive under the Eighth Amendment and Article First, Section 8 of the Connecticut Constitution, as it far exceeds what is necessary to ensure the defendant's appearance given his substantial community ties and lack of criminal history."

When challenging conditions of confinement, counsel should articulate the specific constitutional violation: "Objection, Your Honor. The conditions at the correctional facility, specifically the lack of necessary medical treatment for my client's serious condition, violate the Eighth Amendment prohibition against cruel and unusual punishment and Article First, Section 8 of the Connecticut Constitution."

For disproportionate sentencing objections, reference both general constitutional principles and Connecticut's proportionality jurisprudence: "Objection, Your Honor. The proposed sentence constitutes cruel and unusual punishment under the Eighth Amendment and Article First, Section 8 of the Connecticut Constitution as it is grossly disproportionate to sentences imposed for similar offenses committed by defendants with similar backgrounds."

FOURTEENTH AMENDMENT OBJECTIONS

Fourteenth Amendment objections invoke equal protection, procedural due process, substantive due process, and incorporation of other constitutional rights against state action. Connecticut's Constitution offers parallel protections under Article First, Sections 8 and 20.

Equal protection objections must identify the classification at issue and the appropriate level of scrutiny: "Objection, Your Honor. The prosecution's use of peremptory challenges to strike all African American jurors constitutes racial discrimination in violation of the Equal Protection Clause of the Fourteenth Amendment and Article First, Section 20 of the Connecticut Constitution under Batson v. Kentucky."

Procedural due process objections should specify the protected interest and the process that was due: "Objection, Your Honor. The court's refusal to permit access to potentially exculpatory materials in the complainant's sealed records violates procedural due process under the Fourteenth Amendment and Article First, Section 8 of the Connecticut Constitution. Under State v. Esposito, my client is entitled to an in camera review of these records."

Substantive due process objections address government actions that shock the conscience or intrude upon fundamental rights: "Objection, Your Honor. The prosecution's deliberate destruction of potentially exculpatory evidence violates substantive due process under the Fourteenth Amendment and Article First, Section 8 of the Connecticut Constitution, as it deprives my client of the fundamental right to present a complete defense."

Vagueness challenges assert that statutes fail to provide fair notice or invite arbitrary enforcement: "Objection, Your Honor. Connecticut General Statutes § [section] is unconstitutionally vague as applied to my client's conduct, as it fails to provide fair notice of what conduct is prohibited and invites arbitrary enforcement, violating due process under the Fourteenth Amendment and Article First, Section 8 of the Connecticut Constitution."

PROCEDURAL CONSIDERATIONS

Timing is crucial for constitutional objections. Some must be raised before trial through written motions, while others must be asserted contemporaneously during trial. Generally, Fourth Amendment objections to searches and seizures must be raised pretrial through motions to suppress under Practice Book § 41-12. Fifth Amendment objections to confessions typically require Jackson-Denno hearings before trial. Sixth Amendment confrontation objections, however, are usually raised during trial when the prosecution attempts to introduce testimonial hearsay.

Preservation for appeal requires counsel to raise constitutional objections with specificity at the earliest opportunity. When making constitutional objections, always state: (1) the specific constitutional provision being invoked, including both federal and state constitutional provisions; (2) the specific action or ruling that violates the constitutional provision; and (3) the legal theory supporting the objection, including relevant case law.

Following an adverse ruling on a constitutional objection, consider seeking articulation of the court's ruling to ensure preservation of the issue for appeal. Request that the court make explicit findings of fact and conclusions of law, particularly when the court's ruling involves constitutional standards.

Renewal of constitutional objections may be necessary at multiple stages of proceedings. When a pretrial constitutional objection is overruled, renew the objection when the evidence is introduced at trial to preserve the issue fully. Similarly, constitutional objections raised during trial may need to be renewed after intervening events change the analysis.

Constitutional objections form the backbone of criminal defense practice. By articulating precise constitutional violations under both federal and state constitutions, defense counsel can exclude tainted evidence, secure dismissal of improper charges, and preserve powerful issues for appeal. Connecticut's robust constitutional jurisprudence often provides greater protections than federal counterparts, making state constitutional arguments particularly valuable. Master the substantive constitutional principles and procedural mechanisms described in this section to protect your clients' fundamental rights effectively throughout criminal proceedings.

Proceedings When Rules of Evidence Do Not Apply (or when your objection doesn't matter)

Code of Evidence Sec. 1-1

- Investigative grand juries
- Sentencing
- Probation proceedings
- Summary contempt
- Offers of proof of facts preliminary to admissibility of evidence

Note that if your opponent does not request that the jury be excused for your offer of proof, the jury will hear potentially inadmissible evidence.

Duty to Object

Whenever an objection to the admission of evidence is made, counsel shall state the grounds upon which it is claimed or upon which objection is made, succinctly and in such form as he or she desires it to go upon the record, before any discussion or argument is had. Argument upon such objection or upon any interlocutory question arising during the trial of a case shall not be made by either party unless the judicial authority requests it and, if made, must be brief and to the point.[20]

Duty of Court to Rule on Objection

Whenever evidence offered upon trial is objected to as inadmissible, the judicial authority or committee trying such case shall not admit such evidence subject to the objection, unless both parties agree that it be so admitted; but, if either party requests a decision, such judicial authority or committee shall pass upon such objection and admit or reject the testimony.

CPB sec. 5-6

Relevancy Defined

"Relevant evidence" means evidence having any tendency to make the existence of any fact that is material to the determination of

---

[20] CPB sec. 5-5

the proceeding more probable or less probable than it would be without the evidence.

Conn. Code. Evid. 4-1

Materiality Defined

"Evidence is material when it is offered to prove a fact directly in issue or a fact probative of a matter in issue."

Connecticut Evidence, Colin Tait, (3rd Ed 2001) Sec. 4.1.3

Rule of General Admissibility

All relevant evidence is admissible, except as otherwise provided by the Federal or State Constitutions, or the General Statutes. Irrelevant evidence is inadmissible.

Conn. Code. Evid. 4-2

Prejudice v. Probative Value

There are 4 situations where prejudice could outweigh the probative value of evidence:

1. Where the facts offered may unduly arouse the jury's emotions, hostility or sympathy.
2. Where the proof and answering evidence it provokes may create a side issue that will unduly distract the jury from the main issues.
3. Where the evidence offered and the counterproof will consume an undue amount of time.

4. Where the defendant, having no reasonable ground to anticipate the evidence, is unfairly surprised and unprepared to meet it.

State v. DeMatteo, 186 conn. 696, 702-03 (1982)

Objections to Questions or Exhibits

- Asks for **irrelevant** information,
- Calls for an **immaterial** answer.
- Contrary to the **best evidence** rule/parole rule of evidence.
- **Privileged** communication.
- Calls for an **opinion** (by an incompetent witness).
- Calls for a **narrative** answer (and does not give opportunity for objection).
- Calls for a **hearsay** answer.
- **Leading** (on direct examination).
- **Repetitive** or asked and answered.
- **Beyond the scope** (of the direct, cross, or redirect).
- **Assumes facts** not in evidence.
- **Confusing/misleading**/ambiguous/vague/unintelligible.[21]
- **Speculative.**
- **Form of question.**
- **Argumentative.**
- **Improper Characterization.**
- **Misstates evidence**/misquotes the witness.
- **Cumulative.**

[21] Code Sec. 4-3

- **Improper method** of impeachment.
- **Insufficient foundation**.
- **Prejudice outweighs probative value**.[22]
- **Document speaks for itself**.

<u>**Objections to Answers**</u>

- **Irrelevant.**
- **Non-responsive** to question asked.
- **Privileged.**
- **Conclusion.**
- **Improper opinion.**
- **Hearsay.**
- **Narrative** (question called only for yes or no answer).

[22] Code Sec. 4-3

READY-TO-USE OBJECTION LANGUAGE

RELEVANCE OBJECTIONS

- **Basic Relevance**: "Objection, Your Honor. Irrelevant."
- **Expanded Relevance**: "Objection, Your Honor. This line of questioning is irrelevant to the issues in this case."
- **Materiality**: "Objection, Your Honor. The question calls for immaterial information."
- **Probative Value**: "Objection, Your Honor. Any probative value is substantially outweighed by the danger of unfair prejudice under §4-3 of the Connecticut Code of Evidence."

FORM OF QUESTION OBJECTIONS

- **Compound Question**: "Objection, Your Honor. Compound question."
- **Vague/Ambiguous**: "Objection, Your Honor. The question is vague and ambiguous."
- **Argumentative**: "Objection, Your Honor. Counsel is being argumentative."
- **Asked and Answered**: "Objection, Your Honor. This question has been asked and answered."
- **Assumes Facts Not in Evidence**: "Objection, Your Honor. The question assumes facts not in evidence."
- **Leading on Direct**: "Objection, Your Honor. Counsel is leading on direct examination."

- **Narrative**: "Objection, Your Honor. The question calls for a narrative response."
- **Calls for Speculation**: "Objection, Your Honor. Calls for speculation."

HEARSAY OBJECTIONS

- **Basic Hearsay**: "Objection, Your Honor. Hearsay."
- **Expanded Hearsay**: "Objection, Your Honor. The question calls for hearsay under §8-1 of the Connecticut Code of Evidence."
- **Double Hearsay**: "Objection, Your Honor. This constitutes double hearsay without applicable exceptions for each level."

WITNESS COMPETENCY OBJECTIONS

- **Lack of Personal Knowledge**: "Objection, Your Honor. No foundation establishing personal knowledge has been laid."
- **Improper Opinion - Lay Witness**: "Objection, Your Honor. Improper opinion testimony from a lay witness under §7-1."
- **Improper Expert Opinion**: "Objection, Your Honor. The witness has not been qualified as an expert to offer this opinion."

PRIVILEGE OBJECTIONS

- **Attorney-Client Privilege**: "Objection, Your Honor. This calls for information protected by attorney-client privilege."
- **Fifth Amendment**: "Objection, Your Honor. This question calls for information that may incriminate the witness."
- **Spousal Privilege**: "Objection, Your Honor. This information is protected by spousal privilege."

CHARACTER EVIDENCE OBJECTIONS

- **Improper Character Evidence**: "Objection, Your Honor. Improper character evidence under §4-4."
- **Prior Bad Acts**: "Objection, Your Honor. Improper evidence of prior misconduct under §4-5."
- **Propensity Evidence**: "Objection, Your Honor. This constitutes improper propensity evidence."

DOCUMENTARY/PHYSICAL EVIDENCE OBJECTIONS

- **Lack of Foundation**: "Objection, Your Honor. Insufficient foundation has been laid for this exhibit."
- **Authentication**: "Objection, Your Honor. The exhibit has not been properly authenticated under §9-1."
- **Best Evidence Rule**: "Objection, Your Honor. This violates the best evidence rule under §10-1."
- **Chain of Custody**: "Objection, Your Honor. The chain of custody has not been established."

CONSTITUTIONAL OBJECTIONS

- **Fourth Amendment**: "Objection, Your Honor. This evidence was obtained in violation of my client's Fourth Amendment rights."
- **Fifth Amendment**: "Objection, Your Honor. This violates my client's Fifth Amendment right against self-incrimination."
- **Sixth Amendment**: "Objection, Your Honor. This violates my client's Sixth Amendment right to confrontation."

PROCEDURAL OBJECTIONS

- **Beyond Scope**: "Objection, Your Honor. Beyond the scope of direct examination."
- **Improper Impeachment**: "Objection, Your Honor. Improper impeachment under §6-10."
- **Violates Motion in Limine**: "Objection, Your Honor. This violates the Court's order on our motion in limine."

OBJECTIONS AND RESPONSES

Objection	Supporting Authority	Response to Opposing Counsel's Objection
Relevance	"This evidence does not make any fact of consequence more or less probable." Conn. Code Evid. §4-1	"This evidence is directly relevant to [specific issue] because [reason]."
Unfair Prejudice	"The probative value is substantially outweighed by the danger of unfair prejudice." Conn. Code Evid. §4-3	"The probative value substantially outweighs any prejudicial effect because [reason]."
Leading Questions	"Counsel is leading the witness on direct examination." Conn. Code Evid. §6-8(b)	"This is preliminary information/This witness is hostile/This is a complex matter that requires direction."
Hearsay	"The statement is being offered for the truth of the matter asserted and doesn't fall under any exception." Conn. Code Evid. §8-1, §8-2	"The statement is not being offered for its truth, but to show [effect on listener, etc.]" or "This falls under the [specific] exception because [elements of exception]."

Lack of Foundation	"No foundation has been laid establishing the witness's personal knowledge." Conn. Code Evid. §6-3	"I'll establish the foundation with these additional questions..."
Assumes Facts	"The question assumes facts not in evidence."	"The facts in this question have been established through [witness/exhibit]."
Speculation	"The question calls for speculation beyond the witness's knowledge."	"The witness has sufficient knowledge to provide a non-speculative answer based on [reason]."
Beyond Scope	"This exceeds the scope of direct examination." Conn. Code Evid. §6-8(a)	"This directly relates to [topic] covered during direct examination."
Improper Character	"This constitutes inadmissible character evidence." Conn. Code Evid. §4-4	"This evidence is admissible under §4-5(c) to prove [motive, opportunity, etc.]."
Best Evidence	"This violates the best evidence rule." Conn. Code Evid. §10-1	"The original is [lost/destroyed/not obtainable] through no fault of our client, satisfying §10-3."

Authentication	"The exhibit has not been properly authenticated." Conn. Code Evid. §9-1	"Authentication requirements have been satisfied through [witness testimony/distinctive characteristics/etc.]."
Expert Opinion	"The witness has not been qualified as an expert." Conn. Code Evid. §7-2	"The witness has specialized knowledge based on [education/experience/training] that will assist the trier of fact."
Improper Impeachment	"This constitutes improper impeachment." Conn. Code Evid. §6-10	"This is proper impeachment by [prior inconsistent statement/bias/etc.]."

STRATEGIC DECISION TREES FOR OBJECTIONS

WHEN TO OBJECT VS. WHEN TO ALLOW TESTIMONY

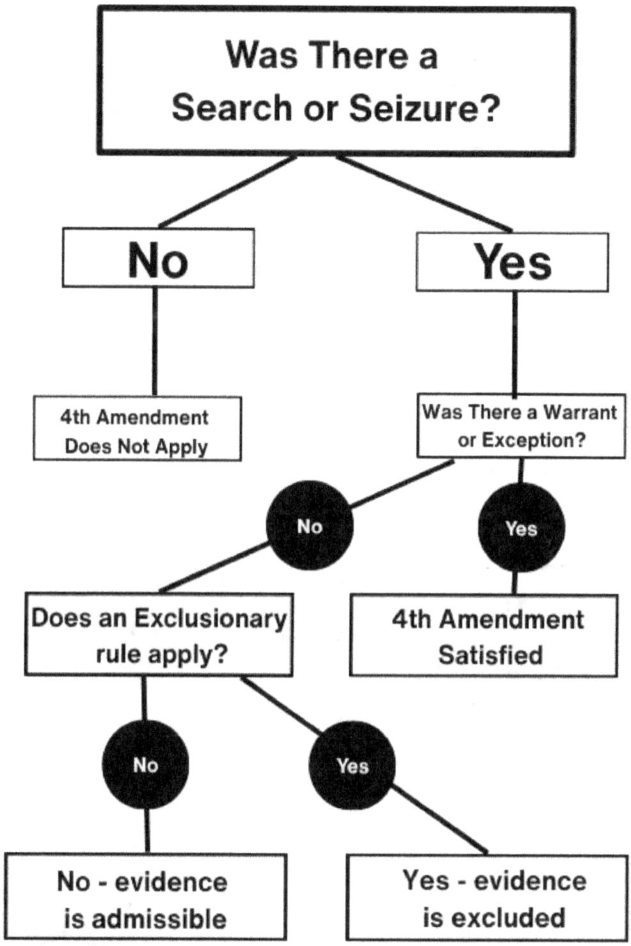

HEARSAY OBJECTION DECISION TREE

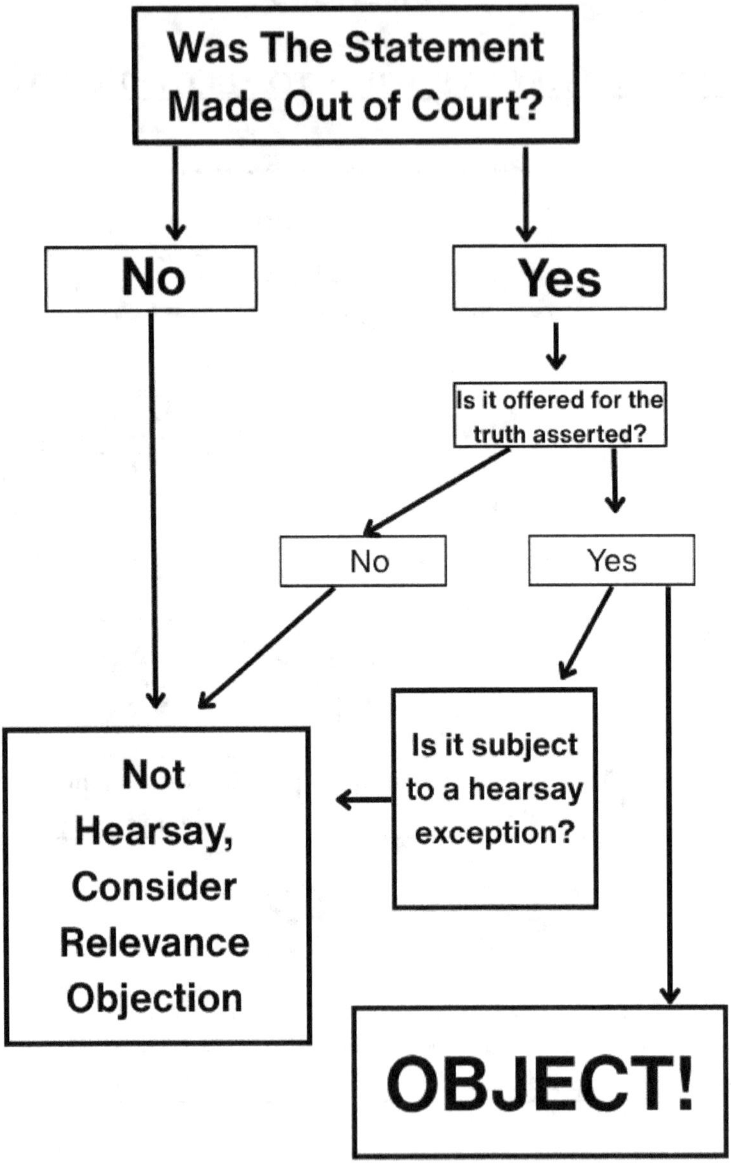

EXPERT TESTIMONY OBJECTION DECISION TREE

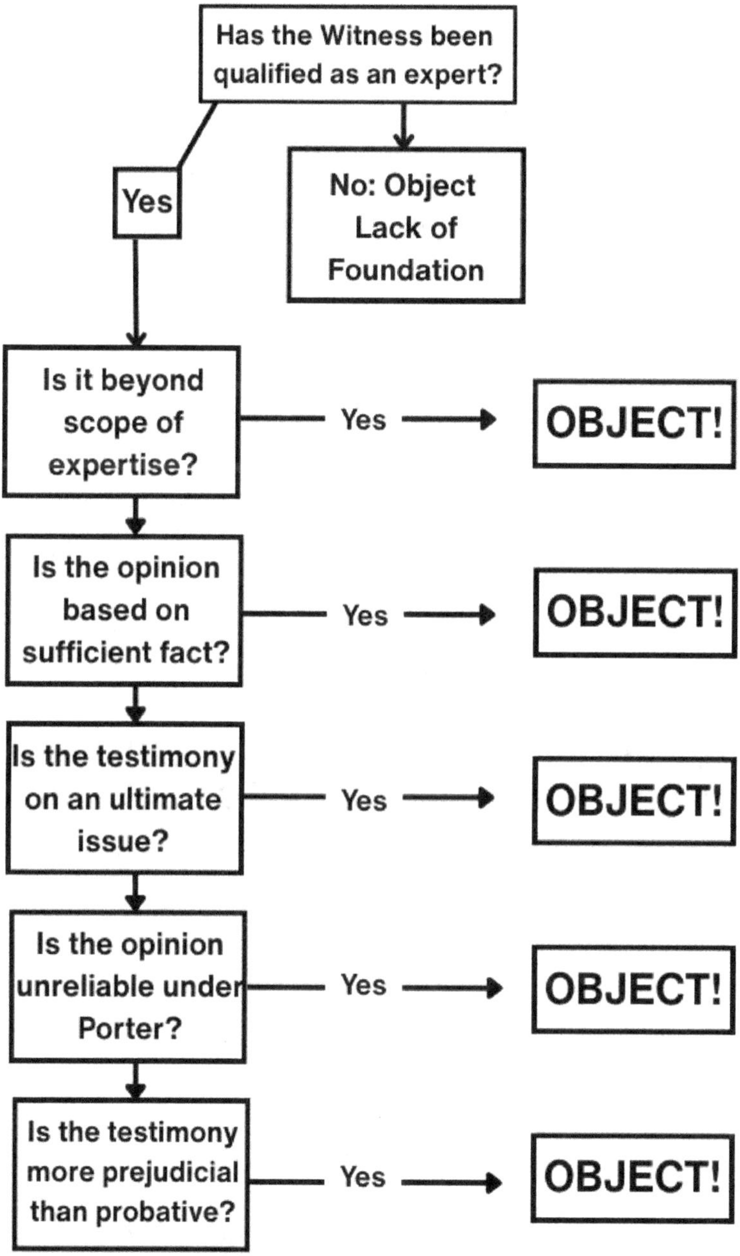

STRATEGIC SIDEBAR REQUESTS

When making a complex objection or addressing sensitive matters, request a sidebar with language such as:

- "Your Honor, may we approach the bench?"
- "Your Honor, I have a matter I'd like to address outside the hearing of the jury."
- "Your Honor, I request a sidebar to address an evidentiary issue."

At sidebar, be concise and specific:

1. State the specific objection
2. Cite the relevant evidence rule or case
3. Explain briefly why the testimony is inadmissible
4. Request specific relief (sustaining objection, striking testimony, limiting instruction)

WHEN TO REQUEST A JURY INSTRUCTION FOLLOWING SUSTAINED OBJECTION

After a sustained objection to particularly prejudicial evidence, consider requesting a curative instruction:

"Your Honor, I request that the jury be instructed to disregard the [question/testimony/comment] as it is [improper/prejudicial/not evidence]."

For more serious violations, consider:

"Your Honor, may we approach? I believe a stronger curative instruction is necessary to address the prejudicial impact of that [question/testimony/comment]."

CHAPTER 7

DUI

One of the most common crimes charged in our lower courts that make it to trial are DUI trials. When preparing a DUI case for trial, there are dozens of scientific and evidentiary issues you must be prepared to face. DUI cases are the most complicated of criminal trials. In no other crime charges do you have the main witness for the prosecution being a 1. Trained professional, and, 2. Actually witnesses the crime being conducted most of the time. The hurdles for the introduction of evidence is high given the scientific nature of the evidence and regulations governing the application of tests conducted.

When approaching a DUI case, care should be taken to completely address all the issues which may arise during the actual trial, and that starts, of course, by well conducted preparation in the office in advance of the trial date.

MOTIONS YOU MAY CONSIDER:

Motion for Discovery (Breath, Blood or Urine test)

- This should be filed so that you have access to scrutinize the results and reliability as part of your case.

Motion in Limine, if you're concerned that:

- The cop may try to give unfounded expert opinions, such as "DUI dealers always say they only had 2 drinks"
- The cop may try to sneak in your client's record or misconduct: "I recognized him from when I arrested him before"

- Note: the officer may offer opinion on the ultimate issue in a DUI case.[23]

Motion in Limine (Number of drinks irrelevant)

- If you're concerned that the State may proffer evidence by a witness or expert witness concerning the number of drinks the Accused would have had to consume to achieve the blood alcohol level contained/reported in the Chemical test results. Tuttle v. Russell

Motion to Exclude Evidence of Refusal of Chemical Test and/or SFSTs

- It would be highly prejudicial and unfair to inform Defendant that he has a right to refuse to submit to a test and then use the evidence of refusal against him at his criminal trial. Defendant was informed of what penalties would be incurred should he refuse. He took the risk and incurred the penalties.

DUI VOIR DIRE

DUI voir dire is a challenging part of any DUI defense case. There are a number of reasons why that you must consider when planning your questions. First, nobody will ever say in voir dire that they are OK with DUI. But more importantly, in most DUI cases, the only witnesses will be police officers. When you have professionally trained police officers, you are fighting an uphill battle because the

[23] State v. Lamme, 19 Conn. App. 594, 604, 563 A.2d 1372, 1377 (1989)

general juror relies on a world view that police are good, do their job correctly, and only arrest guilty people. If they don't believe that, especially if they live in suburban or rural Connecticut, their entire world view is shaken. The natural tendency for them then, is to just simply trust in the police in DUI cases, because they would have to throw out all they believe in to accept the alternative. Know this as you begin to Voir Dire in a DUI case and build a defense that accepts that world view as the fundamental framework that every juror brings to the case. It is then you can fashion a defense that can win.

<u>Sample DUI Voir Dire Questions</u>

- Do you believe in an arbitrary number of drinks that means no driving whatsoever?
- Do you realize that it is not against the law to drink and drive?
- Do you realize that in order for my client to be found guilty he must have had a sufficient amount to drink to cause him to be under the influence to an extent that it rendered him incapable of safely operating his motor vehicle?
- Do you disagree with this law?
- Do you feel that a person who drinks alcohol and then drives a car has violated the law, regardless of the effect that alcohol had on him?
- Will my client's admission that he was drinking and driving lead you to believe that he is guilty of the crime charged?

- Do you think that my client should be punished because he was drinking and driving, even if he was not intoxicated?
- Do you realize that you must make your decision based on whether the facts prove my client's guilty beyond a reasonable doubt? You will be given certain opinions by the police officer, by the State's chemical expert, and in a sense by the breath testing machine. Are you willing to look beyond those opinions, to examine the facts which allegedly support those opinions, and require that the facts prove guilty beyond a reasonable doubt, before voting for a guilty verdict?
- Have you ever heard of a Dräger 9250?
- Do you have any understanding of how the machine works? (Note: always use the word "machine" rather than "instrument" - jurors know about machines and how they can malfunction. On the other hand, "instrument" sounds more scientific. See Tarantino: "Words that Condition the Jury's Perceptions," 5 DWI JOURNAL: LAW & SCIENCE 11 (November 1990); Tarantino, "Bad Habits Can Sabotage Your Communication With Jurors," 6 DWI JOURNAL: LAW AND SCIENCE 7 (July 1991).
- Do you have any preconceived ideas that the Breathalyzer test is scientific and accurate?
- Do you believe that the test result ought to be accepted because it is scientific and accurate?

- Will you allow the chemical latest result to substitute for your own opinion based upon the facts that you will hear in this case?
- Regardless of the machine's test reading, will you still presume my client to be innocent until proven guilty beyond a reasonable doubt?
- Do you believe that a police officer has probable cause to arrest someone for driving under the influence merely because the person had the odor of an alcoholic beverage on his breath and was driving his car?
- Have you had any friends, relatives or acquaintances arrested for DWI?
    - What about field tests? Know anyone pulled over and not arrested?

- Have you had any friends, relatives, or acquaintances who were hurt or had their property damaged by a drunk driver?
- Would you be offended if the arresting officer were vigorously cross examined?
- If you were to vote, "not guilty," would you think that your verdict was a criticism and an indictment of the arresting officers?
- Have you ever challenged or wanted to challenge a traffic citation?
- Do you believe that alcohol affects different people in different ways?

- What do you understand the term "tolerance to alcohol" to mean?
- Do you have any experience with Community Groups, such as MADD?
- If you were to have an operation, would you require a second medical opinion?
- Do you realize that a Dräger 9510 takes only one test or renders only one opinion, even though it has the ability to run a second test?
- Have you (or someone you have talked to) ever "talked" their way out of a ticket?
- Do you have any problem with people trying to do that?
- If give the opportunity to try to talk your way out of a ticket, would you do so?
- On a scale of 1-10, would you say you are pro defense or pro prosecution?
- Play sports - hit the ball the first time you tried? Got easier the more you did it?
- Does exhaustion affect your coordination?

DIRECT EXAMINATION

In a DUI case it may not be wise to have your client testify, so your ONLY witness may be an expert you employ. If you bring in any witness, it should be one that can combat the state's scientific evidence. If you wish to have your client testify, you should review the Chapter on Direct Examination.

FOUNDATIONAL QUESTIONS FOR DEFENSE WITNESSES:

Foundation for Qualifying a Toxicologist

- What is your occupation?
- Where do you work?
- Is your laboratory certified/accredited?
- What is your position?
- What are your job responsibilities?
- How long have you worked at your current position?
- Have you held similar positions in your field prior to your current job?
- What is your educational background?
- Have you performed laboratory work?
- Have you published any articles in any professional journals?
- Have you peer reviewed articles?
- What specialized training or experience do you have on the effects of alcohol or drugs on the human body?
- What specialized training or experience do you have on the effects of alcohol or drugs on the ability of a person to operate an automobile?
- Have you testified as an expert in the effects of alcohol on the human body?

Foundation for a Toxicologist to Testify about Chemical Test Results

- Are you familiar with the method of determining alcohol content used in this case?
- What is that method?
- Can you explain how that method works?
- Is that a method generally accepted by the scientific community?
- Was the testing performed in accordance with established operating procedure?
- What were the results of the testing?

Admission of a Chemical Test (Breath)

- Was defendant given an opportunity to contact an attorney?
- Did defendant consent to the test?
- Was a copy of test results given to the defendant or mailed to the defendant within 24 hours?
- Was test performed at direction of police officer?
- Was test performed in accordance with methods approved by Department of Public Safety?
- Was test performed on equipment approved by the Department of Public Safety?
- Was machine tested for accuracy?
- Was additional test given at least 15 minutes after the initial test was performed?
- Was test conducted within 2 hours of operation?

Admission of a Chemical Test (Blood)

- Was the sample drawn by a person licensed to practice medicine and surgery, a phlebotomist, a qualified laboratory technician, an emergency medical technician II or a registered nurse?
- Was the sample collected using a sterile syringe and needle?
- Was the area of the puncture sterilized with a solution that did not contain ethyl alcohol?
- Did the container preserve the integrity of the sample until testing?
- Was the sample container sealed and labeled?
- Were the results performed in duplicate?
- Did the duplicate results correspond to plus or minus 0.01 percent?
- Does the analysis indicate the determined or equivalent blood alcohol concentration in terms of hundredth of a percent by weight?

Admission of a Chemical Test (Urine)

- Did a police officer monitor the collection of the sample to prevent adulteration or misidentification?
- Was that police officer a member of the same gender as the person providing the sample?
- Did the container preserve the integrity of the sample?
- Was the sample container sealed and labeled?
- Was the test conducted on the sealed container?

- Did the duplicate results correspond to plus or minus 0.01 percent?
- Does the analysis indicate the determined or equivalent blood alcohol concentration in terms of hundredth of a percent by weight?

Admission of the Horizontal Gaze Nystagmus (HGN)

- Check for eyeglasses/contact lenses
- Verbal instructions to the subject
- Position the stimulus 12-15 inches away from eyes
- Check for equal tracking
- Check for equal pupil size
- Check for the lack of smooth pursuit, repeat
- Check for distinct nystagmus at maximum deviation, repeat (hold for 4 seconds at max on each side, both times)
- Check for onset of nystagmus prior to 45, repeat
- Total the clues
- Check for vertical nystagmus

Admission of the Standardized Field Sobriety Tests - Walk & Turn

Since the tests are standardized, the NHTSA protocols require that the administration of the tests and the instructions are given identically in every case. The standard instructions are:

Instructions for Instruction Stage:

- "Place your left foot on the line."

- "Place your right foot on the line ahead of the left foot, with the heel of the right foot against the toe of the left foot."
- "Place your arms down at your side."
- "Maintain this position until I tell you to begin. Do not start to walk until I tell you to do so."
- "Do you understand the instructions so far?"

Instructions for the Walking Stage:

- "When I tell you to start, take 9 heel to toe steps down the line, turn around and take 9 heel to toe steps back up the line."
- "When you turn, keep the front foot on the line, and turn by taking a series of small steps with the other foot, like this (demonstrate)."
- "While you are walking, keep your arms at your side, watch your feet at all times and count your steps out loud."
- "Once you start walking, don't stop until you have completed the test."
- "Do you understand the instructions?"
- "Begin, and count your first step form heel to toe position as 'One.'"

Admission for the Standardized Field Sobriety Tests - One Leg Stand

Since the tests are standardized, the NHTSA protocols require that the administration of the tests and the instructions are given identically in every case. The standard instructions are:

Instructions for the Instruction Stage:

- "Please stand with your feet together and your arms down by your side, like this (demonstrate)."
- "Do not start the test until I tell you to do so."
- "Do you understand the instructions so far?"

Instructions for the Balance and Counting Stage:

- "When I tell you to start, raise one leg, either leg, approximately 6 inches off the ground, toes pointed out."
- "You must keep both legs straight, arms at your sides."
- "While holding this position, count out loud for thirty seconds in the following manner: one thousand and one, one thousand and two, until told to stop."
- "Keep your arms at your side at all times and keep watching your raised foot."
- "Do you understand?"
- "Go ahead and perform the test."

Foundation Questions for Police Officers as Expert Witnesses

Officer can give expert opinion on ultimate issue if 3 prongs are met:[24]

1. Special skills
2. Information is beyond juror's knowledge
3. It is helpful to the jury

Officer is an expert based on his training and the results of the Standardized Field Sobriety Tests,[25] **but,** "Field sobriety tests, unlike the horizontal gaze nystagmus test, are within the common knowledge of lay jurors."[26] So, if jurors can assess one-leg-stand and walk-and-turn, then the basis for the expert opinion as stated in Lamme is undercut because the information is not beyond the juror's knowledge.

CROSS EXAMINATION IN DUI CASES

The chapter method of cross examination is ideal for the DUI defense lawyer, because you can segregate your issues into clearly distinct moments in time: The driving, the first contact, the SFSTs, post arrest behavior, mental acuity, etc. The critical issue, however, in a DUI defense case is to not cross examine chronologically. If you do that, you merely stack the inferences a juror can make until ultimately your client is arrested. Never cross examine

[24] State v. Lamme, 19 Conn. App. 594 (1989)
[25] State v. Pjura, 68 Conn. App. 119 (2002)
[26] State v. Garcia, 51 Conn. App. 4 (1998)

chronologically, the state will have done that in direct examination to make their case, and rightfully so. Instead identify the strongest chapters for your defense and bookend them into your cross examination. This way you utilize the primacy and recency effect and leave the jurors remembering the GOOD things your client may have done.

There is a sample cross examination for a DUI case located in Appendix 4.

DRUG DUI CASES AND THE SCIENCE OF DRUG DUI DETECTION.

Following the legalization of cannabis, several amendments were introduced to the regulations pertaining to Operating Under the Influence. These modifications will inherently influence the manner in which such cases are pursued, consequently affecting the approach taken for their defense. For those who are unfamiliar the type of witnesses in a Drug DUI case, a D.R.E. refers to a drug recognition expert who, "is a trained and certified police officer who is called in to examine persons suspected of operating a motor vehicle while under the influence of drugs. The examination almost always takes place at a police station after the suspect has been arrested…." Commonwealth v. Ineson, NO. 1148CR0642 (Mass. Dist. Ct.).

We will provide a brief overview and tools, but the D.R.E. Manual is over 1,000 pages long. Hopefully this is enough to get you started.

THE 12 STEP D.R.E. TEST

<u>Every step must be conducted to be a valid DRE test.</u>

1. Breath Alcohol Test: Preliminary test to determine alcohol impairment.
2. Interview with Arresting Officer: Gathering details about the driver's behavior and appearance.
3. Preliminary Examination: Assessing the individual's overall appearance and behavior.
4. First Pulse Measurement: Measuring the individual's initial pulse rate.
5. Eye Examination: Tests such as Horizontal Gaze Nystagmus, Vertical Gaze Nystagmus, and Lack of Convergence.
6. Divided Attention Tests: Includes Walk and Turn, One-Leg Stand, and Finger-to-Nose tests.
7. Vital Signs Check: Measuring blood pressure and a second pulse rate.
8. Dark Room Examination: Checking pupils for size, light reaction, and near-point reaction with a penlight.
9. Muscle Tone Examination: Assessing muscle tone and looking for involuntary tremors.
10. Injection Site and Third Pulse Check: Examining for recent drug use signs and taking a third pulse measurement.
11. Evaluator Analysis: Forming an opinion on drug impairment and identifying potential drug categories.

12. Toxicological Examination: Sending blood or urine samples for lab analysis to confirm drug presence and concentration.

"The process is systematic because it relies on a comprehensive set of observable signs and symptoms that are proven to be dependable indicators of drug impairment. DRE evaluation is standardized as it follows the same procedure, conducted uniformly by every drug recognition expert, for each suspect whenever feasible." Clearly, the evaluation is grounded in a physical examination; Steps 3 through 10 involve direct observation or assessment of the defendant by the DRE.

Challenges to the D.R.E.

Naturally, a defense attorney will be to limit the introduction of D.R.E. testimony to the greatest extent feasible. However, it appears highly improbable that we can prevent all or even the majority of its inclusion. Nonetheless, presented here are several potential strategies to consider in addressing this testimony. Some possible challenges to consider are: The Porter (Daubert) Challenge, Lack of Foundation, Opinion on the Ultimate Issue

Offering a Suggested BAC in Behavioral Case

In Connecticut, the admission of Blood Alcohol Concentration (BAC) evidence is stringently governed by statutes and the Code of Evidence. If the state attempts to infer a BAC or BAC equivalent from the defendant's behavior (which they frequently do), immediate objection is advised.

C.G.S. § 14-227a(b) exclusively allows evidence derived from chemical tests of the defendant's blood alcohol level at the time of the offense. This is permissible provided certain conditions are met, including the defendant's opportunity to consult with an attorney, prompt testing, accurate reporting, adherence to regulations, calibration checks, commencement of testing within two hours of operation, and a second test after ten minutes to ensure reliability. Failure to comply with these safeguards may render the evidence inadmissible.

C.G.S. § 14-227a(c) further restricts the use of BAC evidence in behavioral subsection cases (like the one at hand). It stipulates that reliable evidence concerning the defendant's alcohol content, as indicated by chemical analysis, is admissible only at the defendant's request.

The legislative history of C.G.S. § 14-227a underscores the strict enforcement of these limitations. Concerns about establishing an irrefutable presumption of guilt led to these stringent requirements, which seek to strike a balance between different methods of proof for DUI cases.

In cases such as State v. Cooper and State v. Gracia, adherence to these statutory restrictions has been pivotal. Cooper's reversal highlighted the mandatory nature of the defendant's request for BAC evidence admission. However, in cases where the defendant introduces BAC evidence, as demonstrated by State v. Wynne, admission of related evidence is possible.

Forensic toxicologists in Connecticut courts have been allowed to draw some conclusions about blood alcohol content. For instance, State v. Hood endorsed a toxicologist's opinion on the number of drinks required to reach a specific BAC. This demonstrated the potential use of BAC conclusions by such experts.

The extrapolation of BAC levels from behavior remains a novel issue in Connecticut, with persuasive authority from other jurisdictions deeming it impermissible. Courts have highlighted due process concerns, legislative restrictions, and the unreliability of behavior-based conclusions.

In summary, challenging the admissibility of D.R.E. testimony and the introduction of BAC evidence based on behavior necessitates a comprehensive understanding of the legal parameters and relevant case law in Connecticut courts.

FIELD SOBRIETY TESTS

Important Cases to Consider

- State v. Popeleski, 291 Conn. 769 (2009). Substantial compliance is enough.

One Leg Stand / Walk and Turn Test:

- State v. Merritt, 36 Conn. App. 90 (1994)
- State v. Garcia, 51 Conn. App. 4 (1998). Not specific but within common knowledge of jurors.

Finger Dexterity

- State v. Tenay, 150 Conn. App. 140, 155 (2014). Not specific.

Horizontal Gaze Nystagmus

- State v. Merrit, 233 Conn. 302 (1995). HGN is scientific.
- State v Commins, 86 Conn. App. 496 (2004). Satisfies Porter.
- State v. Kelly, 95 Conn. App. 423 (2006). Even though the test requires terms such as "pass," "fail," "points," these are not scientific terms.
- State v. Popeleski, 291 Conn. 769 (2006). "Substantial" compliance with testing protocol is all that is needed.

<u>**The Non-Sequitur of Connecticut Law**</u>

First, the Appellate Court says, "The State must lay a proper foundation with regard to the qualifications of the individual administering the test and demonstrate that the test was conducted in accordance with generally accepted standards such as those specified in the relevant sections of the National Highway Traffic Safety Administration's manual. State v. Merritt."

State v. Balbi, 89 Conn. App. 567 (2005)

Then, the Appellate Court says, "There is no authority, however, for the defendant's claim that the horizontal gaze nystagmus test must be administered in accordance with the standards set forth by the traffic safety administration."

State v. Weed, 188 Conn. App. 654 (2009)

Refusal of Test

A continued request for counsel can be a refusal.

State v. Weed, 118 Conn. App. 654 (2009)

A refusal is not a statement in response to interrogation.

State v. Burns, 140 Conn. 347 (2013)

A defendant must be given a chance to talk to a lawyer prior to the test.

Conn. Gen. Statute 14-227a(b)

Besides the HGN, oftentimes counsel will be dealing with one or more standardized or non-standardized field sobriety tests as the basis of the evidence offered against a DUI defendant.

The law in Connecticut with respect to field testing has become well settled in the last 25 years. Knowledge of the following cases which deal with field testing is essential for the effective handling of DUI cases, both prosecution and defense.

SFST's are Non-Custodial in Nature and Do Not Require Miranda Warnings

"The United States Supreme Court has held that questioning at the scene and conducting field sobriety tests does not involve custody for purposes of Miranda. See Pennsylvania v. Bruder, 488 U.S. 9, 109 S. Ct. 205, 102 L. Ed. 2d 172 (1988). Indeed, we have noted that our case law presumes that such testing is "incident to the initial stop, based on the officer's reasonable suspicion, rather than on the subsequent arrest." State v. Lamme, 19 Conn. App. 594, 601, 563 A.2d 1372 (1989), aff'd, 216 Conn. 172, 579 A.2d 484 (1990). We concluded that such roadside testing and questioning based on "a reasonable, articulable suspicion in the absence of probable cause is 'clearly warranted' within the meaning of the Connecticut constitution."

State v. Gracia, 51 Conn. App. 4 (1998)

Field Tests are Not Scientific Tests and Do Not Require Porter Hearing

The Court in *Gracia* also addressed whether field sobriety tests constitute scientific evidence. Prior to our Supreme Court's decision in state v. Porter, 241 Conn. 57, 698 A.2d 739 (1997) (en banc), cert. denied, 523 U.S. 1058, 118 S. Ct. 1384, 140 L. Ed. 2d 645 (1998), Connecticut courts used the test outlined in Frye v. United States, 293 F. 1013 (D.C. Cir. 1923), for determining the admissibility of scientific evidence. While the events at issue occurred prior to the *Porter* decision, we conclude that the *Frye* test is inapplicable to the field sobriety tests used in this case.

The *Frye* test was found to be appropriate when the "nature of the scientific evidence had the 'potential to mislead lay jurors awed by an aura of mystic infallibility surrounding scientific techniques, experts and the fancy devices employed.'" State v. Borrelli, 227 Conn. 153, 164 A.2d 1105 (1993), quoting State v. Hansen, 205 conn. 485, 490, 534 A.2d 877 (1987). Satisfaction of the *Frye* test, however, was not required in cases where "the jury is in position to weigh the probative value of the testimony without abandoning common sense and sacrificing independent judgment to the expert's assertions based on his special skill or knowledge…Furthermore, where understanding of the method is accessible to the jury, and not dependent on familiarity with highly technically or obscure scientific theories, the expert's qualifications, and the logical bases of his opinions and conclusions can be effectively challenged by cross-examination and rebuttal evidence.'" *Id.,* quoting State v. Hasan, supra, 491. Such a situation exists in this case. The field sobriety tests administered here assessed the defendant's balance, coordination and ability to follow directions. The tests were neither highly technical, nor did they require special skills or knowledge in order to be understood. As we previously stated in State v. Merritt, 36 Conn. App. 76, 90-91, 647, A.2d 1021 (1994), appeal dismissed, 233 Conn. 302, 659 A.2d 706 (1995), such field sobriety tests, unlike the horizontal gaze nystagmus test, are within the common knowledge of lay juror. In the present case, the trial court admitted evidence of the field sobriety tests but limited the evidence to observations of the defendant's behavior made by the arresting officer. Additionally, the court instructed the jury that the roadside sobriety tests were not scientific evidence, and that it should consider the observations made during the tests and use its common experience in determining whether the defendant was intoxicated.

Because the field sobriety tests did not require expert testimony as a precondition of admission, the trial court did not abuse its discretion by admitting evidence concerning those tests.

Police Officers May Testify to Ultimate Issue If Qualified as Expert

In State v. Lamme, 19 Conn. App. 594 (1989), the Appellate Court examined the issue of police testimony as expert testimony concerning a defendant's sobriety when his intoxication was the ultimate issue. The defendant in Lamme contended that the trial court improperly admitted a police officer's opinion testimony about intoxication because that was the ultimate issue in the case.

The officer in Lamme testified that the defendant was driving without his headlights on when he was stopped. The officer also testified that when he approached the defendant's car, he had to bang on the window before the defendant opened it and that there was a strong odor of alcohol in the car. The testimony also related to the officer's administration of field sobriety tests and his interpretation of those tests. Finally, the officer testified that on the basis of his observations and the sobriety tests, he believed that the defendant was intoxicated.

Affirming the decision of the trial court, the Appellate Court stated that "(the officer's) testimony, which included a description and interpretation of and conclusions regarding the roadside sobriety tests, was necessary for the jury intelligently to make a finding as to whether the defendant violated General Statutes $ 14-227a (a) by 'operating] a motor vehicle while under the influence of intoxicating liquor or any drug or both?' The opinion portion of (the officer's) testimony differed from any other opinion testimony regarding the sobriety of an individual because it was based in great part on knowledge and skill beyond the ken of the average juror." Id., 603-604. We concluded that the officer's testimony in Lamme met the previously stated requirement of the trier of facts needing expert assistance so as to permit the testimony's admission as expert testimony on the ultimate issue of fact.

Police Officer Cannot Testify as Expert about Intoxication Unless Information Was Gathered in Course of Professional Duties Using SFST's (lay observations do not rise to level of expert simply because expert observed them).

In State v. McNally, 39 Conn. App. 419, 665 A.2d 137 (1995), the defendant was an off-duty police officer who was charged with assault after an altercation outside a bar. He argued on appeal that the trial court improperly excluded his expert testimony, as a police officer, that the victim was intoxicated at the time of the event.

In affirming the trial court's decision, the Appellate Court stated that, "Lamme is distinguishable from this case because in Lamme the officer's opinion was based on field sobriety tests and the officer's interpretation of those tests. In this case, however, the witness did not conduct held sobriety tests, but rather relied solely on his observation of the victim and his companions to formulate his opinion." They concluded that "Ithe expert opinion was properly excluded on the ground that a determination of a person's intoxication based solely on observation and not on ah interpretation of sobriety tests is within the general knowledge of the jury." McNally indicates that testimony based solely on observations of another's behavior that might indicate intoxication is not beyond the jury's understanding and therefore does not meet the three-pronged test for admitting expert testimony.

The Reconciliation of McNally and Lamme

When Lamme and McNally are read together, there is a clear distinction. Expert testimony is improper if it is based solely on general observations by themselves because in that situation an officer need not invoke or rely on the skill and knowledge garnered from his training. Expert testimony is permissible, however, in the context of an official roadside investigation because in that situation, an officer is required to administer tests and to observe the driver. Those related tasks require the officer to use his specialized skill and knowledge to determine whether the driver is intoxicated.

The defendant argued further that the trooper's testimony, which included both his general observations and discussion of the field sobriety tests, should not have been admitted as proper expert testimony. The defendant asserted that McNally should apply to this situation because the trooper's opinion was based, in part, on his observations and general knowledge of intoxicated people.

First, the trooper's opinion was based on more than his general observations. Second, the observations discussed in McNally arose in a factual context too remote from those we consider presently. McNally concerned an off-duty officer, charged with a crime, who observed a person in a social setting. Here, the trooper observed the defendant in the context of an authorized roadside intoxication investigation.

The defendant's claim was governed by *Lamme* rather than by *McNally*. The Appellate Court applied *Lamme* here for two reasons. First, the officer's testimony that was admitted in that case is similar to the testimony in dispute in this case. Second, whereas *McNally* discusses testimony about observations alone, *Lamme* addresses expert testimony that concerns both observations and the interpretation of field tests.

As we determined in *Lamme*, an officer properly may testify as an expert when his opinion is based on the specialized skill and knowledge he has derived from his training. Specifically, we referred to the application of that specialized knowledge to the interpretation of field sobriety tests in our disposition of that appeal. Because we concluded, however, that all of the officer's testimony constituted expert testimony, we implicitly determined that testimony based on the application of that same skill and knowledge to his observations made during a roadside investigation is also admissible expert testimony.

The Lamme decision recognized, without specifically stating, that in the context of roadside sobriety tests, there is an interrelationship between what the officer observes about the defendant's demeanor and behavior, and how the officer interprets the defendant's performance on the sobriety tests. The roadside investigation must therefore be viewed in light of all the circumstances because the officer's observations generally provide the basis for, and are an integral part of, his decision to field test the driver and his interpretation of the field tests.

When a police officer's opinion testimony involves an overall interpretation of observations and field tests that is based on his skill and knowledge, which is beyond the jury's general knowledge because the officer has special training, that opinion properly may be admitted as his expert opinion. We conclude accordingly that consistent with Lamme, a police officer's observations concerning a defendant and his actions, along with the officer's interpretation of field tests, may be admitted as part of the officer's expert opinion testimony when they are interpreted by the officer as an integral part of his opinion.

Officers Who Apply Their Specialized Training to Evaluate a Suspect May Testify as to the Ultimate Issue in a DUI Case, i.e., that the defendant was intoxicated

In State v. Pjura, 68 Conn. App. 119, 789 A. 2d 1124 (2002), the defendant appealed from the judgment of conviction, rendered after a jury trial, of operating a motor vehicle while under the influence of intoxicating liquor in violation of General Statutes $ 14-227a (a) (1). The defendant claimed that the trial court improperly (1) allowed opinion testimony by a state police trooper that the defendant was under the influence of alcohol and (2) admitted evidence of the horizontal gaze nystagmus (HGN) test.

In State v. Lamme, discussed supra, the Appellate Court determined the nature of the off-cer's testimony in the context of the principal question about expert testimony on the ultimate issue. The Appellate Court noted that despite the trial court's categorization of the officer's testimony as lay opinion, his testimony constituted expert testimony.

In assessing the officer's testimony in Lamme, the Appellate Court first noted his training. The officer had received instruction that provided him with specialized skill and knowledge to assess and determine whether a person is intoxicated. We therefore stated that "the officer's opinion ... was based on this training. As such, his opinion qualified as that of an expert and should have been accorded that status."

Although the Appellate Court did not provide detailed analysis for that conclusion, implicit was the idea that because the officer applied the skill and knowledge derived from his training to interpret the field sobriety tests, his testimony met the three-pronged test for expert testi-mony. That knowledge and skill, which is not common to the layman, allowed the officer to provide assistance to the jury in its decision concerning the defendant's intoxication.

THE MECHANICS OF THE STANDARDIZED FIELD SOBRIETY TESTS

Caveat for Officers in Administration of Field Tests

- Remain motionless while the test is being conducted.

- Be at least 3 feet away.

Standardized Steps for the Walk and Turn

Have the suspect assume a heel-to-toe stance by both giving the following verbal instructions and demonstrating them.

Instructions for Instruction Phase

1. "Place your left foot on the line."
2. “Place your right foot on the line ahead of the left foot, with the heel of the right foot against the toe of the left foot.”
3. "Place your arms down at your side."[27]
4. "Maintain this position until I tell you to begin. Do not start to walk until I tell you to do so."[28]
5. "Do you understand the instructions so far?"

Instructions for the Walking Stage

1. "When I tell you to start, take 9 heel to toe steps down the line, turn around and take 9 heel to toe steps back up the line.
2. When you turn, keep the front foot on the line, and turn by taking a series of small steps with the other foot, like this (demonstrate).”[29]

---

[27] Only after this instruction is given may an officer count a raised arm as a clue.
[28] Many officers fail to give the last part of this instruction which is critical in that a person may start the test too soon if not otherwise instructed.
[29] Confirm that the turn was demonstrated, as an improper turn is frequently a clue documented in the report. If the turn was not demonstrated properly a Defendant should not be penalized for improper turn.

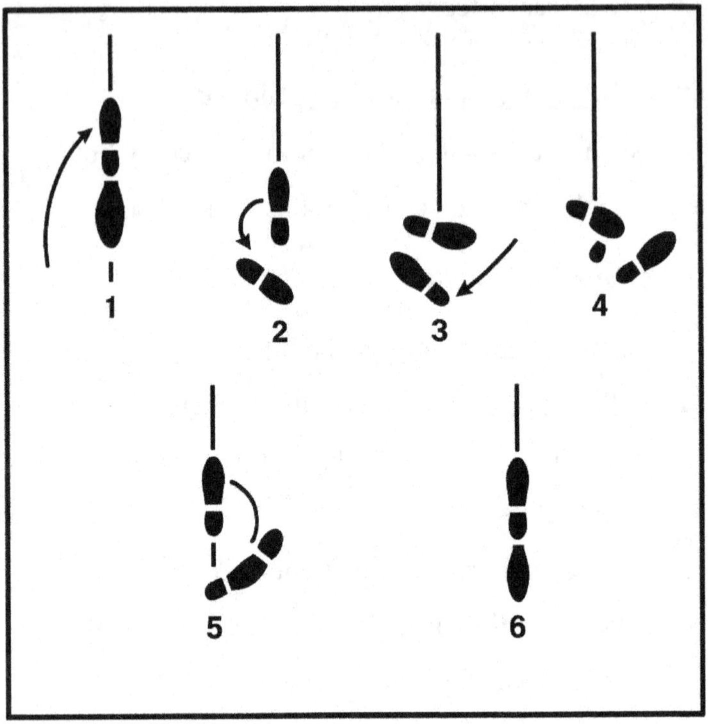

3. "While you are walking, keep your arms at your side, watch your feet at all times, and count your steps out loud."
4. "Once you start walking, don't stop until you have completed the test."
5. "Do you understand the instructions?"
6. "Begin, and count your first step from the heel to toe position as One."

Standardized Clues/Points

1. Cannot keep balance while listening to instructions.
2. Starts before instructions are finished.

3. Stops while walking to steady self.
4. Does not touch heel to toe (Note: the distance must be more than one half inch - some space is permissible).
5. Steps offline (one foot must be entirely off line).
6. Uses arms to balance (more than 6 inches; less is acceptable).
7. Improper turn.
8. Incorrect number of steps.

2 or more clues is considered a failure of this test

Standardized Steps for the One Leg Stand

This test requires a reasonably level, smooth surface and adequate lighting for the suspect to have a visual frame of reference.

Instructions for the Instruction Stage:

1. "Please stand with your feet together and your arms down by your side, like this."
2. "Do not start the test until I tell you to do so."
3. "Do you understand the instructions so far?"

Instruction for the Balance and Counting Stage:

1. "When I tell you to start, raise one leg, either leg, approximately 6 inches off the ground, toes pointed out."
2. "You must keep both legs straight, arms at your sides."
3. "While holding this position, count out loud for thirty seconds in the following manner: one thousand and one, one thousand and two, until told to stop."

4. "Keep your arms at your side at all times and keep watching your raised foot."
5. "Do you understand?"
6. "Go ahead and perform the test."

Standardized Clues/Points

1. Suspect sways while balancing.
2. Uses arms for balance (more than 6 inches, less than 6 is acceptable).
3. Hopping.
4. Puts foot down.

2 or more clues is considered a failure of this test

Note: A clue may appear several times during the administration of the field tests, but it will constitute only one distinct clue, except for the One Leg Stand clue of "Puts foot down," which is graded on the whole number of times it is put down.

Note: The Appellate Court in State v. Kelley, 95 Conn. App. 423 (2006) permitted the use of the terms "pass," "fail, "points, "results," "clues" and "tests" by officers when testifying about the Standardized Field Sobriety Tests. The decision states: "words (such as those above) are commonly used by the average person to describe unscientific topics. In this context the language is nothing more than descriptive and does not automatically imply that the topic is scientific in nature."

HORIZONTAL GAZE NYSTAGMUS

Nystagmus is an involuntary jerking of the eyes. Alcohol, which is a central nervous system depressant, has an impact on the eye's ability to track smoothly. Normally, the muscles of the eyes, when tracking a stimulus, will move smoothly side-to-side, and not "jerk." When under the influence of CNS depressant, the eyes will track the stimulus slower, then jerk forward to catch up to the correct position. Also, the eye muscles will "bounce" when taken beyond a 45-degree angle. All persons have some degree of nystagmus, and it increases with age. A certain percentage of the population will have pathological nystagmus not induced by alcohol.

Admissibility of HGN Test Results into Evidence

In State v. Popeleski, 291 Conn. 769 (2009), the defendant, in part, claimed on appeal that the trial court had improperly admitted into evidence the results of a HGN test, because it had not been administered according to "strict" standards established by the National Highway Traffic Safety Administration (NHTSA).

Up until *Popeleski*, the Supreme Court of Connecticut had never before addressed the standards required for the admissibility of HGN test results into evidence. However, in State v. Merritt, 36 Conn. App. 76 (1994) at 91, our Appellate court articulated a three-part test for such evidence to be admissible. Under the test, the State must:

1. Satisfy criteria for the admission of scientific evidence.

2. Lay the proper foundation with regard to qualification of the individual administering the test, and
3. Demonstrate that the test was conducted in accordance with relevant procedures.

Ultimately, the Supreme Court held that the HGN test results were admissible because the evidence showed that the officer had advanced training from NHTSA and complied substantially with the standards for administering the test.

Porter Hearing Not Required

"Our determination in Commins that horizontal gaze nystagmus evidence satisfies the Porter test for the admission of scientific evidence rendered it unnecessary for the court in the present case to conduct its own Porter hearing prior to admitting evidence about the test. The trial court's thorough consideration of the issue in Commins sufficiently demonstrated to this court that horizontal gaze nystagmus evidence satisfies Porter, and we see no compelling reason to put the state to the burden of having to reestablish, in case after case, the same proposition. Requiring our trial judges to repeatedly hold Porter hearings would serve no legitimate purpose and would needlessly squander judicial resources.

We emphasize that this determination does not relieve the state of its burden to satisfy the remaining two prongs of the Merritt test in every case in which horizontal gaze nystagmus evidence is proffered. The state still must lay a proper foundation with regard to the qualifications of the individual administering the test and demonstrate that the test was conducted in accordance with generally accepted standards such as those specified in the relevant sections of the National Highway Traffic Safety Administration's manual." **Merritt**, at 91.

State v. Balbi, 89 Conn. App. 567 (2005)

Standard Administrative Procedures

1. Check for eyeglasses/contact lenses.
2. Verbal instructions to the subject.
3. Position the stimulus 12-15 inches from eyes.
4. Check for equal tracking.
5. Check for equal pupil size.
6. Check for the lack of smooth pursuit.
7. Check for distinct nystagmus at maximum deviation, repeat (hold for 4 seconds at max on each side, both times).
8. Check for onset of nystagmus prior to 45, repeat.
9. Total the clues.
10. Check for vertical nystagmus.

There are 7 Complete Passes needed to comply with the guidelines.

Other Types of Nystagmus

1. Acquired
2. Anticipatory
3. Arthrokinetic
4. Associated
5. Audio kinetic
6. Bartel's
7. Brun's
8. Centripetal

9. Cervical
10. Circular/elliptical
11. Congenital
12. Convergence
13. Convergence (evoked)
14. Dissociated
15. Down beat
16. Epileptic
17. Flash induced
18. Gaze (evoked)
19. Induced
20. Intermittent vertical
21. Jerk
22. Latent
23. Labral medullary
24. Lid
25. Miner's
26. Musculo-paretic
27. Opto-kinetic
28. Opto-kinetic after induced
29. Pendicular
30. Periodic alternating
31. Physiologic
32. Pursuit after-effect
33. Pursuit defect
34. Pseudo-spontaneous
35. Rebound
36. Reflect
37. See-saw
38. Somatosensory
39. Spontaneous
40. Sleeping around
41. Torsional
42. Unocular
43. Upbeat
44. Vestibular

CHAPTER 8

SEXUAL ASSAULT

Introduction by Ioannis Kaloidis

Sexual assault cases present among the most challenging, complex, and emotionally fraught matters a criminal defense attorney will encounter. The stakes could not be higher for the accused, who faces not only significant prison sentences but also collateral consequences that permanently alter life trajectories: sex offender registration, housing restrictions, employment barriers, and profound social stigma. Defending these cases demands mastery of specialized procedural tools, evidentiary frameworks, and strategic approaches unique to sexual assault prosecutions. This chapter aims to equip Connecticut defense attorneys with practical knowledge to navigate these treacherous waters.

The landscape of sexual assault prosecutions has shifted dramatically over the past three decades. Connecticut, like many jurisdictions, has enacted significant statutory changes expanding the scope of criminal liability, extending statutes of limitations, creating specialized evidentiary frameworks, and enhancing penalties. Simultaneously, cultural movements have transformed juror perspectives and increased public awareness of sexual violence. These changes necessitate defense strategies calibrated to contemporary realities.

Recent amendments to Connecticut's sexual assault statutes have eliminated the statute of limitations for many sexual offenses, particularly those involving minors. As outlined in Public Act 19-16, prosecutors may now bring charges decades after alleged incidents. This temporal expansion creates profound challenges for defense attorneys, who must investigate allegations where physical evidence has deteriorated, memories have faded, and witnesses have disappeared. The extended reach of these statutes demands heightened scrutiny of charging decisions and amplifies the importance of pretrial motion practice.

Few practice areas involve such profound evidentiary tensions as sexual assault defense. The rules of evidence—designed to ensure reliability and fairness—bend considerably in sexual assault prosecutions. Connecticut's statutory framework creates specialized paths for admitting evidence that would otherwise be excluded under traditional evidentiary principles. The tension between these specialized rules and fundamental constitutional rights creates the central battleground for pretrial litigation and trial strategy.

Connecticut's rape shield statute, codified at C.G.S. § 54-86f, exemplifies this tension. The statute appropriately protects complainants from unwarranted invasions of privacy but simultaneously creates hurdles for defendants seeking to introduce evidence crucial to their defense. The four enumerated exceptions to the shield—evidence concerning the source of physical evidence, testimony about sexual conduct introduced by the complainant, evidence of sexual conduct with the defendant, and evidence so relevant that exclusion would violate constitutional rights—require defense counsel to master procedural and substantive frameworks for offering such evidence.

The statute creates a paradox: to introduce evidence under the fourth exception, counsel must make a sufficient offer of proof, yet building that offer often requires access to the very evidence being sought. The strategic challenge becomes apparent—how does counsel construct an offer of proof sufficient to trigger in camera review without access to the underlying information? This handbook provides practical guidance for navigating this procedural labyrinth.

Conversely, Connecticut's specialized rules regarding prior misconduct evidence create asymmetries favoring the prosecution. While traditional evidentiary principles exclude propensity evidence, State v. DeJesus and its progeny create a specialized framework permitting prosecutors to introduce evidence of uncharged sexual misconduct to establish propensity in sexual assault cases. This exception to the prohibition against character evidence dramatically alters the defense landscape, requiring counsel to develop strategies for limiting, contextualizing, or counterbalancing such evidence.

Beyond these evidentiary frameworks, sexual assault cases involve complex procedural mechanisms that do not appear in other criminal matters. The Jarzbek procedure for child testimony outside the defendant's physical presence, the Bruno-Esposito framework for accessing confidential records, and specialized rules for constancy of accusation testimony create a procedural architecture unique to sexual assault prosecution. Mastering these mechanisms is essential for effective representation.

Sexual assault prosecutions frequently turn on issues of consent, credibility, and memory—matters that implicate both expert testimony and cross-examination strategy. The admissibility of expert testimony regarding the general characteristics of sexual assault victims creates challenging strategic considerations. While such testimony cannot directly address the credibility of a particular complainant, it can powerfully influence juror assessment of complainant behavior that might otherwise seem counterintuitive. The line between permissible general characteristic testimony and impermissible commentary on witness credibility has become increasingly blurred, requiring defense counsel to develop nuanced approaches to expert cross-examination and strategic use of objections.

Perhaps most challenging is the intensely emotional nature of sexual assault allegations. These cases evoke powerful reactions from jurors, judges, witnesses, and even defense counsel. Traumatic narratives, disturbing details, and cultural preconceptions about sexual violence create an emotional backdrop that can overwhelm rational evaluation of evidence. The effective defense attorney must acknowledge these emotional dimensions while creating space for methodical assessment of evidence and application of the presumption of innocence.

The presumption of innocence—cornerstone of our criminal justice system—faces its sternest test in sexual assault cases. Cultural movements have rightly brought attention to sexual violence but have simultaneously created pressure to "believe all victims." This pressure can subtly erode the presumption of innocence, creating environments where accusation alone carries devastating weight. Defense counsel must navigate this tension with sensitivity and strategic acumen, honoring the experiences of complainants while vigorously protecting the accused's constitutional rights.

The challenges of sexual assault defense extend beyond the courtroom. Prosecutors often bring specialized expertise to these cases, with dedicated units staffed by attorneys who have developed significant experience in sexual assault litigation. Many jurisdictions employ vertical prosecution models, where a single prosecutor handles the case from charging through trial. Defense attorneys must match this expertise and continuity, developing specialized knowledge and building cases with comparable strategic depth.

Pretrial motion practice assumes heightened importance in sexual assault cases. Motions in limine regarding admissibility of prior acts, rape shield evidence, and expert testimony can fundamentally alter the trial landscape. Motions to dismiss based on statute of limitations, constitutional challenges, or insufficiency of evidence may terminate prosecutions before trial. Motions to suppress statements, identifications, or physical evidence can neutralize the prosecution's most compelling evidence. The outcome of these pretrial battles frequently determines whether cases proceed to trial and shapes the narrative framework for those that do.

Jury selection in sexual assault cases requires particular attention to potential juror biases and preconceptions. Voir dire must explore attitudes toward sexual violence, reporting delays, consent standards, and witness credibility without appearing insensitive or adversarial. Identifying jurors who can truly maintain impartiality despite powerful emotional reactions demands both strategic questioning and careful assessment of verbal and non-verbal responses. This chapter provides guidance for developing voir dire approaches that identify problematic jurors while laying groundwork for trial themes.

Trial presentation in sexual assault cases demands careful calibration of tone, narrative structure, and evidentiary focus. Cross-examination of complainants requires particular sensitivity—effective challenges to credibility or accuracy must avoid appearing unnecessarily adversarial or victim-blaming. Defense counsel must develop approaches that test reliability of testimony without alienating jurors through perceived insensitivity. Similarly, the presentation of defense evidence must acknowledge the emotional weight of allegations while methodically establishing reasonable doubt. This chapter offers practical guidance for developing trial narratives that respect complainant dignity while vigorously defending the accused.

The terminology employed in sexual assault cases carries significant strategic implications. Even neutral terms like "victim" versus "complainant" or "alleged victim" frame juror perceptions. Connecticut courts have restricted judicial use of the term "victim" in cases where victimization itself is contested, but the linguistic battlefield extends beyond this single term. Defense counsel must consider how language choices throughout trial—from opening statement through closing argument—shape juror perceptions and evaluations of evidence.

Recent Connecticut cases have refined frameworks for assessing the admissibility of statements made by complainants to medical providers, social workers, and other professionals. State v. Maguire, State v. Arroyo, and related cases have clarified when such statements constitute testimonial evidence implicating the Confrontation Clause versus non-testimonial statements potentially admissible under hearsay exceptions. These distinctions create complex strategic considerations regarding pretrial motions, objections, and cross-examination approaches.

Technological developments have transformed sexual assault prosecutions, introducing new forms of evidence including digital communications, social media records, GPS data, and video recordings. The authentication, admissibility, and interpretation of such evidence create new battlegrounds requiring defense counsel to develop technological literacy and strategic approaches to digital evidence. This chapter addresses emerging issues in handling technological evidence in sexual assault prosecutions.

Jury instructions in sexual assault cases merit particular attention, as specialized instructions regarding constancy of accusation, prior misconduct evidence, tender years hearsay, and delayed reporting can significantly influence how jurors evaluate evidence. Defense counsel must advocate for balanced instructions that reflect both specialized rules of sexual assault prosecution and fundamental principles of the presumption of innocence and proof beyond reasonable doubt. Preserving instructional issues for appeal requires precise objections and alternative proposed language.

Finally, sentencing advocacy in sexual assault cases demands specialized approaches addressing risk assessment, sex offender treatment, and the complex interplay between incarceration and registration requirements. Defense counsel must develop sentencing strategies that address legitimate public safety concerns while advocating for proportionate punishment and meaningful rehabilitation opportunities. The collateral consequences of conviction—particularly sex offender registration—often outweigh direct sentencing penalties, requiring integrated approaches to plea negotiations and sentencing advocacy.

This chapter is designed to provide practical guidance while acknowledging that sexual assault prosecution and defense continue to evolve in response to legislative changes, judicial interpretations, and cultural developments. The materials offered here provide foundational knowledge and strategic approaches, but effective representation requires ongoing education and adaptation to this rapidly changing landscape. Above all, defense counsel must balance zealous advocacy with ethical practice, recognizing the profound human dimensions of these cases for both accusers and accused. By mastering the specialized procedural tools, evidentiary frameworks, and strategic approaches outlined in this chapter, defense attorneys can fulfill their constitutional mandate to provide effective representation in these most challenging cases.

Statute of Limitations Framework

Connecticut's approach to sexual assault prosecutions reflects a careful balance between protecting victims and ensuring defendants' rights. The state has established varying limitation periods based on the severity of the offense, the age of the victim, and the availability of DNA evidence.

CASES WITH NO STATUTE OF LIMITATIONS

Class A Felony Sexual Assault

The most serious sexual assault offenses can be prosecuted at any time under Connecticut General Statute § 54-193 (2022), as amended by PA 19-16 § 17. These include first degree sexual assault when force or threat of force is used and the victim is under the age of 16 (CT Gen Stat § 53a-70), or when the victim is under age 13 and the alleged offender is more than two years older. Additionally, first degree aggravated sexual assault when the victim is under the age of 16 (CT Gen Stat § 53a-70a), aggravated sexual assault of a minor (CT Gen Stat § 53a-70c), commercial sexual abuse of a minor when the victim is under the age of 15 (CT Gen Stat § 53a-83b), trafficking in persons (CT Gen Stat § 53a-192a), and employing a minor in an obscene performance (CT Gen Stat § 53a-196a) all carry no limitation period.

Perhaps most significantly, any other offense involving sexual abuse, sexual exploitation, or sexual assault of a minor, including risk of injury to a minor involving intimate contact with a victim under the age of 16 (CT Gen Stat § 51-21(a)(2)), can be prosecuted indefinitely.

DNA Evidence Cases

Connecticut has eliminated statute of limitations for specific sexual assault crimes when two conditions are met: the victim reports the crime to police or a prosecutor within five years after it is committed, and the alleged offender's identity is established using DNA evidence collected at the time of the offense (CT Gen Stat § 54-193b, as amended by PA 19-16 § 22 & PA 19-189 § 37). This provision applies to first, second or third degree sexual assault (CT Gen Stat § 53a-70, 71, 72), first degree aggravated sexual assault (CT Gen Stat § 53a-70a), and third degree sexual assault with a firearm (CT Gen Stat § 53a-72b).

CASES WITH STATUTES OF LIMITATIONS

Sexual Assault of Victims Aged 18 to 20

PA 19-16 created a special category for young adult victims. For any offense involving sexual abuse, sexual exploitation or sexual assault of a person age 18, 19 or 20, the statute of limitations extends until the victim's 51st birthday, unless there would be no statute of limitations under the categories described above.

Other Felony Cases

Under PA 19-16, the statute of limitations is 20 years for other felony sexual assault crimes where the victim is age 21 or older, unless there would be no statute of limitations under existing law. This applies to first degree sexual assault and first degree aggravated sexual assault in cases where either crime is a class B felony, as well as second degree sexual assault and third degree sexual assault with a firearm in cases where either crime is a class C felony, and third degree sexual assault in cases where the crime is a class D felony.

Misdemeanor Fourth Degree Sexual Assault

Under PA 19-16, the statute of limitations is 10 years for fourth degree sexual assault in cases where the crime is a class A misdemeanor and the victim is age 21 or older.

CIVIL CASES

Connecticut provides extensive protection for civil remedies in sexual assault cases. There is no limitation on bringing a personal injury action to recover damages caused by sexual assault when the offender has been convicted of first degree sexual assault or first degree aggravated sexual assault (CT Gen Stat § 52-577e).

For other cases involving victims under age 18 at the time of assault that occurred before October 1, 2019, the victim has until their 48th birthday to file a personal injury action for damages caused by sexual assault, sexual abuse, or sexual exploitation (CT Gen Stat § 52-577d). Under PA 19-16, if the victim was under the age of 21 at the time of an assault that happened on or after October 1, 2019, the victim has until his or her 51st birthday to file the action.

In civil cases not subject to these provisions, the three-year statute of limitations that applies to other civil tort cases would generally apply (CGS § 52-577).

Strategic Motion Practice in Sexual Assault Cases

Sexual assault cases demand a comprehensive and aggressive motion practice unlike almost any other criminal matter. The strategic deployment of pretrial motions can fundamentally reshape the evidentiary landscape, secure crucial information otherwise unavailable to the defense, and in some instances, lead to outright dismissal. In sexual assault prosecutions, the battle is often won or lost before trial begins, making mastery of specialized motion practice essential for effective representation.

The Unique Evidentiary Framework

The unique evidentiary frameworks governing sexual assault cases create both challenges and opportunities for defense counsel. Connecticut's rape shield statute, tender years exception, constancy of accusation doctrine, and specialized rules for prior misconduct evidence establish procedural hurdles that can only be overcome through carefully crafted motions. Success requires not merely familiarity with standard motion practice but intimate knowledge of the specialized statutory and case law frameworks specific to sexual assault litigation.

Motion practice in sexual assault cases serves multiple strategic functions beyond their stated legal objectives. Well-crafted motions educate the court about the defense theory, preserve issues for appeal, create settlement leverage, and establish a foundation for trial themes. Even when motions ultimately fail to achieve their primary objective, they frequently yield valuable information about the prosecution's case, expose weaknesses in their evidence, and shape the trial court's understanding of contested issues.

Timing and Strategic Considerations

The timing of motions in sexual assault cases requires particular attention. Some motions must be filed within specific statutory periods, while others strategically benefit from earlier or later filing. Defense counsel must develop a comprehensive motion strategy that accounts for both procedural requirements and tactical considerations. This strategy must integrate both constitutional challenges and statutory frameworks, as the interplay between constitutional rights and specialized evidentiary rules creates the central tension in sexual assault litigation.

Motions to access sensitive records exemplify this tension. The Bruno-Esposito framework for accessing confidential records requires defense counsel to establish both that the records are likely to contain material information and that failure to review them would impair confrontation rights. Threading this procedural needle demands specific language, procedural precision, and strategic timing. Similarly, motions under the rape shield statute require carefully constructed offers of proof that establish relevance without access to the very information being sought—a paradox requiring particular strategic acumen.

Constitutional Challenges in Context

Constitutional motions in sexual assault cases often raise novel issues at the intersection of confrontation rights, due process, and specialized evidentiary frameworks. Defense counsel must craft arguments that acknowledge legitimate privacy interests while vigorously asserting constitutional protections. Motions challenging the admissibility of forensic interviews, Jarzbek testimony procedures, tender years hearsay, and constancy of accusation testimony frequently require integrated constitutional and evidentiary analyses.

Discovery motions assume heightened importance in sexual assault prosecutions, where crucial evidence may be scattered across multiple agencies, treatment providers, and digital platforms. Standard discovery requests rarely suffice; defense counsel must craft targeted motions addressing specific categories of information essential to the defense. This often requires interlocking motions addressing materials held by prosecutors, law enforcement agencies, social service departments, medical providers, and educational institutions.

Motion Hearings as Strategic Opportunities

Motion hearings in sexual assault cases frequently involve testimony from multiple witnesses, creating opportunities for discovery and cross-examination before trial. Defense counsel must approach these hearings not merely as procedural steps but as critical opportunities to lock in testimony, test prosecution theories, and develop impeachment material for use at trial. Preparation for motion hearings should mirror trial preparation in depth and strategic focus.

The following sections detail specific motions essential in sexual assault defense, providing both the legal frameworks and strategic considerations for each. Mastery of these specialized motions equips defense counsel to navigate the procedural complexities of sexual assault litigation while creating the strongest possible foundation for favorable outcomes, whether through pretrial dismissal, advantageous settlement, or trial victory.

Voir Dire in Sexual Assault Cases

When defending a sexual assault case, it's essential to ask voir dire questions that help identify potential biases and attitudes of prospective jurors that could impact their ability to be fair and impartial. The goal is to uncover preconceived notions while educating the panel about defense principles.

ESSENTIAL AREAS OF INQUIRY

General Background and Experience

Begin with standard background questions about occupation, prior jury service, and familiarity with the criminal justice system. These foundational inquiries help establish rapport while gathering basic information about potential jurors' backgrounds and experiences that might influence their decision-making.

Preconceived Notions About Sexual Assault

Address whether jurors have formed opinions about sexual assault cases based on media, television shows, or other sources of information. Equally important is determining whether they can set aside any preconceived notions and evaluate the case based solely on the evidence presented in court. This line of questioning helps identify jurors who may have been influenced by external sources or who harbor biases that could affect their judgment.

Understanding Core Legal Principles

Explore jurors' understanding of the principle of "innocent until proven guilty" and their willingness to apply this principle by presuming the defendant's innocence at the start of trial. Additionally, assess their familiarity with common defense strategies in sexual assault cases, such as exploring the credibility of witnesses or raising issues related to consent, and whether they can consider such strategies without automatically assuming the defendant's guilt.

Consent and Credibility Assessment

Question how jurors define consent in the context of sexual activity and whether they can assess evidence related to consent without making assumptions about the parties involved. Similarly, explore what factors they consider when evaluating witness credibility and how they would approach assessing the credibility of the alleged victim and other witnesses in a sexual assault case.

Media Exposure and External Influences

Determine whether jurors have been exposed to media coverage or discussions about the specific case prior to jury selection, and whether they can avoid seeking additional information about the case outside the courtroom during trial. This helps identify potential contamination from pretrial publicity.

Sensitivity to Evidence and Testimony

Address whether jurors can remain objective when presented with graphic or explicit evidence that may be introduced during trial, avoiding being unduly influenced by such material. If expert witnesses or mandatory reporters such as medical professionals or counselors will testify, determine whether jurors can treat their testimony like any other witness without giving it special weight.

Personal Bias and Prejudice

Finally, explore whether there is anything in jurors' backgrounds or personal experiences that they believe might affect their ability to be fair and impartial in the case, and whether they are aware of any biases or prejudices they may need to set aside when considering the evidence.

Remember that voir dire questions should be tailored to the specific circumstances of the case and the potential biases that may exist in the jury pool. These questions can help ensure that selected jurors are capable of being fair and unbiased in their evaluation of the evidence presented during the sexual assault defense.

Direct Examination Considerations

CHILD WITNESS COMPETENCY AND CREDIBILITY

Competency Standards

Connecticut law establishes that "No witness shall be automatically adjudged incompetent to testify because of age and any child who is a victim of assault, sexual assault or abuse shall be competent to testify without prior qualification. The weight to be given the evidence and the credibility of the witness shall be for the determination of the trier of fact" (CT Gen Stat § 54-86h (2022)).

The Connecticut Supreme Court has clarified that trial courts are not required to conduct competency hearings for child witnesses. In State v. Aponte, 249 Conn. 735, 738 A.2d 117 (1999), the court noted that "The trial court denied the defendant's request to conduct a hearing into the competency of the [victim]" before allowing a four-year old child victim to testify, under CT Gen Stat § 54-86h.

Statements of Incompetent Child Witnesses

When a child is found incompetent to testify, their out-of-court statements may still be admissible under certain circumstances. In State v. Dollinger, 20 Conn. App. 530 (1990), a 28-month-old child victim was found incompetent to testify at a pretrial hearing but had made statements to her physician and mother. The statements to a treating physician identifying the defendant as her abuser were admissible under the medical treatment exception to the hearsay rule, while statements made to the child's mother were admissible under the residual exception.

Jury Instructions on Child Credibility

In State v. James, 211 Conn. 55 (1989), the Connecticut Supreme Court overruled previous precedent and held that instruction on the credibility of a child witness was not required, but left to the discretion of the court. The court stated: "We conclude, nevertheless, that Anderson should be overruled in holding that it is essential to grant a requested charge that denigrates a child as usually less worthy of belief than an adult, especially when it treats all children uniformly regardless of differences in age or intelligence and also omits any reference to factors commonly recognized as enhancing the credibility of a child."

SPECIAL COURTROOM PROCEDURES FOR CHILD TESTIMONY

Testimony Outside the Courtroom

Connecticut General Statute § 54-86g discusses procedures available in criminal prosecutions involving assault, sexual assault, or abuse of a child aged twelve years or younger. The statute focuses on ensuring the comfort and well-being of the child during testimony. Under subsection (a), the court has authority to order that the child's testimony be taken in a separate room, away from the courtroom, with the trial judge present to supervise proceedings. The testimony can be either televised in the courtroom through closed circuit equipment or recorded for later viewing by the court.

Only specific individuals are allowed in the room with the child during testimony, including the judge, the defendant, attorneys for both sides, equipment operators, and any person who would contribute to the child's welfare and well-being. However, the court may exclude or screen the defendant from the child's sight and hearing if proven by clear and convincing evidence that the child would be intimidated or inhibited by the defendant's physical presence. In such cases, the defendant is still allowed to observe and hear the child's testimony and consult with their attorney privately. If the child's testimony is taken in this manner, they are not required to testify in court during the actual proceeding.

Additional Protective Procedures

Subsection (b) provides additional procedures that may be ordered by the court when the child's testimony is taken. These include prohibiting individuals from entering or leaving the courtroom during the child's testimony, allowing a trusted adult known to the child to sit close by without obstructing the defendant or fact-finder's view, permitting the use of anatomically correct dolls by the child, and requiring attorneys to question the child while seated at a table in front of them, remaining seated during objections and posing questions in a non-intimidating manner.

State v. Jarzbek addresses whether a minor victim may testify through videotape made outside the physical presence of the defendant in criminal prosecutions involving alleged sexual abuse of children. The Connecticut Supreme Court emphasized that this accommodation is not automatic: "We emphatically reject the proposal of the state that, in every case allegedly involving the sexual abuse of children, we should presume that the credibility of a minor victim's testimony will be improved by excluding the defendant from the witness room during that witness's testimony. There is no constitutional justification for automatically depriving all criminal defendants of the right of physical confrontation during the videotaping of a minor victim's testimony. We instead mandate a case-by-case analysis, whereby a trial court must balance the individual defendant's right of confrontation against the interest of the state in obtaining reliable testimony from the particular minor victim in question" (State v. Jarzbek, 204 Conn. 683, 704, 529 A.2d 1245, 1255 (1987)).

Procedural Requirements for Excluding Defendant

The Jarzbek framework establishes specific requirements that must be met before a defendant can be excluded from the room during a child's testimony. The child must be of "tender years," meaning the court must conclude that the case involves "criminal prosecutions involving the alleged sexual abuse of children of tender years." The child must be the "victim," as "the practice of videotaping the testimony of a minor victim outside the physical presence of the defendant is, in appropriate circumstances, constitutionally permissible."

There must be an evidentiary hearing where "a trial court must determine, at an evidentiary hearing..." the appropriateness of the procedure. The defendant has the right to be physically present at that evidentiary hearing, and the State must prove that there is a compelling need for the special procedure.

Proving "Compelling Need"

To satisfy its burden of proving compelling need, "the state must show that the minor victim would be so intimidated, or otherwise inhibited, by the physical presence of the defendant that the trustworthiness of the victim's testimony would be seriously called into question. Furthermore, the state bears the burden of proving such [a] compelling need by clear and convincing evidence" (State v. Jarzbek, 204 Conn. 683, 704-05, 529 A.2d 1245, 1255 (1987)).

Expert Testimony Not Required

The Connecticut courts have clarified that expert testimony is not required to establish compelling need. In State v. Spigarolo, 210 Conn. 359, 372, the court stated: "We reject the defendant's argument that Jarzbek contemplates that expert testimony is necessary to establish the state's burden of proof. Nothing in Jarzbek indicates any such requirement. Indeed, such a requirement would ignore the unusual and unfortunate circumstances of cases of sexual abuse of children. The family or guardians of a sexually abused child obviously occupy a unique position to assess the mental and emotional impact of a courtroom confrontation on the minor. We have no doubt that the testimony of such individuals may provide critical insight on a minor's ability or inclination to speak truthfully in the physical presence of an alleged perpetrator. We therefore refuse to construe Jarzbek as requiring the state to present expert testimony in order to meet its burden of proof."

However, courts have found that experts are not required to testify that a child will lie in the presence of the defendant. Various cases have established the types of testimony sufficient to meet the compelling need standard. In State v. Bonello, 210 Conn. 51 (1989), a social worker and psychiatrist testified that the witness would be intimidated by the defendant and confused and overstimulated by the courtroom environment, which would render the testimony unreliable. In State v. Hydock, 51 Conn. App. 753 (1999), a grandmother, social worker, nurse and teacher testified that the witness was fearful and intimidated enough to show possible distortion of truth while testifying. In State v. Alterisi, 47 Conn. App. 199 (1997), a social worker and an uncle testified that the witness was frightened by the defendant and would be unable to talk about the events in his presence.

"Tender Years" Definition

Importantly, "tender years" refers to the age of the victim at the time of the offense, not at the time of trial or testimony. In State v. Wegman, 70 Conn. App. 171 (2002), the court concluded: "We conclude that the plain language of the statute is unambiguous. The statute refers to the child's age at the time of the offense and makes no reference to the child's age at the time testimony is given. 'We are constrained to read a statute as written . . . and we may not read into clearly expressed legislation provisions which do not find expression in its words'" (citing Giaimo v. New Haven, 257 Conn. 481, 494 (2001)).

The concept of "tender years" may also apply to "mental age." In State v. Wegman, the court found: "We conclude that under the circumstances, the state met its burden of proving a compelling need by clear and convincing evidence. The court found, and the evidence supports the finding, that 'the child does not have the mental or social or emotional abilities of a child twelve years or older'" (State v. Wegman, 70 Conn. App. 171, 182, 798 A.2d 454, 464 (2002)).

Defense Expert Examination Rights

When the state's motion is supported by expert testimony, the defendant may, upon the trial court's discretion, have an expert of their choosing examine the witness. In State v. Marquis, 241 Conn. 823, 829, 699 A.2d 893, 897 (1997), the court asked: "May a trial court, in exercising its discretion under State v. Jarzbek and General Statutes § 54-86g take into account the fact that the state's motion is supported by expert testimony and, therefore, order the child witness to be examined by the defendant's expert?"

The court answered affirmatively, explaining: "'In the absence of a strong showing of state interests to the contrary, discovery must be a two-way street.' In the present case, the state moved for a procedure that called into question R's ability to testify in the presence of the defendant, yet denied the defendant the opportunity to obtain evidence in opposition to the motion, evidence that the trial court deemed necessary to make a fully informed decision. For the state to take such a position is antithetical to the constitutional underpinnings of a Jarzbek hearing" (State v. Marquis, 241 Conn. 823, 837, 699 A.2d 893, 900 (1997), citing Wardius v. Oregon, 412 U.S. 475, 93 S. Ct. 2208, 37 L. Ed. 2d 82 (1973)).

ADMISSIBILITY OF FORENSIC INTERVIEWS

Frequently, following an initial complaint, the individual making the complaint is interviewed by a social worker or similar professional who is part of a "multi-disciplinary team." This team usually includes police officers, DCF workers, a nurse, other social workers, and the parents of the complainant as observers during the interview. The social worker's primary role is to ask questions aimed at eliciting details about the alleged crime from the complainant, following a nationally established protocol. To minimize trauma, usually only the social worker conducts the questioning. After the interview, the complainant is typically escorted to a nurse for a medical examination.

During trial, the prosecution will attempt to present this recorded interview, conducted outside the courtroom, as substantive evidence of the crime, in addition to the complainant's testimony. The key issue in determining whether the recorded interview should be admitted as evidence at trial is whether the statements made during the interview were testimonial.

The Crawford Framework

Under Crawford v. Washington, 541 U.S. 36, 68-69 (2004), "the hearsay statements of an unavailable witness that are testimonial in nature may be admitted under the sixth amendment's confrontation clause only if the defendant has had a prior opportunity to cross-examine the declarant."

"Hearsay statements that are nontestimonial in nature are not governed by the confrontation clause, and their admissibility is governed solely by the rules of evidence. Thus, the threshold inquiry for purposes of the admissibility of such statements under the confrontation clause is whether they are testimonial in nature" (State v. Slater, 285 Conn. 162, 169-70 (2008)).

Determining Primary Purpose

The focus is on the intent of the interrogator for purposes of determining whether the primary purpose of the statement is testimonial (State v. Maguire, 310 Conn. 535, 568-69 (2013); Michigan v. Bryant, 562 U.S. 344 (2011)).

Statements taken by government actors who are not members of law enforcement are testimonial if the interview is the functional equivalent of police interrogation with the primary purpose of establishing or proving past events potentially relevant to later criminal prosecution (State v. Arroyo, 284 Conn. 597, 629 (2007)).

A victim's statements during a forensic interview may be deemed nontestimonial only if the essential purpose of the interview is to provide medical assistance to the victim (State v. Maguire, 310 Conn. 569 (2013)).

When Testimonial Statements Are Admissible

If the out-of-court statement is testimonial, its admissibility depends on whether the witness is available for cross-examination. If the witness is unavailable, then the statement is inadmissible. If the witness is available, then it depends on whether the statement qualifies as a prior inconsistent statement under State v. Whelan, 200 Conn. 743 (1986).

In State v. Cameron M., 307 Conn. 504 (2012), the Connecticut Supreme Court affirmed the admission of an out-of-court statement for substantive purposes because it satisfied the Whelan requirements and the witness was available at trial for cross-examination.

ADMISSIBILITY OF NONTESTIMONIAL STATEMENTS

Nontestimonial statements are subject to the Rule Against Hearsay. If an exception exists, then the statement may be admissible. Three of the most common exceptions in sexual assault cases are spontaneous utterance, medical treatment exception, and the tender years doctrine.

Spontaneous Utterance

Code of Evidence Section 8-3(2) establishes the requirements for a spontaneous utterance. The statement must follow a startling occurrence, be related to that occurrence, be made by someone having an opportunity to observe the occurrence (State v. Wargo, 255 Conn. 113 (2000)), and be made under circumstances that indicate it is a spontaneous utterance caused by the excitement of the declarant and that negates an opportunity for deliberation and fabrication.

Courts have found relatively short time periods sufficient for spontaneous utterances. In State v. Cayouette, 25 Conn. App. 384 (1991), the court held that 30 minutes was sufficiently close in time. In State v. Kelly, 256 Conn. 23 (2001), a period of 10 to 15 minutes was held to be sufficient.

Medical Treatment Exception

State v. Arroyo, 284 Conn. 597, 635, 935 A.2d 975, 999 (2007), is the primary precedent addressing the medical treatment exception concerning statements made by complainants of sexual abuse. The court found: "There is no evidence in the record to indicate that the victim's interviews with Montelli were at the instruction or request of law enforcement. Instead, the record reflects that Hammie, an investigator with the department, initially brought the victim and the victim's mother to the clinic for examinations. Moreover, there is no indication that Montelli was in the employ of a law enforcement agency and no evidence that she cooperated or assisted in the investigation of the defendant. The purpose of her interviews was related solely to securing the welfare of the child. As she explained during her testimony: '[T]he purpose of my interview was to obtain information that would help us in determining what happened and what steps need to take place at that point.' When questioned regarding what those 'steps' would include, she clarified: 'Medical treatment to secure her safety. Mental health treatment, if necessary.' On the basis of these facts, we conclude that the primary purpose of the interviews was not to build a case against the defendant, but to provide the victim with assistance in the form of medical and mental health treatment. Therefore, the statements were nontestimonial, and the admission of those statements did not violate the defendant's right to confrontation."

Tender Years Doctrine

Connecticut General Statute 54-86L (and Code of Evidence 8-10) provides that a statement by a child twelve years of age or younger at the time of the statement relating to a sexual offense committed against that child, or an offense involving physical abuse committed against that child by the child's parent or guardian or any other person exercising comparable authority over the child at the time of the offense, shall be admissible in a criminal or juvenile proceeding if specific requirements are met.

Tender Years Exception Requirements

First, the tender years exception must be read consistently with the sixth amendment bar against testimonial hearsay, as explained in Crawford. The prohibition against statements made in preparation of a legal proceeding is simply another way of saying that, to be admissible, the statement must be nontestimonial for purposes of Crawford (State v. Cameron M., 307 Conn. 504, 514-15 (2012)).

When a child does not testify and the statement is determined to be non-testimonial, specific procedural requirements must be followed. There must be an evidentiary hearing where the court finds that the circumstances of the statement, including its timing and content, provide particularized guarantees of its trustworthiness. The statement must not have been made in preparation for a legal proceeding, and there must be independent, non-testimonial corroborative evidence of the alleged act. Finally, the out-of-court statement must have been made before the defendant's arrest for the act.

Identity of Abuser in Medical Treatment Context

In cases of sexual abuse in the home, hearsay statements made in the course of medical treatment which reveal the identity of the abuser are reasonably pertinent to treatment and are admissible. If the sexual abuser is a member of the child victim's immediate household, it is reasonable for a physician to ascertain the identity of the abuser to prevent recurrences and to facilitate the treatment of psychological and physical injuries (State v. DePastino, 228 Conn. 552, 565 (1994)).

This principle may also apply to adults. The Connecticut Supreme Court concluded that "in any sexual assault, the identity of the perpetrator undoubtedly is relevant to the physician to facilitate the treatment of psychological and physical injuries" (State v. Kelly, 256 Conn. 23, 45 (2001); see also State v. Cruz, 260 Conn. 1 (2002)).

The definition of a treating physician has been extended to psychologists and psychiatrists who have been treating the declarant's psychological and emotional injuries. If a social worker is acting within the chain of medical diagnosis and treatment, then the statements would also be admissible (State v. Cruz, 260 Conn. 1 (2002)). As long as the person is in the chain of medical diagnosis or treatment, and the declarant's motive is consistent with the purpose of obtaining medical diagnosis or treatment, the statement would be admissible under this exception. It does not matter that the interview takes place in the presence of police officials.

CONSTANCY OF ACCUSATION AS SUBSTANTIVE EVIDENCE

If a witness whose testimony would typically be restricted by the constraints of constancy of accusation has provided an out-of-court statement that meets the criteria of the Tender Years Doctrine, that statement can be admitted as substantive evidence. In State v. Maguire, 310 Conn. 535, 576 (2013), the court explained: "That the drafters intended for testimony admitted under the tender years exception to be treated like all other evidence admissible under a hearsay exception—i.e., as substantive evidence that is admissible to prove the truth of the matter asserted—is demonstrated by the fact that tender years evidence is not admissible unless two significant conditions have been met, namely, that the evidence is trustworthy and that it was not generated in preparation of litigation. Although the tender years exception is a relatively new addition to the Connecticut Code of Evidence, there is nothing in its language to suggest that its drafters intended tender years evidence to be limited by the constancy of accusation doctrine. Accordingly, because there is nothing in the text of § 8-10 of the Connecticut Code of Evidence or its accompanying commentary to suggest that tender years evidence is admissible solely to corroborate the victim's testimony, it would be manifestly improper for us to read such a limitation into that provision."

Challenging this Holding

The law as it currently stands allows constancy testimony as substantive evidence under certain circumstances. However, a close reading of the Tender Years statute indicates that there may be room for debate. The language of both C.G.S. §54-86L and §8-10 of the Code of Evidence are identical in substance and state: "Notwithstanding any other rule of evidence or provision of law, a statement by a child twelve years of age or younger at the time of the statement relating to a sexual offense committed against that child, or an offense involving physical abuse committed against that child by the child's parent or guardian or any other person exercising comparable authority over the child at the time of the offense, shall be admissible in a criminal or juvenile proceeding."

The Court in Maguire applied this to admit constancy testimony as substantive evidence. However, both the statute and the Code contemplate the admission only of statements by the child against whom the abuse is alleged. It is unclear whether this distinction was raised in Maguire, and the court made no mention of this limitation, so it remains open for challenge.

Constancy of Accusation Doctrine

Framework and Requirements

The Connecticut Code of Evidence permits constancy of accusation testimony under specific circumstances. Section 6-11(c) provides that "A person to whom a sexual assault victim has reported the alleged assault may testify that the allegation was made and when it was made, provided the victim has testified to the facts of the alleged assault and to the identity of the person or persons to whom the assault was reported. Any testimony by the witness about details of the assault shall be limited to those details necessary to associate the victim's allegations with the pending charge. The testimony of the witness is admissible only to corroborate the victim's testimony and not for substantive purposes."

This section codifies the ruling of the Connecticut Supreme Court in State v. Troupe, 237 Conn. 284 (1996).

Who Qualifies as a Constancy Witness

A constancy witness is a person to whom a sexual assault victim has reported the assault. However, this applies only to witnesses to whom the assault was reported prior to any report to law enforcement (State v. Samuels, 273 Conn. 541, 552 (2005)). The court explained: "If the purpose of the doctrine is to combat stereotypes held by jurors regarding nonreporting victims, once a victim has officially reported the crime to the police, we do not believe any reasonable function can be further served by the admission of postcharge constancy testimony" (State v. Samuels, 273 Conn. 552 (2005)).

Restrictions on Constancy Testimony

"Any testimony by the witness regarding the details surrounding the assault must be strictly limited to those necessary to associate the victim's complaint with the pending charge" (State v. Troupe, 237 Conn. 284, 304 (1996)). This is limited to the fact and timing of the victim's complaint, the time and place of the attack, and the identity of the alleged perpetrator.

The testimony is not admitted for substantive purposes, but merely for corroboration unless admissible as substantive evidence under another hearsay exception. The complainant must first have testifie

d concerning the facts of the sexual assault and the identity of the person or persons to whom the incident was reported. The testimony is also subject to a 4-3 prejudice analysis (State v. Troupe, 237 Conn. 303-305).

Victim's Testimony Not Required Regarding Constancy Statement

The Connecticut courts have clarified that the victim does not need to explicitly testify about making the constancy statement. In State v. Orhan, 52 Conn. App. 231 (1999), the court noted: "The state concedes that the trial court was mistaken as to the requirements of Troupe but argues that although the victim did not explicitly testify that she told her mother what the defendant did to her, there was sufficient circumstantial evidence to lay the foundation necessary for her constancy of accusation testimony. We agree with the state."

Modification of the Constancy Doctrine

In State v. Daniel W. E., 322 Conn. 593, 595, 142 A.3d 265, 267 (2016), the Connecticut Supreme Court modified the traditional constancy doctrine: "The [Constancy] doctrine should continue to be employed in Connecticut to counter implicit juror bias against victims, including children, who delay in reporting sexual abuse, but in a modified form ... if defense counsel thereafter challenges the victim's credibility by inquiring about, for example, the victim's out-of-court complaints or delayed reporting, the state will be permitted to call constancy of accusation witnesses subject to the limitations established by applicable case law."

The court established new jury instructions: "If defense counsel does not challenge the victim's credibility on these points, the trial court shall not permit the state to introduce constancy testimony and shall instruct the jury that there are many reasons why sexual assault victims may delay in officially reporting the offense and that, to the extent the victim delayed in reporting the offense, the jury should not consider the delay in evaluating the victim's credibility."

The court further explained: "...to ensure clarity in future cases in which constancy of accusation evidence is admitted, § 6-11 (c) of the Connecticut Code of Evidence and Connecticut's standard criminal jury instruction on constancy evidence, 7.2-1, should be modified to conform more closely to the language used in New Jersey's model instruction on fresh complaint evidence, which explains that evidence of a sexual assault victim's complaint to other persons is admissible only for the purpose of negating any inference that, because there was a delay in reporting the offense, the offense did not occur, and that such evidence may be used only in considering whether the complaint was made and not to corroborate the substance of the complaint or to bolster the credibility of the victim with respect to any other issue."

Rape Shield Protections and Exceptions

General Framework

Connecticut General Statute § 54-86f establishes comprehensive protections limiting the admissibility of evidence concerning a sexual assault victim's sexual conduct. In any prosecution for sexual assault under sections 53a-70, 53a-70a, and 53a-71 to 53a-73a, inclusive, no evidence of the sexual conduct of the victim may be admissible unless such evidence falls within specific statutory exceptions.

Recognized Exceptions

The statute provides four specific exceptions where evidence of sexual conduct may be admitted. First, evidence may be offered by the defendant on the issue of whether the defendant was, with respect to the victim, the source of semen, disease, pregnancy or injury. Second, evidence may be offered by the defendant on the issue of credibility of the victim, provided the victim has testified on direct examination as to his or her sexual conduct. Third, any evidence of sexual conduct with the defendant offered by the defendant on the issue of consent by the victim, when consent is raised as a defense by the defendant, may be admissible. Finally, evidence that is otherwise so relevant and material to a critical issue in the case that excluding it would violate the defendant's constitutional rights may be admitted.

Such evidence shall be admissible only after a hearing on a motion to offer such evidence containing an offer of proof.

Burden of Proof and Offers of Proof

A defendant who seeks to introduce evidence under one of the exceptions of § 54-86f bears the burden of establishing the relevance of proffered testimony (State v. Martinez, 295 Conn. 758, 771 (2010)).

An offer of proof consists of "allegations by the attorney ... in which he represents to the court that he could prove them if granted an evidentiary hearing. Additionally, an offer of proof should contain specific evidence rather than vague assertions and sheer speculation ..."

Alternative Source of Sexual Knowledge

One significant application of the rape shield exceptions involves cases where a child victim demonstrates age-inappropriate sexual knowledge. In State v. Rolon, 257 Conn. 156 (2001), the court recognized: "If the jury is not allowed to learn of the [prior sexual] offenses against [the] complainants, then [it] will inevitably conclude that the complainants' highly age-inappropriate sexual knowledge could only come from [the] defendant having committed such acts."

Prior to trial, the defendant must make an offer of proof showing that the prior acts clearly occurred, that the acts closely resembled those of the present case, that the prior act is clearly relevant to a material issue, that the evidence is necessary to defendant's case, and that the probative value of the evidence outweighs its prejudicial effect.

Alternative Source of Physical Injuries

General Statute § 54-86f(1) recognizes and protects defendant's constitutional rights to confrontation and to present a defense by permitting evidence of sexual conduct of the complainant when the evidence is "offered by the defendant on the issue of whether the defendant was, with respect to the victim, the source of...injury."

When evidence is proffered under one of the exceptions in the rape shield statute to support an alternative theory concerning the source of the victim's injuries, "it will almost always be deemed more probative than prejudicial because it implicates the defendant's constitutional right of confrontation" (State v. Shaw, 312 Conn. 85 (2014)).

The Rolon test does not apply to an offer of proof on whether there is an alternative explanation for the victim's injuries (State v. Brisco, 84 Conn. App. 120, 138-39, 852 A.2d 746, cert. denied, 271 Conn. 944, 861 A.2d 1178 (2004)).

Prior False Claims

Prior false claims of rape, if relevant, are admissible evidence under C.G.S. § 54-86f(4) exception (State v. Manini, 38 Conn. App. 100, 115 (1995)). The evidence does not need to prove the prior accusation is false; it merely needs to support the premise that the accusation is false (State v. Rolon, 257 Conn. 156, 177 (2001)).

There is an argument that allegations of prior false claims of rape are not covered by the Rape Shield statute. Other states have held this to be the case (State v. Sullivan, 244 Conn. 640, 657-8 (1998) (Berdon, J., dissenting); Miller v. State, 105 Nev. 497, 501 (1989); State v. Guenther, 181 N.J. 129, 152-155 (2004)).

Bruno-Esposito Framework for Accessing Protected Records

Categories of Protected Records

Connecticut has established broad protections for various types of confidential communications and records. These include psychiatrist-patient privilege protecting confidential communications or records of a patient seeking diagnosis and treatment (52-146d), DCF records which are confidential under General Statutes § 17a-28, school records which are confidential under General Statutes § 10-15b (State v. George J., 280 Conn. 551 (2006)), clinical social worker records (54-146q), and licensed professional counselor records (54-146s).

The Connecticut Supreme Court has held that records and communications between a sexual assault victim and a sexual assault counselor are similarly protected and subject to the Esposito-Bruno procedure before such information may be disclosed to the defendant (State v. Allen, 140 Conn. App. 423 (2013); see also 52-146k).

Defendant's Constitutional Rights

The victim's right to privacy in such cases often directly conflicts with the defendant's right to confront the state's witnesses. The right to confrontation is fundamental to a fair trial under both the federal and state constitutions, expressly protected by the sixth and fourteenth amendments to the United States constitution and by article first, § 8, of the Connecticut constitution.

In Pennsylvania v. Ritchie, 480 U.S. 39, 58 (1987), the United States Supreme Court held that the fourteenth amendment's due process clause provides a right to exculpatory information contained in confidential materials.

The Esposito Balance

In Esposito, 192 Conn. 166 (1984), the Connecticut Supreme Court struck a balance between the confidentiality of psychiatric records and the defendant's right to confrontation and established a procedure for disclosure of these records.

Preliminary Showing by Defendant

First, a defendant must make a preliminary showing that there is a reasonable ground to believe that failure to review the records likely would impair the defendant's right to confrontation (State v. Kulmac, 230 Conn. 58-59).

To meet this burden, the defendant must do more than assert that the privileged records may contain information that would be useful for impeaching a witness' credibility (State v. Colon, 272 Conn. 106, 264-65 (2004)). The defendant's offer of proof should be specific and should set forth the issue in the case to which the confidential information sought will relate (State v. George J., 280 Conn. 599).

The linchpin of the determination of the defendant's access to the records is whether they sufficiently disclose material especially probative of the ability to comprehend, know and correctly relate the truth so as to justify breach of their confidentiality and disclosing them to the defendant in order to protect his right of confrontation (State v. Stephen J. R., 309 Conn. 586 (2013); State v. Slimskey, 257 Conn. 842, 856-57 (2001)).

To compel an in camera review under the due process clause, the defendant "must at least make some plausible statement of how the information would be both material and favorable to his defense" (State v. Leduc, 40 Conn. App. 233, 248).

Materiality and Favorability Standards

Favorable evidence is that evidence which might have led the jury to entertain a reasonable doubt about guilt and this doubt must be one that did not otherwise exist. Evidence is material only if there is a reasonable probability that, had the evidence been disclosed to the defense, the result of the proceeding would have been different. A reasonable probability is a probability sufficient to undermine confidence in the outcome (United States v. Bagley, 473 U.S. 667, 682(1985); State v. Rasmussen, 225 Conn. 55, 92,(1993)).

The defendant "of course, may not require the trial court to search through the [department] file without first establishing a basis for his claim that it contains material evidence" (Pennsylvania v. Ritchie, 480 U.S. 58 n.15).

The Bruno-Esposito Procedure

The established procedure requires several sequential steps (State v. Esposito, 192 Conn. 179-80; see also State v. Bruno, 197 Conn. 329-30). If the claimed impeaching information is privileged, there must be a showing that there is reasonable ground to believe that the failure to produce the information is likely to impair the defendant's right of confrontation such that the witness' direct testimony should be stricken.

Upon such a showing, the court may then afford the state an opportunity to secure the consent of the witness for the court to conduct an in camera inspection of the claimed information and, if necessary, to turn over to the defendant any relevant material for the purposes of cross-examination.

If the defendant does make such showing and such consent is not forthcoming, then the court may be obliged to strike the testimony of the witness. If the consent is limited to an in camera inspection and such inspection, in the opinion of the trial judge, does not disclose relevant material, then the resealed record is to be made available for inspection on appellate review.

If the in camera inspection does reveal relevant material, then the witness should be given an opportunity to decide whether to consent to release of such material to the defendant or to face having her testimony stricken in the event of refusal.

However, the Connecticut Supreme Court has clarified important limitations on this procedure. In State v. Kemah, 289 Conn. 411 (2008), the court held: "Therefore, the trial court improperly ordered disclosure to the defendant merely because the complainant had waived her statutory privilege with respect to state law enforcement officials."

Prior Misconduct Evidence in Sexual Assault Cases

General Rule Against Propensity Evidence

Evidence of prior misconduct is not admissible for the purpose of establishing a defendant's propensity to engage in criminal conduct (Conn. Code Evid. § 4-5 (a); State v. Randolph, 284 Conn. 328, 340 (2007)).

Exception for Sexual Assault Cases

Evidence of uncharged sexual misconduct is admissible only if it is relevant to prove that the defendant had a propensity or a tendency to engage in the type of aberrant and compulsive criminal sexual behavior with which he or she is charged (State v. DeJesus, 288 Conn. 418, 470-74 (2008)).

Requirements for Admissibility

For uncharged sexual misconduct evidence to be admissible, it must be relevant to prove that the defendant had a propensity or a tendency to engage in the crime. The evidence is relevant if the act is not too remote in time, is similar to the offense charged, and was committed upon persons similar to the prosecuting witness. Additionally, the probative value must outweigh the prejudicial effect.

State v. Antonaras, 137 Conn. App. 703 (2012), provides detailed analysis of the caselaw and parameters surrounding these three relevancy requirements.

No Requirement of Sexual Assault Charge

The defendant does not need to be charged with a sexual assault crime for this evidence to be admissible. In State v. Snelgrove, 288 Conn. 742, 760 (2008), the court explained: "Whenever the evidence establishes that both the prior misconduct and the offense with which the defendant is charged were driven by an aberrant sexual compulsion, regardless of whether the prior misconduct or the conduct at issue resulted in sexual offense charges."

There must be an accompanying limiting instruction to the jury (State v. DeJesus, Criminal Jury Instruction 2.6-13).

Use of Comfort Items During Testimony

THERAPY/SERVICE/COMFORT DOGS

Statutory Authority

Connecticut law does not provide explicit statutory authority for the use of therapy dogs during testimony. In State v. Devon D., 150 Conn. App. 514, cert. granted, 314 Conn. 909 (2014), the court explained: "The text of this statute clearly states what special courtroom procedures it permits for child victims who were under the age of twelve when they suffered abuse: a court may prohibit persons from entering and leaving the courtroom, require attorneys to remain seated, permit the use of anatomically correct dolls to elicit testimony, and permit an adult with whom the child is familiar to sit in close proximity to the child during testimony; the statute also forbids intimidating questioning or objections. The use of a live dog is not listed as a special procedure. Prior judicial interpretation of the statute has narrowly limited it to its terms. Accordingly, we conclude that the court did not have the authority, pursuant to the plain and unambiguous text of § 54-86g (b), to permit a dog to sit beside C1 while she testified."

Discretionary Authority

Despite the lack of specific statutory authority, courts do possess inherent discretionary authority. The same court in State v. Devon D. noted: "Under the facts of this case, we conclude that the court did have such inherent general discretionary authority to do so despite the absence of specific authority pursuant to § 54-86g (b). Moreover, [t]he [ability] of a witness [to testify reliably] is a matter peculiarly within the discretion of the trial court and its ruling will be disturbed only in a clear case of abuse or of some error in law."

OTHER COMFORT ITEMS

Fiancé or Support Person

In State v. Torres, 60 Conn. App. 562, 569-70 (2000), cert. denied, 255 Conn. 925 (2001), the trial court permitted the fiancé of the witness to sit beside her while she testified.

Dolls and Stuffed Animals

Connecticut case law draws important distinctions regarding comfort objects. In State v. Aponte, 249 Conn. 735, 745 (1999), the Connecticut Supreme Court determined that the defendant's right to a fair trial was jeopardized by the prosecutor's gifting of a Barney doll to a child victim to hold while she testified.

However, the court stated in dicta that a child bringing a special doll from home would be permissible. The court explained: "The defendant acknowledges that it would have been proper to allow the victim to bring a doll from home to hold as a comfort object during her testimony. See, e.g., State v. Palabay, supra, 9 Haw. App. 417."

The reasoning behind this distinction relates to the psychological function of comfort objects: "Many children derive comfort from a favorite toy or stuffed animal. A child witness should be permitted to bring their particular favorite object with them. These comforting objects are more than mere toys. They symbolically represent a little bit of a mother's ability to soothe the child when frightened or nervous. Their presence helps children calm themselves when parents are not immediately on hand" (J. Myers, K. Saywitz & G. Goodman, Psychological Research on Children as Witnesses: Practical Implications for Forensic Interviews and Courtroom Testimony, 28 Pac. L.J. 3, 71 (1996)).

"Therefore, had the victim simply brought a favorite object from home, there would have been no basis for objection" (State v. Aponte, 249 Conn. 744-745 (1999)).

Courts have permitted stuffed animals in other cases. In State v. McPhee, 58 Conn. App. 501 (2000), the complainant was allowed to hold a stuffed animal while testifying.

Expert Testimony on Sexual Abuse Victim Behavior

Trial Court Discretion and General Standards

The trial court has wide discretion in ruling on the qualification of expert witnesses and the admissibility of their opinions (State v. Kemp, 199 Conn. 473, 476 (1986)). Generally, expert testimony is admissible if the witness has a special skill or knowledge directly applicable to a matter in issue, that skill or knowledge is not common to the average person, and the testimony would be helpful to the court or jury in considering the issues (State v. Rodgers, 207 Conn. 646, 651(1988)).

Helpfulness of Expert Testimony in Sexual Assault Cases

Expert testimony on the behavior of sexual abuse victims is considered helpful to the jury because "the consequences of the unique trauma experienced by minor victims of sexual abuse are matters beyond the understanding of the average person. Consequently, expert testimony that minor victims typically fail to provide complete or consistent disclosures of the alleged sexual abuse is of valuable assistance to the trier in assessing the minor victim's credibility" (State v. Spigarolo, 210 Conn. 359, 379 (1989)).

Distinction Between General and Specific Testimony

The cases that have considered this issue have noted the critical distinction between admissible expert testimony on general or typical behavior patterns of minor victims and inadmissible testimony directly concerning the particular victim's credibility (State v. Spigarolo, 210 Conn. 359, 379 (1989)).

When Expert Testimony is Admissible

In State v. Spigarolo, the Connecticut Supreme Court established the framework for when such testimony is appropriate: "We hold that, where defense counsel has sought to impeach the credibility of a complaining minor witness in a sexual abuse case, based on inconsistency, incompleteness or recantation of the victim's disclosures pertaining to the alleged incidents, the state may offer expert testimony that seeks to demonstrate or explain in general terms the behavioral characteristics of child abuse victims in disclosing alleged incidents. We express no opinion on the state's use of such expert testimony in the absence of the defendant's impeachment of the victim's credibility."

Porter/Daubert Challenges

In Porter, 241 Conn. at 68, the Connecticut Supreme Court explicitly adopted the Daubert test to determine the admissibility of scientific evidence but did not explicitly overrule Connecticut precedent regarding the evidence to which such a test should apply. Courts apply the Daubert standard only when such testimony involves innovative scientific techniques (State v. Reid, 254 Conn. at 546).

Connecticut courts determine if the testimony is based on obscure scientific theories that have the potential to mislead the trier of fact awed by an aura of mystic infallibility surrounding scientific techniques, experts and the fancy devices employed (State v. Hasan, 205 Conn. 485, 490 (1987)).

The answer to whether this testimony is subject to a Porter challenge seems to be no. In State v. Vumback, 68 Conn. App. 313 (2002), the court found: "We find, on the basis of the circumstances of this case, that the court was in a position to weigh the probative value of the testimony without abandoning common sense and sacrificing independent judgment to the expert's assertions based on his special skill or knowledge, and that this evidence was not based on obscure scientific theories that were potentially misleading to the trier of fact. We conclude, therefore, that Leventhal's testimony was not scientific."

If an expert's testimony concerns a method, the understanding of which is accessible to the trier of fact and the value of the expertise lay in its assistance to the trier of fact in viewing and evaluating the evidence, the testimony is not scientific even though an expert's skill and training are based on science (State v. Reid, 254 Conn. 540, 547 (2000)).

Limits on Expert Testimony

General Testimony Permissible

Following State v. Spigarolo, general testimony is permissible where defense counsel has sought to impeach the credibility of a complaining minor witness in a sexual abuse case, based on inconsistency, incompleteness or recantation of the victim's disclosures pertaining to the alleged incidents, allowing the state to offer expert testimony that seeks to demonstrate or explain in general terms the behavioral characteristics of child abuse victims in disclosing alleged incidents.

Indirect Validation Prohibited

Indirect assertions by an expert witness regarding the ultimate issue in a case can serve inappropriately to validate the truthfulness of a victim's testimony. In State v. Grenier, 257 Conn. 797 (2001), the Connecticut Supreme Court found problematic both direct and indirect validation of a victim's credibility.

The court explained: "As the Appellate Court concluded, the statements of Herwerth and McGeehan reflected their view that S was telling the truth when she testified that the defendant had abused her sexually. The Appellate Court correctly characterized Herwerth's testimony that '[S's] statements were very credible'" as "a direct assertion that validated the truthfulness of S's testimony."

"With respect to McGeehan's statement that her treatment of S was for 'the trauma of the abuse that [she] experienced', the Appellate

Court agreed that that testimony constituted 'an indirect assertion that validated the truthfulness of S's testimony.' The Appellate Court further noted that, although McGeehan's 'testimony was not a literal statement of her belief in S's truthfulness, such testimony had the same substantive import and could be perceived as a conclusive opinion that S had testified truthfully.' Thus, the testimony of Herwerth and McGeehan, to which the defendant timely objected, was improper and should have been stricken."

The court reaffirmed that "[w]e have recognized the 'critical distinction between admissible expert testimony on general or typical behavior[al] patterns of minor victims and inadmissible testimony directly concerning the particular victim's credibility.'"

Opinion on Specific Victim Credibility Prohibited

It is not permissible for an expert to testify as to his opinion of whether a victim in a particular case is credible or whether a particular victim's claims are truthful. In State v. Iban C., 275 Conn. 624 (2005), the court explained: "In cases that involve allegations of sexual abuse of children, we have held that expert testimony of reactions and behaviors common to victims of sexual abuse is admissible. See State v. Spigarolo, 210 Conn. 380. Such evidence assists a jury in its determination of the victim's credibility by explaining the typical consequences of the trauma of sexual abuse on a child. In this regard, we have found expert testimony stating that a victim's behavior was generally consistent with that of a victim of sexual or physical abuse to be admissible, and have distinguished such statements from expert testimony providing an opinion as to whether a particular victim had in fact suffered sexual abuse."

The court noted the particular danger of expert diagnosis: "In light of Ron-Priola's expertise, and in view of the fact that the victim's statements provided the only evidence of the defendant's guilt, it is reasonable to presume that the jurors would conclude that, if Ron-Priola believed the victim's allegations enough to reach a diagnosis of 'child sexual abuse,' then they should as well."

Credibility Determinations Based on Victim Statements

When an expert reaches a conclusion on the ultimate issue in part based upon statements made by the victim, it constitutes a credibility determination. In State v. Apostle, 8 Conn. App. 216, 232-33 (1986), the court concluded that a physician's opinion that intercourse was nonconsensual was inadmissible because it went beyond his physical examination and was based on the victim's description of the incident. Such credibility determinations are more properly within the sole province of the jury.

Form of Questions Irrelevant

The form of the questions asked to the expert has no substantial bearing on admissibility. In State v. Grenier, the court explained: "[W]e disagree . . . that the form of [the] questions has any substantial bearing on the extent or degree of the prejudice that flowed from the answers. Our resolution of the defendant's claim does not depend on the precise context in which the improper testimony was given, but, rather, the substance of that testimony."

The "Duck Test" from Favoccia

In State v. Favoccia, 306 Conn. 770 (2012), the Connecticut Supreme Court established clear limits on how expert testimony can connect general characteristics to specific victims: "An expert witness may not testify in a way that connects or links, either directly or indirectly, a complainant's testimony or allegations of abuse to general characteristics of children who have been sexually abused."

The court explained the risk: "This is because there is a risk that the jury will 'improperly us[e testimony about general characteristics] offensively as substantive proof that the complainant was sexually assaulted, rather than properly to respond defensively to impeachment by explaining behaviors that might otherwise impact her credibility.'"

The court articulated the famous "duck test": "There is no material distinction between express testimony that the child has been sexually abused, and implicit testimony that outlines the unreliable behavioral reactions found with sexually abused victims, followed by a list of the complainant's own behavioral reactions, that points out that the two are consistent, and then invites the jury to add up the points to conclude that the child has been sexually abused."

This principle is "particularly true where the expert offering testimony about general characteristics is familiar with the complainant's allegations, or has treated or evaluated the complainant."

The Supreme Court observed that the facts in Favoccia "present a delicate middle ground between the generalized behavioral testimony held admissible in [State v. Spigarolo, 210 Conn. 359 (1989)] and the more pointed diagnoses held inadmissible in [State v. Grenier, 257 Conn. 797 (2001) and State v. Iban C., 275 Conn. 624 (2005)]." The court ultimately concluded that "permitting an expert witness to make that connection, but not opine directly on a complainant's credibility or diagnosis, is the logical equivalent or permitting an expert to testify that the bird acts, walks and quacks like a duck, but then precluding that expert from opining that a particular bird is, in fact, a duck."

Current Framework for Expert Testimony

Expert testimony about general, behavioral characteristics of child abuse victims is permissible where the defense has sought to impeach the complainant and such testimony is necessary to explain behaviors that "might otherwise reflect adversely on the complainant's credibility if not explained by the expert" (State v. Favoccia, 306 Conn. 770, 787, 796 n.31 (2012)). However, an expert witness may not testify in a way that connects or links, either directly or indirectly, a complainant's testimony or allegations of abuse to general characteristics of children who have been sexually abused. This is because there is a risk that the jury will "improperly us[e testimony about general characteristics] offensively as substantive proof that the complainant was sexually assaulted, rather than properly to respond defensively to impeachment by explaining behaviors that might otherwise impact her credibility."

Specificity Requirements for Date of Offense

General Principles

Connecticut law recognizes that precise dating of offenses may not always be possible, particularly in cases involving ongoing abuse. In State v. Spigarolo, 210 Conn. 359, 386 (1989), the court established: "'The state has a duty to inform a defendant, within reasonable limits, of the time when the offense charged was alleged to have been committed. The state does not have a duty, however, to disclose information which the state does not have. Neither the sixth amendment [to] the United States constitution nor article first, § 8 of the Connecticut constitution requires that the state choose a particular moment as the time of an offense when the best information available to the state is imprecise.'"

Time as Non-Essential Element

Time is not an element of the offense of sexual assault. The general rule in Connecticut is that time is not an essential ingredient of the crime of sexual assault (State v. Saraceno, 15 Conn. App. 222, 236 (1988)).

Alibi Defense Considerations

An alibi defense cannot supersede the State's inability to provide an exact date. In State v. Vumback, 68 Conn. App. 313, 321 (2002), the court addressed this issue: "In addition, the defendant asserts that he was impermissibly precluded from presenting an alibi defense by the state's inability to provide exact dates of the offenses. Our Supreme Court has rejected this precise claim several times. See State v. Evans, 205 Conn. 528, 535 (1987)."

The court explained: "That a defendant may offer an alibi defense is a factor to be considered by the court in deciding whether to grant a motion [for a bill of particulars], but an alibi defense does not create a per se requirement that the state limit the times in the information more narrowly than the evidence available warrants" (State v. Spigarolo, supra, 210 Conn. at 387).

"On the basis of Evans and our previous discussion in this opinion, we conclude that the defendant was not impermissibly precluded from presenting an alibi defense by the state's inability to provide exact dates of the offenses."

Jury Unanimity Requirements

General Unanimity Principles

"It is settled doctrine in Connecticut that a valid jury verdict in a criminal case must be unanimous" (State v. Daniels, 207 Conn. 374, 388 (1989)). "The possibility of disagreement by the jury is implicit in the requirement of a unanimous verdict and is part of the constitutional safeguard of trial by jury" (State v. Sawyer, 227 Conn. 566, 576 (1993)). The jury is required to agree on the factual basis of the offense (State v. Suggs, 209 Conn. 733, 761 (1989)).

The Multipartite Test

The Connecticut Supreme Court has articulated the "multipartite test" for determining whether a specific unanimity charge is required "to be given in [a] case in which criminal liability may be premised on the violation of one of several alternative subsections of a statute" (State v. Martinez, 278 Conn. 598, 608-610 (2006), quoting State v. Famiglietti, 219 Conn. 605, 619-20 (1991)).

The test requires courts to first review the instruction that was given to determine whether the trial court has sanctioned a nonunanimous verdict. If such an instruction has not been given, that ends the matter. Even if the instructions at trial can be read to have sanctioned such a nonunanimous verdict, however, courts will remand for a new trial only if there is a conceptual distinction between the alternative acts with which the defendant has been charged, and the state has presented evidence to support each alternative act with which the defendant has been charged.

Continuing Offense Theory

If the State cannot allege specific dates and instances, a unanimous verdict is not required. In State v. Spigarolo, 210 Conn. 359 (1989), the State was unable to list specific dates on which the alleged acts occurred and instead had to rely on calling the acts a continuous assault over a period of a year. Under those circumstances, jury unanimity was not required.

The court explained: "Because the state was unable to specify with greater precision the times of the alleged incidents, it necessarily proceeded under a theory that the defendant's conduct was in the nature of a continuing offense. Cf. State v. Hauck, [172 Conn. 140, 150-51 (1976)]; but see State v. Snook, [210 Conn. 244, 261 (1989)]. Under these circumstances, the acts specified in the counts were not conceptually distinct within the meaning of Gipson. State v. Mancinone, [15 Conn. App. 251, 277 (1988)]. The defendant's right to a unanimous

verdict, therefore, was not violated by the trial court's failure to provide a specific unanimity instruction with respect to counts three and seven."

This can be contrasted with State v. Snook, 210 Conn. 244, 262 (1989), where the Connecticut Supreme Court held that "[a] distinct repetition of an act prohibited by § 53-21 constitutes a second offense."

Alternative Methods of Committing Same Crime

Force and threat of force are two methods of committing the same crime and do not require unanimity instructions. In State v. Tucker, 226 Conn. 618 (1993), the court explained: "The use of force and the threat of the use of force are quite simply two alternative methods of compulsion used by an actor to commit the one crime of sexual assault in the first degree."

Unanimity in Risk of Injury Cases

"Placing in a situation" and "doing any act" likely to impair the health or morals of a child may require a unanimity instruction as to how the harm was accomplished because they are conceptually different (State v. Ostolaza, 20 Conn. App. 40 (1989)). However, no unanimity instruction is required as to the type of harm caused, i.e. health or morals (State v. Thomas, 19 Conn. App. 44 (1989)).

Intent Requirements in Sexual Assault Cases

Sexual Assault as General Intent Crime

It is well settled that first degree sexual assault is a general intent crime (State v. Johnson, 185 Conn. 163, 176 (1981), aff'd, 460 U.S. 73(1983); State v. Truppi, 182 Conn. 449, 455 n.4 (1980)). "Sexual assault in the first degree requires proof of general intent, that is that the defendant intended to perform the physical acts that constitute the crime of sexual assault" (State v. Jackson, 30 Conn. App. 281, 290 (1993)).

"Sexual assault in the second degree is a general intent crime that requires only that the actor possess a general intent to perform the acts that constitute the elements of the offense" (State v. Blake, 63 Conn. App. 536, 542 (2001)).

No Knowledge of Age Required in Statutory Rape

"The only intent required for a violation of § 53a-71 is a general intent to perform the acts that constitute the offense" (State v. Pierson, 201 Conn. 211, 216 (1986)). "Thus, under § 53a-71 (a)(1), the state is not required to establish that the accused knew that the person with whom he had sexual intercourse was under the age of sixteen; the state must prove only that the accused knowingly engaged in sexual intercourse with a person who, in fact, had not attained the age of sixteen" (State v. Sorabella, 277 Conn. 155, 169 (2006)).

Risk of Injury as General Intent Crime

Risk of injury is also a general intent crime (State v. McClary, 207 Conn. 233, 240 (1988); State v. Reid, 85 Conn. App. 802, 809-10 (2004)). "Thus, 'it is not necessary, to support a conviction under § 53-21, that the [accused] be aware that his conduct is likely to impact a child younger than the age of sixteen years. Specific intent is not a necessary requirement of the statute. Rather, the intent to do some act coupled with a reckless disregard of the consequences … of that act is sufficient to [establish] a violation of the statute'" (State v. Davila, 75 Conn. App. 432, 438 (2003)).

Attempted Sexual Assault as Specific Intent Crime

In contrast to completed sexual assault offenses, attempted sexual assault is a specific intent crime. "The state must prove that the defendant acted with the specific intent to commit sexual assault in the first degree which in turn included the intent to have sexual intercourse" (State v. Green, 194 Conn. 258, 273 (1984)).

State's Burden on Consent Issues

When consent is raised as an issue, the state must prove lack of consent beyond a reasonable doubt. "A finding that a complainant had consented would implicitly negate a claim that the actor had compelled the complainant by force or threat to engage in sexual intercourse. Consent is not made an affirmative defense under our sex offense statutes, so, as in the case of the defense of alibi, the burden is upon the state to prove lack of consent beyond a reasonable doubt whenever the issue is raised" (State v. Smith, 210 Conn. 132, 140-41 (1989)).

Objective Standard for Consent

Connecticut employs an objective standard for determining consent. "While the word 'consent' is commonly regarded as referring to the state of mind of the complainant in a sexual assault case, it cannot be viewed as a wholly subjective concept. Although the actual state of mind of the actor in a criminal case may in many instances be the issue upon which culpability depends, a defendant is not chargeable with knowledge of the internal workings of the minds of others except to the extent that he should reasonably have gained such knowledge from his observations of their conduct."

"[W]hether a complainant has consented to intercourse depends upon her manifestations of such consent as reasonably construed. If the conduct of the complainant under all the circumstances should reasonably be viewed as indicating consent to the act of intercourse, a defendant should not be found guilty because of some undisclosed mental reservation on the part of the complainant."

"We agree, however, with the California courts that a defendant is entitled to a jury instruction that a defendant may not be convicted of this crime if the words or conduct of the complainant under all the circumstances would justify a reasonable belief that she had consented" (State v. Smith, 210 Conn. 132, 140-41 (1989)).

Use of the Word "Victim" in Court Proceedings

General Inappropriateness

The repeated use of the word victim with reference to the complaining witness is inappropriate when the issue at trial is whether a crime has been committed (State v. Thompson, 146 Conn. App. 249 (2013)).

Trial Court Usage Guidelines

Connecticut courts have established clear guidelines for when trial courts may appropriately use the term "victim." In cases in which the fact that a crime has been committed against the complaining witness is not contested, but only the identity of the perpetrator is in dispute, a court's use of the term "victim" is not inappropriate.

However, in cases in which the fact that a crime has been committed is contested, and where the court's use of the term "victim" has been the subject of an objection and has not been the subject of a subsequent curative instruction, a court's use of the term may constitute reversible error.

"The danger in the latter type of case is that the court, having used the term without specifically instructing the jury as to its intention in using the term, might convey to the jury, to whatever slight degree, its belief that a crime has been committed against the complainant" (State v. Cortes, 84 Conn. App. 70, 86 (2004)).

Prosecutorial Usage Limitations

Connecticut's Supreme Court has expressly admonished prosecutors to refrain from making excessive use of that term because of its obvious potential for prejudice (State v. Warholic, 278 Conn. 354, 370 n.7 (2006)). The court cautioned: "We caution the state, however, against making excessive use of the term 'victim' to describe a complainant when the commission of a crime is at issue because prevalent use of the term may cause the jury to draw an improper inference that the defendant committed a crime against the complainant."

Trial Court Authority for Motions in Limine

Under these authorities, in order to avoid the risk of prejudice naturally arising from a prosecutor's reference to the complainant as the victim, a trial court obviously has the power to order a prosecutor not to use the term "victim" in reference to the complainant during trial (State v. Thompson, 146 Conn. App. 249, 270 (2013)).

Sample Direct and Cross-Examination Questions

Direct Examination Approach

When preparing direct examination questions for a sexual assault case, it's crucial to be sensitive to the nature of the crime and the potential trauma experienced by the victim. The examination should progress logically from establishing the witness's identity and relationship to the case, through the background and relationship between the victim and defendant, to the context and details of the incident itself.

Key areas of inquiry include identifying the witness and establishing their relationship to the case by having them state their name and occupation for the record and explaining how they are connected to the case. The examination should establish the background and relationship between the victim and the defendant, including how they knew each other and the nature of their relationship.

The context of the incident should be established by describing the time and place of the incident and any specific circumstances surrounding it. When describing the incident itself, questions should seek a detailed account of what happened and what the defendant did, while also addressing how the defendant's actions made the victim feel.

Establishing the victim's lack of consent requires asking whether consent was given to the defendant's actions, how lack of consent was indicated, and whether the victim was able to resist or say "no" to the defendant. The emotional and physical impact should be addressed by exploring how the incident affected the victim emotionally, whether any physical injuries resulted, and whether medical or psychological treatment was sought.

Finally, addressing potential corroboration or evidence involves asking whether the victim told anyone about the incident shortly after it occurred, whether there were any witnesses present, and whether any evidence or documentation was preserved.

Cross-Examination Strategy

Cross-examination in sexual assault cases must be conducted with sensitivity while still challenging the witness's testimony effectively. The approach should be respectful and within the bounds of legal and ethical guidelines while exploring potential weaknesses in the prosecution's case.

Challenging the witness's credibility or perception might involve exploring whether the witness was under the influence of alcohol or drugs during the incident, whether they were wearing corrective lenses, and whether their memory of events might be flawed or distorted.

Exploring inconsistencies or contradictions in testimony could address discrepancies between different accounts of timing, descriptions of clothing or other details, and variations between current testimony and previous statements.

Questioning the witness's actions or behavior following the incident might explore whether friendly interactions continued with the defendant after the alleged assault, and why there might have been a delay in reporting the incident.

When consent is an issue, cross-examination might address whether lack of consent was clearly communicated to the defendant and whether there had been consensual sexual activity between the parties on previous occasions.

Highlighting potential ulterior motives or bias could involve exploring whether there are personal vendettas against the defendant or recent relationship issues that might provide alternative explanations for the allegations.

Questioning the accuracy of physical evidence or lack thereof might address the absence of DNA evidence linking the defendant to the alleged assault or the lack of visible injuries from the incident.

Finally, challenging the witness's interpretation of events could explore whether actions might have been misinterpreted as assault when they were actually consensual, or whether certain details of the incident might have been misremembered or exaggerated.

Remember that these approaches must be tailored to the specific circumstances of each case and the witness's testimony, always conducted respectfully and within proper legal and ethical bounds.

CHAPTER 9

SEARCHES

Introduction by Timothy Greene

"The right of the people to be secure in their persons, houses, papers, and effects, against unreasonable searches and seizures, shall not be violated, and no warrants shall issue, but upon probable cause, supported by oath or affirmation, and particularly describing the place to be searched, and the persons or things to be seized."

USCS Const. Amend. 4

When Defending clients, the Fourth Amendment to the United States Constitution is a crucial component of the Bill of Rights that protects the rights of individuals against unreasonable searches and seizures by the government.

To understand the fourth amendment, it is important to understand what is known as a "general warrant." A general warrant was a type of warrant British authorities often utilized during colonial times. These broad warrants allowed law enforcement officers to search any place and seize any property they believed might be connected to criminal activity, without specifying the exact location or items to be searched or seized. This practice was frequently used to suppress political dissent and target individuals who were critical of the British government's policies.

General warrants essentially gave authorities unchecked power to invade homes, confiscate property, and arrest individuals without clear evidence or probable cause. This abuse of power was one of the grievances that contributed to the American Revolution and the eventual drafting of the Bill of Rights, including the Fourth Amendment.

The framers of the Constitution, having experienced the harm caused by general warrants, were determined to ensure that such abuses of power would not continue in the newly formed United States. The Fourth Amendment was a direct response to the colonial experience with general warrants and was designed to protect individuals from unreasonable searches and seizures. It sought to establish a clear and specific process for obtaining search warrants, requiring that warrants be issued by a judge or neutral magistrate, based on probable cause, supported by oath or affirmation, and describing with particularity the place to be searched and the items or individuals to be seized.

The Fourth Amendment stands as perhaps the most frequently litigated constitutional protection in criminal defense practice. For cases involving drug offenses and contraband, successful Fourth Amendment challenges often represent the difference between conviction and dismissal. While all criminal defense attorneys recognize the importance of Fourth Amendment litigation, mastering the complex and ever-evolving jurisprudence surrounding searches and seizures requires specialized knowledge and strategic acumen. This chapter provides Connecticut practitioners with practical tools to identify, articulate, and successfully litigate Fourth Amendment violations in the context of drug cases and other contraband offenses.

The landscape of Fourth Amendment jurisprudence has shifted dramatically in recent decades, with courts increasingly recognizing exceptions to the warrant requirement while simultaneously developing more nuanced approaches to privacy in the digital age.

Connecticut courts have often interpreted our state constitution to provide greater protections than those afforded under federal law, creating a dual-track system that defense counsel must navigate strategically. Understanding when to invoke federal versus state constitutional protections—and how to frame arguments under each—represents a critical strategic decision in Fourth Amendment litigation.

Drug cases present particularly fertile ground for Fourth Amendment challenges. From the initial police encounter through the search of persons, vehicles, and digital devices, drug investigations typically involve multiple potential constitutional violations. The pressure on law enforcement to produce arrests and seizures in drug cases often leads to aggressive tactics that push—and sometimes cross—constitutional boundaries. The defense attorney who thoroughly understands Fourth Amendment principles can identify these violations and translate them into suppression of evidence and case dismissals.

Police encounters with citizens exist on a constitutional continuum, with different levels of suspicion required for different levels of intrusion. The distinction between consensual encounters, investigative detentions, and arrests forms the foundation of Fourth Amendment analysis. Each category triggers different legal standards and strategic considerations. In consensual encounters, officers require no suspicion whatsoever, but any show of authority that would make a reasonable person feel unfree to leave elevates the interaction to a seizure requiring reasonable suspicion. Recognizing when a seemingly "consensual" encounter has transformed into a seizure often represents the first step in identifying Fourth Amendment violations.

Traffic stops, the most common police-citizen interaction leading to drug charges, involve particularly complex Fourth Amendment considerations. While courts have approved pretextual stops based on minor traffic violations, Connecticut follows the Rodriguez principle that stops cannot be extended beyond the time necessary to address the traffic violation absent independent reasonable suspicion of criminal activity. The strategic approach to challenging traffic stops begins with scrutinizing the initial basis for the stop, proceeds through analyzing the duration and scope of the detention, and culminates in examining the justification for any searches that followed. Each step presents distinct constitutional questions and litigation opportunities.

Vehicle searches represent a frequent battleground in drug cases. The automobile exception permits warrantless searches of vehicles based solely on probable cause, without the exigent circumstances required for most other warrantless searches. However, Connecticut practitioners should note that our state constitution sometimes provides enhanced protections in this area. The scope of permissible searches incident to arrest in the vehicle context has been significantly narrowed by Arizona v. Gant, which permits such searches only when the arrestee remains within reaching distance of the passenger compartment or when it is reasonable to believe evidence of the offense of arrest will be found in the vehicle. This limitation creates powerful suppression opportunities when officers conduct vehicle searches following arrests for offenses unrelated to contraband.

The relationship between the Fourth Amendment and consent presents particularly thorny issues in drug cases. While valid consent obviates the need for a warrant or exception, the state bears the burden of proving voluntariness. Strategic litigation of consent issues requires thorough investigation of the circumstances surrounding the purported consent, including officer demeanor, show of force, failure to inform defendants of their right to refuse, and language barriers. Connecticut courts have sometimes found state constitutional violations even where federal standards for valid consent were satisfied, creating additional avenues for suppression.

Technological developments have dramatically transformed Fourth Amendment jurisprudence. The use of drug-detection canines, GPS tracking devices, cell phone searches, and digital data extraction requires specialized knowledge of rapidly evolving case law. The Supreme Court's recognition in Riley v. California that cell phones contain "the privacies of life" has led to enhanced protection for digital information, while cases like Carpenter v. United States have begun to address location data and third-party records. Connecticut courts have sometimes provided enhanced protection for digital privacy under our state constitution, creating additional litigation opportunities for defense counsel.

Challenging searches and seizures requires not merely legal knowledge but strategic vision. The timing of suppression motions, the decision to request evidentiary hearings, the strategic use of officer testimony, and the deployment of expert witnesses all impact litigation outcomes. Counsel must develop comprehensive suppression strategies that account for both the legal and factual dimensions of Fourth Amendment violations, incorporating witness interviews, scene investigations, and thorough review of body camera footage and other documentary evidence. The effective practitioner anticipates prosecution responses and prepares counter-arguments addressing inevitable claims of inevitable discovery, good faith, and attenuation.

Standing doctrine presents particular challenges in drug cases, especially those involving vehicle searches where passengers may lack sufficient possessory interest to mount direct Fourth Amendment challenges. However, even passengers have standing to challenge their own seizure during traffic stops following Brendlin v. California, and may challenge searches as fruits of unlawful seizures even when lacking direct standing to contest the search itself. Creative litigators can often overcome apparent standing barriers through careful framing of constitutional claims.

The exclusionary rule—the primary remedy for Fourth Amendment violations—has faced increasing limitations in federal courts, with expanded good faith exceptions and cost-benefit analyses that sometimes favor admission even when constitutional violations have occurred. Connecticut courts have sometimes rejected these limitations under our state constitution, maintaining stronger exclusionary principles that better protect constitutional rights.

Defense counsel must carefully frame suppression arguments to invoke these stronger state protections where appropriate, while addressing federal limitations when proceeding under the United States Constitution.

Connecticut's accelerated rehabilitation and other diversion programs create additional strategic considerations in drug cases involving Fourth Amendment violations. When suppression motions present close questions, these programs may provide acceptable alternative resolutions that avoid both the risks of trial and the collateral consequences of drug convictions. Counsel must balance the strength of suppression arguments against the benefits of diversionary programs, considering the client's criminal history, immigration status, employment concerns, and risk tolerance.

The sections that follow provide detailed guidance for challenging specific types of searches and seizures common in drug cases, from Terry stops through automobile searches, consent scenarios, and technological surveillance. Each section includes relevant federal and state precedent, practical guidance for spotting issues, and strategic considerations for litigation. By mastering these frameworks, defense counsel can transform Fourth Amendment principles from abstract constitutional guarantees into powerful tools for protecting clients and securing favorable case outcomes.

Common Searches

- **Automobile Exception:** The exception to the warrant requirement in an automobile search demands that the searching officer have probable cause to believe that the vehicle contains contraband.

  Carroll v. United States, 267 U.S. 132 (1925); State v. Badgett, 200 Conn. 412 (1986).

- **Stop and Frisk (Terry Stop):** First, the investigatory stop must be lawful. That requirement is met when the police officer reasonably suspects that the person apprehended is committing or has committed a criminal offense. Second, to proceed from a stop to a frisk, the police officer must reasonably suspect that the person stopped is armed and dangerous.
  Terry v. Ohio, 392 U.S. 1 (1968).

- **Terry Stop of Car Seizes Passengers:** *Brendlin v. California* held that a passenger is seized, just as the driver is, "from the moment [a car stopped by the police comes] to a halt on the side of the road." A passenger therefore has standing to challenge a stop's constitutionality.
  Arizona v. Johnson, 555 U.S. 323 (2009).

- **Remedy for Violation:** If the initial stop is found to be in violation of the defendant's constitutional rights, the "fruits," or evidence seized as a result of the stop, must be suppressed.
  Terry v. Ohio, 392 U.S. 1 (1968).

A Brief Overview of the Law of Car Searches

Foundation Principles

The automobile exception to the warrant requirement demands that the searching officer have probable cause to believe that the vehicle contains contraband. Carroll v. United States, 267 U.S. 132 (1925); State v. Badgett, 200 Conn. 412 (1986). The Terry stop framework establishes a two-step analysis: first, the investigatory stop must be lawful, which requires that the police officer reasonably suspect that the person apprehended is committing or has committed a criminal offense; second, to proceed from a stop to a frisk, the police officer must reasonably suspect that the person stopped is armed and dangerous. Terry v. Ohio, 392 U.S. 1 (1968).

A traffic stop seizes all occupants of the vehicle. Brendlin v. California established that a passenger is seized, just as the driver is, "from the moment [a car stopped by the police comes] to a halt on the side of the road." Arizona v. Johnson, 555 U.S. 323 (2009). This seizure gives passengers standing to challenge a stop's constitutionality. If the initial stop violates the defendant's constitutional rights, the "fruits," or evidence seized as a result of the stop, must be suppressed under Terry v. Ohio, 392 U.S. 1 (1968).

Traffic Stop Authority and Reasonable Suspicion

Justification for Vehicle Stops

A police officer has the right to stop a motor vehicle operating on a Connecticut highway even if the reason for the stop is only an infraction under traffic laws. State v. Dukes, 209 Conn. 98 (1988). However, there must be an actual infraction. Stopping a vehicle to check the driver's license and automobile registration, where neither traffic or equipment violations nor suspicious activity preceded the stop, is unreasonable under the Fourth Amendment. Delaware v. Prouse, 440 U.S. 648 (1979).

The Fourth Amendment also permits brief investigative stops, including traffic stops, when a law enforcement officer has "a particularized and objective basis for suspecting the particular person stopped of criminal activity." United States v. Cortez, 449 U.S. 411; Navarette v. California, 134 S. Ct. 1683 (2014).

Nature of Seizure

Stopping an automobile and detaining its occupants constitute a seizure within the meaning of the fourth and fourteenth Amendments, even though the purpose of the stop is limited and the resulting detention is quite brief. State v. Sailor, 33 Conn.App. 409 (1994); Delaware v. Prouse, 440 U.S. 648 (1979). The law is settled that in Fourth Amendment terms a traffic stop entails a seizure of the driver "even though the purpose of the stop is limited and the resulting detention quite brief." Delaware v. Prouse, 440 U.S. 648 (1979); Whren v. United States, 517 U.S. 806 (1996).

A traffic stop necessarily curtails the travel a passenger has chosen just as much as it halts the driver, diverting both from the stream of traffic to the side of the road, and the police activity that normally amounts to intrusion on "privacy and personal security" does not normally distinguish between passenger and driver. Brendlin v. California, 551 U.S. 249 (2007).

Standard for Reasonable and Articulable Suspicion

Reasonable and articulable suspicion is an objective standard that focuses not on the actual state of mind of the police officer, but on whether a reasonable person, having the information available to and known by the police, would have had that level of suspicion. This standard is based not on the officer's inchoate and unparticularized suspicion or hunch, but on the specific reasonable inferences which he is entitled to draw from the facts in light of his experience. What constitutes reasonable and articulable suspicion depends on the totality of the circumstances. State v. Tuck, 90 Conn.App. 872 (2005).

When engaging in a fourth amendment reasonableness inquiry, courts ask whether the facts available to the officer at the moment of the seizure warrant a man of reasonable caution in the belief that the action taken was appropriate. State v. Nash, 278 Conn. 620 (2006). In the context of a Terry stop, simple good faith on the part of the arresting officer is not enough. If subjective good faith alone were the test, the protection of the Fourth Amendment would evaporate, and the people would be secure in their persons, houses, papers and effects, only in the discretion of the police. Terry v. Ohio, 392 U.S. 1 (1968).

Reasonable suspicion is a less demanding standard than probable cause not only in the sense that reasonable suspicion can be established with information that is different in quantity or content than that required to establish probable cause, but also in the sense that reasonable suspicion can arise from information that is less reliable than that required to show probable cause. State v. Cofield, 220 Conn. 38 (1991).

Scope and Duration of Traffic Stops

Permissible Scope

Questions related to the traffic stop are permissible, including "a check of the driver's license, vehicle registration, and criminal history, and the writing of the citation or warning," as well as background questions about the destination and purpose of the driver's trip. State v. Jenkins, 298 Conn. 209 (2010). Inquiries incident to a traffic stop typically "involve checking the driver's license, determining whether there are outstanding warrants against the driver, and inspecting the automobile's registration and proof of insurance. These checks serve the same objective as enforcement of the traffic code: ensuring that vehicles on the road are operated safely and responsibly." Rodriguez v. United States, 135 S.Ct. 1609 (2015).

Questions permissible under Terry during a routine traffic stop include inquiries about whether the car or driver are carrying contraband, as well as concomitant requests for consent to search the vehicle so long as the questions do not measurably extend the stop beyond the time necessary to complete the investigation of the traffic violation and issue a citation of warning. State v. Jenkins, 298 Conn. 209 (2010).

An officer's inquiries into matters unrelated to the justification for the traffic stop do not convert the encounter into something other than a lawful seizure, so long as those inquiries do not measurably extend the duration of the stop. Arizona v. Johnson, 555 U.S. 323 (2009); Muehler v. Mena, 544 U.S. 93 (2005). The critical question is whether the stop is unnecessarily prolonged, not whether the officer has yet issued a ticket or not. Rodriguez v. United States, 135 S.Ct. 1609 (2015).

Duration Limitations

A police stop exceeding the time needed to handle the matter for which the stop was made violates the Constitution's shield against unreasonable seizures. A seizure justified only by a police-observed traffic violation becomes unlawful if it is prolonged beyond the time reasonably required to complete the mission of issuing a ticket for the violation. Rodriguez v. U.S., 135 S.Ct. 1609 (2015). Because addressing the infraction is the purpose of the stop, it may last no longer than is necessary to effectuate that purpose. Authority for the seizure ends when tasks tied to the traffic infraction are or reasonably should have been completed.

In determining the reasonable duration of a stop, it is appropriate to examine whether the police diligently pursued the investigation. United States v. Sharpe, 470 U.S. 675 (1985). An officer may conduct certain unrelated checks during an otherwise lawful traffic stop, but he may not do so in a way that prolongs the stop, absent the reasonable suspicion ordinarily demanded to justify detaining an individual. Rodriguez v. U.S., 135 S.Ct. 1609 (2015); State v. Jenkins, 298 Conn. 209 (2010).

The stop must still be considered through the lens of the time reasonably necessary to effectuate the initial purpose of the traffic stop, and expansions of the stop beyond that time are constitutionally impermissible in the absence of an independent basis of objectively reasonable, articulable suspicion. State v. Jenkins, 298 Conn. 209 (2010).

Authority to Order Occupants from Vehicle

Driver Exit Orders

A vehicle stop based on reasonable articulable suspicion encompasses the authority to order the driver out of the car. The additional step of ordering driver out of the car is a de minimis intrusion. Pennsylvania v. Mimms, 434 U.S. 106 (1977).

Passenger Exit Orders

A vehicle stop based on reasonable articulable suspicion also encompasses the authority to order the passenger out of the car based on concerns for officer safety. Maryland v. Wilson, 519 U.S. 408 (1997); State v. Kelly, 313 Conn. 1 (2014).

Pat-Down and Frisk Authority

Two-Part Inquiry

The determination of whether a pat-down or frisk is permitted requires a two-part inquiry: first, was the officer justified in initially detaining the individual based on specific and articulable facts, and second, did specific and articulable facts exist that suggested that the individual presented a harm to the officers or others so as to justify the patdown. State v. Wilkins, 240 Conn. 489 (1997).

The stop must be lawful, meaning the officer must rightfully be in the presence of the party that is ultimately frisked. Com. v. Johnson, 908 N.E.2d 729 (Mass. 2009); Speten v. State, 185 P.3d 25, 33 (Wyo. 2008); People v. Batino, 367 N.Y.S.2d 784 (1975); cf. Sibron v. New York, 392 U.S. 40, 64 (1968).

Armed and Dangerous Requirement

If, during the course of a lawful investigatory detention, the officer reasonably believes that the detained individual might be both armed and dangerous, the officer may undertake a patdown search of the individual to discover weapons. State v. Nash, 278 Conn. 620 (2006); State v. Trine, 236 Conn. 216 (1996); Terry v. Ohio, 392 U.S. 1 (1968); Adams v. Williams, 407 U.S. 143 (1972).

Scope Limitations

Because a patdown search is intended to secure the safety of the investigating officer, it is strictly limited to a search for weapons. The officer cannot conduct a general exploratory search for whatever evidence of criminal activity he might find. State v. Davis, 85 Conn. App. 755 (2004); State v. Trine, 236 Conn. 216 (1996). A patdown search for weapons that is justified at its inception becomes constitutionally infirm if the search becomes more intrusive than necessary to protect the safety of the investigating officer. State v. Clark, 255 Conn. 268 (2001); State v. Trine, 236 Conn. 224 (1996).

Vehicle Compartment Searches

An officer conducting a Terry stop of an automobile may search the passenger compartment of the automobile for weapons, limited to areas where the weapon might be hidden, if he or she reasonably believes the suspect is potentially dangerous. Michigan v. Long, 463 U.S. 1032 (1983); State v. Wilkins, 240 Conn. 489 (1997). If officers have reason to believe a driver or passenger is armed and dangerous, the officer may frisk the individuals and conduct a limited search of the interior of the car immediately within the suspects control even if the suspect is already out of the car.

However, the protective search of the vehicle clearly must be limited to those areas in which a weapon may be placed or hidden, as it is justified solely by the danger that weapons stored there might be used against the officers or bystanders. Minnesota v. Dickerson, 508 U.S. 366 (1993).

Passenger Pat-Downs

In the context of a vehicular stop for a minor infraction, an officer may conduct a pat-down search of a passenger when the officer has an articulable basis to believe the passenger might be armed and presently dangerous, even if the officer has no reasonable grounds to believe that the passenger is committing, or has committed, a criminal offense. Arizona v. Johnson, 555 U.S. 323 (2009).

Extending Pat-Down Authority

Plain Feel Doctrine

In the course of a justified pat search for weapons, if an officer feels an object that is immediately recognizable as contraband, the officer is entitled to seize the object. Minnesota v. Dickerson, 508 U.S. 366 (1993); State v. Clark, 255 Conn. 268 (2001). The dispositive question is whether the officer who conducted the search was acting within the lawful bounds marked by Terry at the time he gained probable cause to believe that the lump was contraband.

Prohibited Manipulation

The authority to pat-down is limited to a search for weapons and the officer may not extend the "feel" beyond that necessary to determine if it's a weapon. Minnesota v. Dickerson, 508 U.S. 366 (1993); State v. Clark, 255 Conn. 268 (2001); United States v. Davis, 530 F.3d 1069 (9th Cir.2008). Physically invasive inspection is simply more intrusive than a purely visual inspection. Law enforcement officer's physical manipulation of an opaque bag that a passenger carried onto a cross-country bus and placed in a rack directly above his seat violated the Fourth Amendment prohibition against unreasonable searches of effects. Bond v. U.S., 529 U.S. 334 (2000).

Transition to Full Search

Assuming the object discovered in the pat-down does not feel like a weapon, this only means that a further search may not be justified under a Terry analysis. However, the pat-down may give rise to probable cause. There remains the possibility that the feel of the object, together with other suspicious circumstances, will amount to probable cause that the object is contraband or some other item subject to seizure, in which case there may be a further search based upon that probable cause. United States v. Salazar, 945 F.2d 47 (2d Cir. 1991); United States v. Campbell, 549 F.3d 364 (6th Cir.2008); United States v. Davis, 457 F.3d 817 (8th Cir.2006).

Vehicular Search Exceptions

The Automobile Exception

The U.S. Supreme Court first recognized the automobile exception to the fourth amendment warrant requirement in Carroll v. U.S., 267 U.S. 132 (1925). The automobile exception permits a warrantless search of an automobile whenever the police have probable cause to do so as where the searching officers have probable cause to believe that the vehicle contains contraband. State v. Winfrey, 302 Conn. 195 (2011).

This automobile exception to the warrant requirement applies only to searches of vehicles that are supported by probable cause. The absence of probable cause, despite the exigency created by the ready mobility of automobiles and the lesser expectation of privacy in them, will render any warrantless search unreasonable. Chambers v. Maroney, 399 U.S. 42 (1970); State v. Badgett, 200 Conn. 412 (1986); State v. Federici, 179 Conn. 46 (1979).

Probable Cause Requirements

Probable cause to search exists if there is probable cause to believe that the particular items sought to be seized are connected with criminal activity or will assist in a particular apprehension or conviction and there is probable cause to believe that the items sought to be seized will be found in the place to be searched. State v. Badgett, 200 Conn. 412 (1986); State v. DeChamplain, 179 Conn. 522 (1980).

A warrantless vehicle search does not require a showing of exigent circumstances. Maryland v. Dyson, 527 U.S. 465 (1999); Pennsylvania v. Labron, 518 U.S. 938 (1996); State v. Smith, 257 Conn. 216 (2001). The probable cause determination must be based on objective facts that could have justified the issuance of a warrant by a neutral magistrate at the time the search was made. State v. Winfrey, 302 Conn. 195 (2011); State v. Badgett, 200 Conn. 412 (1986).

Scope of Automobile Exception

If probable cause justifies the search of a lawfully stopped vehicle, it justifies the search of every part of the vehicle and its contents that may conceal the object of the search. United States v. Ross, 456 U.S. 798 (1982); State v. Williams, 311 Conn. 626 (2014). This applies to trunks, Maryland v. Dyson, 527 U.S. 465 (1999); the purse of a passenger, Wyoming v. Houghton, 526 U.S. 295 (1999); paper bag, California v. Acevedo, 500 U.S. 565 (1991); center console, State v. Winfrey, 302 Conn. 195 (2011); safe, State v. Dukes, 209 Conn. 98 (1988); duffel bag; State v. Longo, 243 Conn. 732 (1998).

This rule applies to all containers within a car, without qualification as to ownership and without a showing of individualized probable cause for each container. Wyoming v. Houghton, 526 U.S. 295 (1999). Police may search a container located within an automobile, and need not hold the container pending issuance of a search warrant, even though they lack probable cause to search the vehicle as a whole and have probable cause to believe only that container itself holds contraband or evidence. California v. Acevedo, 500 U.S. 565 (1991).

However, the mere fact that police have probable cause to believe that a container placed in the vehicle contains contraband or evidence does not justify a search of the entire vehicle. Probable cause to search a car does not justify a body search of a passenger. United States v. Di Re, 332 U.S. 581 (1948). This contrasts with Wyoming v. Houghton, which permits search of belongings of passenger.

Search Incident to Arrest

Police may search a vehicle incident to a recent occupant's arrest only if the arrestee is within reaching distance of the passenger compartment at the time of the search or it is reasonable to believe the vehicle contains evidence of the offense of arrest. When these justifications are absent, a search of an arrestee's vehicle will be unreasonable unless police obtain a warrant or show that another exception to the warrant requirement applies. Arizona v. Gant, 556 U.S. 332 (2009); New York v. Belton, 453 U.S. 454 (1981); United States v. Robinson, 414 U.S. 218 (1973); Chimel v. California, 395 U.S. 752 (1969); State v. Shaw, 186 Conn. 45 (1982).

The arrest must be lawful. Among the exceptions to the warrant requirement is a search incident to a lawful arrest. Arizona v. Gant, 556 U.S. 332 (2009); State v. Cobuzzi, 161 Conn. 371, 375 (1971); State v. Thomas, 98 Conn.App. 542 (2006); Frazier v. Com., 406 S.W.3d 448(Ky. 2013).

Possibility of Access Standard

Police are authorized to search a vehicle incident to a recent occupant's lawful arrest only when the arrestee is unsecured and within reaching distance of the passenger compartment at the time of the search. Arizona v. Gant, 556 U.S. 332 (2009). Both requirements (unsecured and within reaching distance) must be met.

The right of a police officer to search the vehicle ceases the instant the arrestee departs the scene because the arrestee's removal forecloses any possibility that he could reach for an article within the vehicle. State v. Badgett, 200 Conn. 412 (1986). The Connecticut Supreme Court refused to extend the fiction that the passenger compartment is always within reach of the arrestee to circumstances where the defendant is no longer at the scene of the arrest when the warrantless search was undertaken.

Evidence of Crime of Arrest

A search incident to a lawful arrest is permitted when it is reasonable to believe evidence relevant to the crime of arrest might be found in the vehicle. Arizona v. Gant, 556 U.S. 332 (2009). Police are not permitted to search cell phones and digital data seized pursuant to an arrest, but must get a warrant. Riley v. California, 134 S. Ct. 2473 (2014).

An officer is permitted to search a vehicle's passenger compartment when he has reasonable suspicion that an individual, whether or not the arrestee, is dangerous and might access the vehicle to gain immediate control of weapons, even in light of Arizona v. Gant. Michigan v. Long, 463 U.S. 1032 (1983); State v. Butler, 296 Conn. 62 (2010). All lawful custodial arrests justify a full search of the person without a warrant, including containers and clothing. United States v. Robinson, 414 U.S. 218 (1973); Gustafson v. Florida, 414 U.S. 260 (1973).

Inventory Searches

An inventory search is a well-defined exception to the warrant requirement. In the performance of their community caretaking functions, the police are frequently obliged to take automobiles into their custody. A standardized procedure for making a list or inventory as soon as reasonable after reaching the stationhouse not only deters false claims but also inhibits theft or careless handling of articles taken from the arrested person. State v. Badgett, 200 Conn. 412 (1986); State v. Gasparro, 194 Conn. 96 (1984); State v. Vallejo, 102 Conn. App. 628 (2007).

Inventory searches have two purposes: to protect the vehicle and the property in it, and to safeguard the police or other officers from claims of lost possessions. It is thus customary for an inventory to extend to all parts of the car where personal property might be found, and to include an inventory of containers found within the vehicle. Illinois v. Lafayette, 462 U.S. 640 (1983); South Dakota v. Opperman, 428 U.S. 364 (1976).

However, in State v. Miller, 227 Conn. 363 (1993), the Connecticut Supreme Court declined to follow the United States Supreme Court's decision in Chambers v. Maroney, 399 U.S. 42 (1970), holding that once an automobile has been impounded at a police station, the factors that justify a warrantless search of the vehicle at the scene (the legitimate safety concerns of police officers and the inherent mobility of automobiles) cease to apply and thus such a warrantless search violates the State Constitution.

Plain View Doctrine

If the police are already lawfully in an area, such as a house or a car, items which are immediately apparent evidence of a crime or contraband may be seized without any further justification. Coolidge v. New Hampshire, 403 U.S. 443 (1971). Two requirements must be met: the initial intrusion that enabled the police to view the items seized must have been lawful; and the police must have had probable cause to believe that these items were contraband or stolen goods. State v. Ruscoe, 212 Conn. 223 (1990); State v. Reddick, 207 Conn. 323 (1988).

At the time of discovery of the contraband or evidence, there must be probable cause to associate the property in plain view with criminal activity without further investigation. Arizona v. Hicks, 480 U.S. 321 (1987); State v. Eady, 249 Conn. 431 (1999); State v. Reddick, 207 Conn. 323 (1988). Since warrantless searches of a car are permitted based on probable cause, if contraband observed in plain view give rise to probable cause of criminality, then a further search is permitted. State v. Thomas, 98 Conn. App. 542 (2006).

Consent Searches

A warrantless search is not unreasonable under either the fourth amendment to the constitution of the United States or article first, § 7, of the constitution of Connecticut if a person with authority to do so has freely consented to the search. State v. Azukas, 278 Conn. 267 (2006).

Voluntariness Standard

The state bears the burden of proving that the consent was free and voluntary. The state must affirmatively establish that the consent was voluntary; mere acquiescence to a claim of lawful authority is not enough to meet the state's burden. State v. Azukas, 278 Conn. 267 (2006).

A court will assess the totality of all the surrounding circumstances, both the characteristics of the accused and the details of the interrogation. Some of the factors taken into account have included the youth of the accused, his lack of education, or his low intelligence, the lack of any advice to the accused of his constitutional rights, the length of detention, the repeated and prolonged nature of the questioning and the use of physical punishment such as the deprivation of food or sleep. Schneckloth v. Bustamonte, 412 U.S. 218 (1973); State v. Schroff, 206 Conn. 182 (1988).

While the defendant's knowledge of a right to refuse is a factor to be taken into account, the prosecution is not required to demonstrate such knowledge as a prerequisite to establishing a voluntary consent. Schneckloth v. Bustamonte, 412 U.S. 218 (1973). The Supreme Court has emphasized that this rule remains applicable to requests for consent to search during traffic stops, calling it unrealistic to require police officers to always inform detainees that they are free to go before a consent to search may be deemed voluntary. Ohio v. Robinette, 519 U.S. 33 (1996); State v. Jenkins, 298 Conn. 209 (2010).

Consent to search an automobile includes search of closed container that could hold contraband unless consent was limited. Florida v. Jimeno, 500 U.S. 248 (1990).

Dog Sniff Searches

A dog sniff conducted during a lawful traffic stop does not violate the Fourth Amendment; no suspicion is needed because a dog detects only drugs and there is no privacy interest at risk in detecting only drugs. Illinois v. Caballes, 543 U.S. 405 (2005) (dog sniff conducted only around exterior of vehicle).

However, a dog sniff conducted during a traffic stop violates the Fourth Amendment when the dog sniff is conducted after time necessary for completion of a traffic stop. Rodriguez v. United States, 135 S.Ct. 1609 (2015) (7-8 minute extension of stop). A dog sniff, in contrast to an inquiry to ensure that vehicles are operated safely and responsibly, is a measure aimed at detecting evidence of ordinary criminal wrongdoing and is not fairly characterized as part of the officer's traffic mission. The critical question is not whether the dog sniff occurs before or after the officer issues a ticket, but whether conducting the sniff prolongs (i.e., adds time to) the stop.

Checkpoint Searches

Sobriety checkpoints operated pursuant to neutral criteria are permissible under the Connecticut Constitution, State v. Mikolinski, 256 Conn. 543 (2001); and the Federal Constitution. Michigan Dept. of State Police v. Sitz, 496 U.S. 444 (1990). However, the Supreme Court has never approved a checkpoint program whose primary purpose was to detect evidence of ordinary criminal wrongdoing. City of Indianapolis v. Edmond, 531 U.S. 32 (2000).

Applying the general principle that law enforcement officers do not violate the Fourth Amendment by merely approaching an individual on the street or in another public place, by asking him if he is willing to answer some questions, or by putting questions to him if the person is willing to listen, Florida v. Royer, 460 U.S. 491 (1983), the Supreme Court held that a police roadblock checkpoint at which all motorists were systematically stopped so that police could ask them for information about a recent fatal hit-and-run accident did not violate the Fourth Amendment. Illinois v. Lidster, 540 U.S. 419 (2004).

Standing to Challenge Searches and Seizures

Both the driver and any passengers are seized for Fourth Amendment purposes when an officer makes a traffic stop and thus have standing to challenge the legality of that stop, i.e. seizure. Brendlin v. California, 551 U.S. 249 (2007); Arizona v. Johnson, 555 U.S. 323 (2009).

In determining whether a defendant has standing to challenge the legality of a search and seizure under both the fourth amendment to the United States constitution and article first, § 7, of the constitution of Connecticut, the defendant must demonstrate that he had a reasonable expectation of privacy in the area or subject of the search. Rakas v. Illinois, 439 U.S. 128 (1978); State v. Davis, 283 Conn. 280 (2007).

Reasonable Expectation of Privacy

The burden of proving the existence of a reasonable expectation of privacy rests on the defendant. State v. Kimble, 106 Conn. App. 572 (2008). In order for the defendant to demonstrate that he had a reasonable expectation of privacy in the subject of the search: he must have manifested a subjective expectation of privacy with respect to the subject of the search; and that expectation must be one that society would consider reasonable. State v. Gonzalez, 278 Conn. 341 (2006). Absent such an expectation, the subsequent police action has no constitutional ramifications. State v. Pink, 274 Conn. 241 (2005).

Passenger Standing

Passengers in an automobile, neither claiming nor demonstrating a possessory interest in the automobile, generally are regarded as lacking a reasonable expectation of privacy in the automobile. State v. Altrui, 188 Conn. 161 (1982); State v. Thomas, 98 Conn.App. 542 (2006). In order to challenge the search of the car and seek suppression of evidence found therein, passengers must have both a possessory interest in the car and in the evidence seized. State v. Kimble, 106 Conn.App. 572 (2008); State v. Thomas, 98 Conn.App. 542 (2006).

Arizona v. Johnson does "not extend Fourth Amendment rights to passengers who challenge only the search of the vehicle in which they were traveling and not their seizure." United States v. Symonevich, 688 F.3d 12 (1st Cir.2012).

However, passengers may challenge search as fruit of an unlawful seizure. If either the stopping of the car, the length of the passenger's detention thereafter, the scope of investigation directed at the passenger, or the passenger's removal from it are unreasonable in a Fourth Amendment sense, then surely the passenger has standing to object to those constitutional violations and to have suppressed any evidence found in the car which is their fruit. United States v. Mosley, 743 F.3d 1317 (10th Cir.2014) (defendant-passenger, to have standing re search of vehicle, "must show that the officer violated his Fourth Amendment rights when they seized him, and that a factual nexus existed between this unlawful seizure and the discovery of the gun under his seat"); United States v. Campbell, 741 F.3d 251 (1st Cir.2013) (passengers "may contest whether the stop of the vehicle meets Fourth Amendment standards"); United States v. Katzin, 732 F.3d 187 (3d Cir.2013) (passengers had standing re search of vehicle "by virtue of being subjected to an illegal stop," as 'the stop and subsequent search of the car was to be treated as a single event").

Impact of Marijuana Decriminalization on Probable Cause

After the passage of Public Act 11-71, which decriminalized the possession of less than one-half of an ounce of marijuana, the odor of marijuana and/or possession of such an infractious amount, without additional evidence of any criminal activity, cannot support probable cause to search a vehicle because a non-criminal amount of marijuana cannot justify the issuance of a warrant by a neutral magistrate.

General Statutes § 54-33a(b) governs the issuance of search warrants in this state and requires probable cause to believe that the property to be searched is being used "as the means of committing any criminal offense," was "stolen or embezzled," or "constitutes evidence of an offense." Connecticut courts have not definitively ruled on whether an officer can search a car without a warrant based on a mere traffic violation and the smell of or possession of an infractious amount of marijuana.

This question has been addressed and resolved in Massachusetts, which in 2008 decriminalized possession of less than one ounce of marijuana. In Commonwealth v. Cruz, 459 Mass. 459, 460 (2011), officers initiated a search based on the smell of burnt marijuana emanating from a parked car. The court concluded that crack cocaine found during the search should have been suppressed, holding in part that it was unreasonable for the police to search the car for criminal contraband under the automobile exception because post-decriminalization "the standard for obtaining a search warrant to search the car could not be met." The court noted that there could have been no suspicion of a "criminal offense" because post decriminalization, the offense of possessing one ounce or less of marijuana changed from being a criminal to a civil offense, which as the voters on the ballot initiative were told "would remove the threat of various criminal 'sanctions' for those who possess one ounce or less of marijuana and instead impose a '$100 fine, similar to a speeding ticket.'"

Connecticut's penalty scheme and status of possession of less than one-half an ounce of marijuana has changed in ways that mirror the changes seen in Massachusetts. The Connecticut Supreme Court concluded in State v. Menditto, 315 Conn. 861, 873 (2015), that P.A. 11–71 "chang[ed] the status of an illegal act from a crime to a minor civil violation," constituting decriminalization for the purposes of the erasure statute.

The Menditto court documented a fundamental change in Connecticut's statutory scheme. When the legislature enacted P.A. 11–71 in 2011, it reduced the maximum penalty for a first offense of possession of less than one-half ounce of marijuana from a fine of up to $1000 and/or imprisonment of up to one year to a fine of $150, and reduced the penalty for subsequent offenses from a fine of up to $3000 and/or imprisonment of up to five years to a fine of between $200 and $500. P.A. 11–71, § 1. It accomplished this by limiting the scope of conduct that constituted criminal possession of marijuana under § 21a–279 and enacting a new statute imposing fines for the conduct excluded from the scope of § 21a–279. See General Statutes § 21a–279a. The legislature then added that new statutory provision proscribing possession of less than one-half ounce of marijuana to the list of minor civil violations in § 51–164n (b); P.A. 11–71, § 6; which are deemed not to be offenses pursuant to § 51–164n (e).

The Supreme Court further emphasized this shift in status to a "minor civil violation," noting that following the enactment of P.A. 11–71, possession of less than one-half ounce of marijuana now holds the same legal status as such minor civil violations as maintaining state records using unapproved paper, ink, or loose-leaf binders. General Statutes §§ 1–9 through 1–11. See General Statutes § 51–164n (b). This is not the sort of conduct to which society attaches substantial moral opprobrium, or which one takes into consideration when making important decisions such as hiring an employee, for which criminal records are often consulted. The legislature has determined that such violations are to be handled in the same manner as civil infractions, such as parking violations.

Given this shift in the status of possession of less than one-half ounce of marijuana, evidence of such a "minor civil violation" cannot satisfy the standard used to determine the validity of a warrantless search, which is that used by a neutral magistrate considering the application for a search warrant pursuant to General Statutes § 54-33a(b).

Search Voir Dire

When defending a case involving an illegal search, it's crucial to identify potential jurors who understand Fourth Amendment rights and can be impartial in evaluating the evidence. Here are some sample voir dire questions for defending an illegal search:

General Background Questions:

- Have you ever served on a jury before? If yes, please describe the case.
- Are you familiar with the Fourth Amendment to the U.S. Constitution, which protects against unreasonable searches and seizures?
- How do you feel about the importance of protecting individual rights and privacy?

Preconceived Notions about Illegal Searches:

- Have you formed any opinions about cases involving illegal searches or the exclusionary rule?
- Can you set aside any preconceived notions and evaluate this case based solely on the evidence presented in court?

Perception of Law Enforcement:

- How do you view law enforcement officers and their role in society?
- Can you remain impartial and not automatically favor the prosecution or law enforcement in this case?

Understanding of the Exclusionary Rule:

- Are you familiar with the exclusionary rule, which generally excludes evidence obtained through illegal searches from trial?
- Can you apply the exclusionary rule as instructed by the court, even if it means excluding potentially incriminating evidence?

Consent and Coercion:

- Can you evaluate the circumstances surrounding the search and determine if the defendant's consent was freely given or if any coercion was involved?
- Are you willing to assess the credibility of witnesses who testify about the consent or lack thereof?

Search Warrants and Probable Cause:

- Do you understand the requirements for obtaining a search warrant, including the need for probable cause?
- Can you differentiate between a lawful search with a valid warrant and an illegal search without a warrant?

Prior Experiences or Biases:

- Have you had any personal experiences with law enforcement or illegal searches that could influence your ability to be fair and impartial?
- Are you aware of any biases that might impact your evaluation of evidence in this case?

Openness to Consider Defense Arguments:

- Can you consider and weigh defense arguments regarding the legality of the search and the implications it may have on the case?
- Are you willing to listen to expert witnesses who may testify about search and seizure issues?

Fairness and Impartiality:

- Do you believe you can be fair and impartial in evaluating the evidence presented during the trial, regardless of the outcome?
- Can you follow the court's instructions and apply the law as explained to you, even if you personally disagree with it?

Remember, these questions should be tailored to the specific facts and circumstances of the case and the potential biases that may exist in the jury pool. The goal is to select jurors who can objectively assess the evidence and consider the legality of the search in a fair and unbiased manner.

Direct Examination

Sample Direct Examination of the Defendant

Witness's Background:

- Can you please state your full name and occupation for the record?
- How long have you lived at your current address?
- Have you ever had any previous encounters with law enforcement before this incident?

Knowledge of the Incident:

- Were you present during the incident that occurred on [Date of the incident]?
- Can you briefly describe the events leading up to the encounter with law enforcement?

Encounter with Law Enforcement:

- How did the law enforcement officers approach you on that day?
- Did they inform you of the reason for the encounter or mention any suspicions they had?
- Were you cooperative and respectful during the encounter?

Awareness of Your Rights:

- Were you aware of your constitutional rights, including the Fourth Amendment protection against unreasonable searches and seizures?

- Did you express your understanding of your rights to the law enforcement officers during the encounter?

Consent to Search:

- Did you voluntarily consent to a search of your person, vehicle, or property?
- If you did not provide consent, did you clearly communicate your objection to the search?

Details of the Search:

- How was the search conducted? Can you describe the officers' actions during the search?
- Did you feel intimidated, coerced, or pressured into allowing the search?

Presence of a Warrant:

- Were the law enforcement officers in possession of a valid search warrant at any point during the encounter?
- Did they present you with a warrant or provide any explanation for searching without one?

Request for Legal Representation:

- Did you request legal representation or express a desire to speak with an attorney during the encounter?
- If so, how did the law enforcement officers respond to your request?

Impact of the Search:

- How did the search and the encounter with law enforcement affect you personally and emotionally?
- Were there any consequences or challenges you faced as a result of this incident?

Inconsistencies or Misconduct:

- Did you notice any discrepancies or inconsistencies in the officers' actions during the encounter?
- Did you observe any behavior by the officers that you found concerning or inappropriate?

Your Understanding of the Search:

- Based on your understanding of the law, do you believe the search conducted by the officers was lawful?
- Why do you believe the search was illegal or violated your rights?

Anything Else to Add:

- Is there any additional information or details that you think is important for the jury to know about this incident?

Remember, as a defense attorney, you should adapt these questions to the specific facts and circumstances of the case and the particular witness's testimony. The goal is to elicit favorable information and present a compelling defense against the alleged illegal search.

Cross Examination

When cross-examining a police officer in an illegal search case, the defense attorney seeks to challenge the officer's actions and establish that the search violated the defendant's Fourth Amendment rights. Here are some sample questions for the cross-examination:

Establishing the Officer's Actions:

- Officer, you were the one who conducted the search on [Date of the incident], correct?
- Can you confirm that you did not have a valid search warrant when conducting the search?

Basis for the Search:

- What was the reason or probable cause you had to conduct the search without a warrant?
- Were you acting on a tip, suspicion, or observation when you decided to initiate the search?

Knowledge of the Fourth Amendment:

- Are you familiar with the Fourth Amendment of the U.S. Constitution, which protects against unreasonable searches and seizures?
- Can you explain the Fourth Amendment's requirements for a lawful search without a warrant?

Details of the Search:

- How did you approach the defendant during the encounter?
- Did you inform the defendant of their rights, including their right to refuse the search?

Consent to Search:

- Did the defendant provide voluntary consent for the search?
- Can you provide any evidence or documentation indicating that the defendant agreed to the search?

Request for Legal Representation:

- Did the defendant request legal representation or ask to speak with an attorney during the encounter?
- How did you respond to the defendant's request for legal representation?

Compliance with Search and Seizure Laws:

- Did you believe, at the time of the search, that you were acting within the boundaries of the law and in compliance with search and seizure regulations?
- Were you aware of any inconsistencies or potential violations of the defendant's rights during the search?

Documentation and Record Keeping:

- Can you provide any written records, reports, or documentation related to the encounter and search?

- Did you document the specific reasons and circumstances that led you to conduct the search?

Impact on the Defendant:

- How would you characterize the defendant's demeanor during the encounter and the search?
- Did the defendant object to the search or express any concerns during the encounter?

Alternatives to the Search:

- Were there any alternative courses of action available to you instead of conducting the search without a warrant?
- Could you have sought a search warrant or taken other steps to obtain evidence legally?

Training on Fourth Amendment Rights:

- Have you received training on the Fourth Amendment and its implications for conducting searches and seizures?
- Can you describe the training you received in relation to this case?

Remember, the cross-examination should be tailored to challenge the officer's credibility and actions during the search while highlighting any potential violations of the defendant's Fourth Amendment rights. The defense attorney aims to create doubt about the legality of the search and any evidence obtained as a result.

CHAPTER 10

FOIA REQUESTS

Introduction by Kevin Smith

The Freedom of Information Act represents one of the most underutilized yet powerful tools in a criminal defense attorney's arsenal. While traditional discovery provides access to materials within the prosecutor's file, FOIA opens doors to a vast landscape of information held by public agencies that may never appear in standard discovery. For the resourceful defense attorney, mastering Connecticut's FOIA framework transforms abstract statutory rights into concrete investigative advantages that can fundamentally alter case outcomes.

Connecticut's FOIA statute, among the most robust in the nation, establishes a presumption that government records are open to public inspection unless specifically exempted. This presumption creates strategic opportunities throughout the criminal defense process, from pre-charge investigation through post-conviction advocacy. The effective practitioner uses FOIA to uncover police disciplinary records, department policies, training materials, internal memoranda, electronic communications, and other materials that may reveal investigative deficiencies, pattern evidence, impeachment material, or exculpatory information never disclosed through traditional channels.

FOIA requests serve multiple strategic functions beyond mere information gathering. They signal to opposing counsel that the defense is conducting thorough investigation. They create contemporaneous documentation of defense diligence that may later support ineffective assistance claims if initial counsel fails to pursue evident leads. They establish timelines for agency knowledge and action that may reveal Brady violations. Perhaps most importantly, they frequently uncover information that no one—not prosecutors, not police, not complaining witnesses—anticipated would become relevant to the case.

Unlike discovery, which operates within established judicial timelines, FOIA follows statutory deadlines that can accelerate access to crucial information. Agencies must respond to requests within specific timeframes, and the FOIA Commission provides an administrative appeal process that often moves more quickly than judicial intervention in discovery disputes. This temporal advantage can provide critical momentum in time-sensitive cases or when standard discovery has stalled.

The sections that follow provide a comprehensive roadmap for integrating FOIA into criminal defense practice. From drafting effective requests through navigating exemptions and pursuing administrative appeals, this chapter equips Connecticut practitioners with practical tools to transform public information rights into powerful advocacy advantages. By mastering these frameworks, defense counsel can access information that remains invisible to less resourceful practitioners, creating meaningful differences in case preparation, negotiation leverage, and trial outcomes.

Part I: Law and History

Connecticut General Assembly unanimously adopted the Connecticut Freedom of Information Act (F.O.I.A) in 1975, which created the Freedom of Information Commission (F.O.I.C), which established the specific administrative agency to process claims of alleged violations and issue orders to redress violations. The F.O.I.A was recodified in 1999, and today can be found at C.G.S. Title 1, Chapter 14 §1-200-259, with 243-259 being reserved for future use.

Who can invoke the law?

Anyone. FOIA provides that "*every person* shall have the right to (1) inspect [public] records promptly during regular office or business hours, (2) copy such records in accordance with subsection (g) of section 1-212, or (3) receive a copy of such records in accordance with section 1-212." C.G.S. §1-210(a) (emphasis added)."

Who can it be invoked against?

Public agencies and any person who is the functional equivalent of a public agency pursuant to law. FOIA applies to all "public agencies" as defined in C.G.S. §1-200(1): "'Public agency' or 'agency' means (A) Any executive, administrative or legislative office of the state or any political subdivision of the state or of any state or town agency, any department, institution, bureau, board, commission, authority or official of the state or of any city, town, borough, municipal corporation, school district, regional district or other district or other political subdivision of the state, including any committee of, or created by, any such office, subdivision, agency, department, institution, bureau, board, commission, authority or official, and also includes any judicial office, official or body or committee thereof but only with respect to its or their administrative functions; (B) Any person to the extent such person is deemed to be the functional equivalent of a public agency pursuant to law; or (C) Any "implementing agency", as defined in section 32-222."

Important exceptions: C.G.S. §1-201 "For the purposes of subdivision (1) of section 1-200, the Division of Criminal Justice shall not be deemed to be a public agency except in respect to its administrative functions." Similarly, the Judicial branch is also subject to F.O.I.A, but only with respect to its administrative functions, per section 1-200(1)(A).

Does the purpose of the request matter?

No. The purpose is irrelevant as the general rule under FOIA is one of disclosure. The Supreme Court has held that records' disclosability under FOIA "does not depend in any way on the status or motive of the applicant for disclosure, because the act vindicates the public's right to know, rather than the rights of any individual." Chief of Police v. FOIC, 252 Conn. 377, 387, 746 A.2d 1264 (2000). See also Groton Police Dep't. v. FOIC, 104 Conn. App. 150, 931 A.2d 989 (2007) (disclosure not dependent upon status or motive of person requesting record).

Nature of Request: Inspection vs. Copy

Public records are available for both inspection and copying under FOIA. C.G.S. §1-210(a). In Conn. Dep't of Pub. Safety v. FOIC, 1992 WL 31931 (Conn. Super. Feb. 5, 1992) aff'd, 29 Conn. App. 821, 618 A.2d 565 (1993), the Superior Court held that a written request for copies is required under C.G.S. §1-212, no written request is necessary to inspect under C.G.S. §1-210(a), so copies must be provided if orally requested as part of the request to inspect under C.G.S. §1-210(a). The same decision required motor vehicle accident reports to be made available for inspection at the originating state police barracks, rather than only at the Central Records Division in Meriden.

Additionally, FOIA provides that any individual may copy a public record using a hand-held scanner. A public agency may establish a fee structure not to exceed ten dollars for an individual to pay each time the individual copies records at the agency with a hand-held scanner. As used in this section, "hand-held scanner" means a battery operated electronic scanning device the use of which (1) leaves no mark or impression on the public record, and (2) does not unreasonably interfere with the operation of the public agency. C.G.S. §1-212(g).

Fees

FOIA provides that, with regard to state agencies, the "fee for any copy provided in accordance with [FOIA] . . . shall not exceed twenty-five cents per page;" for all other public agencies, the fee "shall not exceed fifty cents per page." C.G.S.§1-212(a). There is no fee for inspection of public records. Sales tax is not imposed and certified copies cost one dollar for the first page and fifty cents for each additional page. C.G.S. §1-212(c) and (e). Different fees are imposed for copies of certain motor vehicle records and criminal history searches. See C.G.S. § §14-50 and 29-11. See also Williams v. FOIC, 108 Conn. App. 471, 948 A.2d 1058 (2008) (page refers to each side of a document that is copied; not both sides of a single piece of paper).

Timelines

C.G.S. 1-206 provides a timeline for both the initial request to the public agency holding the records, and the appeal of a denial of such request to the FOIC as follows:

> (a) "Any denial of the right to inspect or copy records provided for under section 1-210 shall be made to the person requesting such right by the public agency official who has custody or control of the public record, in writing, within four business days of such request, except when the request is determined to be subject to subsections (b) and (c) of section 1-214, in which case such denial shall be made, in writing, within ten business days of such request. Failure to comply with a request to so inspect or copy such public record within the applicable number of business days shall be deemed to be a denial.
>
> (b)(1) Any person denied the right to inspect or copy records under section 1-210 or wrongfully denied the right to

attend any meeting of a public agency or denied any other right conferred by the Freedom of Information Act may appeal therefrom to the Freedom of Information Commission, by filing a notice of appeal with said commission. A notice of appeal shall be filed not later than thirty days after such denial, except in the case of an unnoticed or secret meeting, in which case the appeal shall be filed not later than thirty days after the person filing the appeal receives actual or constructive notice that such meeting was held. For purposes of this subsection, such notice of appeal shall be deemed to be filed on the date it is received by said commission or on the date it is postmarked, if received more than thirty days after the date of the denial from which such appeal is taken.

Part II: Using FOIA

What you can get: "[public] records and files:" " 'Public records or files' means any recorded data or information relating to the conduct of the public's business prepared, owned, used, received or retained by a public agency, or to which a public agency is entitled to receive a copy by law or contract under section 1-218, whether such data or information be handwritten, typed, tape-recorded, videotaped, printed, photostated, photographed or recorded by any other method." §1-200 (5).

Impeachment Material: Personnel Files, IA Records, Investigative Materials, Other Records

Disciplinary Records: While there are no specific provisions regarding disciplinary records in general, these should be treated as any other record under FOIA and presumed open unless a record comes within a specific exemption -- for example, if disclosure of the record in question would constitute an "invasion of privacy" under C.G.S. § 1-210(b)(2). See Perkins v. FOIC, 228 Conn. 158, 635 A.2d 783 (1993) (sick leave records).

Accident Reports: See C.G.S. § 14-50a regarding fees for copies of accident reports from the commissioner of motor vehicles. In Calibey v. State Police, Do. #FIC 86-310 (Jan. 28, 1987), the FOIC held that a report of a fatal motor vehicle accident was not exempt from disclosure under FOIA.

Police Blotter: In Town of Trumbull v. FOIC, 5 Conn. L. Trib. No. 34 (1979), the Superior Court held that daily activity sheets were not exempt from disclosure under FOIA, as long as certain exempt material was redacted.

Investigation Records: In City of Hartford v. FOIC, 201 Conn. 421, 518 A.2d 49 (1986), the Supreme Court held that certain police department internal affairs records were not exempt from disclosure under C.G.S. § 1-210(b)(2). See also C.G.S.§ 1-210(b)(3) (law enforcement exemption); Dep't of Pub. Safety v. FOIC, 51 Conn. App. 100, 720 A.2d 268 (1998); Kirschner v. FOIC, No. CV 97-0567162, 1998 WL 27829 (Conn. Super. Jan. 15, 1998)

Active Investigations: FOIA exempts from disclosure any "information to be used in a prospective law enforcement action if prejudicial to such action." C.G.S. § 1-210(b)(3). There are no other specific provisions or reported authorities regarding rules for active investigations. See also C.G.S. § 1-210(b)(3) (law enforcement exemption)

Arrest Records under §1-215: In Gifford v. FOIC, 227 Conn. 641, 631 A.2d 252 (1993) the Supreme Court ruled that reports prepared by police in connection with arrests were not required to be disclosed to the public during the pendency of the related criminal prosecution; and that C.G.S. § 1-215(a) exclusively regulates the disclosure of arrest reports, to the exclusion of § 1-210(b)(3); and as it then existed required the police to disclose only limited data: the name and address of the person arrested, the date, time and place of the arrest, and the offense for which the person was arrested. In 1994 § 1-215 was amended to provide that in addition to the aforesaid required disclosures, the police must, subject to the provisions of C.G.S. § 1-210(b)(3), also disclose one of the following: "arrest report, incident report, news release or other similar report of the arrest of a person." See however, C.G.S. § 1-216, mandating destruction of records of uncorroborated allegations of criminal activity upon review one year after compilation.

Prison, Parole, and Probation Reports: There are no specific provisions or reported court decisions on these records. Therefore, they should be treated as any other record and are presumed open unless a specific exemption applies.

Review and Destruction of Records Consisting of Uncorroborated allegations of criminal activity under §1-216: "Except for records the retention of which is otherwise controlled by law or regulation, records of law enforcement agencies consisting of uncorroborated allegations that an individual has engaged in criminal activity shall be reviewed by the law enforcement agency one year after the creation of such records. If the existence of the alleged criminal activity cannot be corroborated within ninety days of the commencement of such review, the law enforcement agency shall destroy such records."

Manuals: These should be treated as any other record and presumed open, unless they fall under a specific exemption, such as presenting a safety concern. C.G.S. §1-210 (18) and (19).

Records of Meetings: Board of Police Commissioners, Committees, Sub-committees.

Exemptions: FOIA contains twenty-eight specific exemptions. See C.G.S. §1-210(b). These exemptions are to be narrowly construed in light of the general rule of disclosure under FOIA. See Wilson v. FOIC, 181 Conn. 324, 435 A.2d 353 (1980); Maher v. FOIC, 192 Conn. 310, 472 A.2d 321 (1984). The exemptions reflect "a legislative intention to balance the public's right to know what its agencies are doing, with the governmental and private needs for confidentiality." Wilson, 181 Conn. at 328. The burden of proving the applicability of an exemption rests upon the agency claiming it. Id. at 329; Maher, 192 Conn. at 315. The exemptions are in general discretionary with the public agency, such that the agency may disclose material that is exempt but need not. See C.G.S. §1-210(b). The Connecticut exemptions are to some degree patterned after the federal Freedom of Information Act, such that the federal act can be a guide to interpretation. See Bd. of Trustees v. FOIC, 181 Conn. 544, 436 A.2d 266 (1980).

In May 2024, Connecticut expanded the law enforcement exemption to include the identity of mandated reporters, sworn witness statements, and visual depictions of victims of sexual or domestic abuse, homicide, suicide, or fatal accidents if such depiction would constitute an unwarranted invasion of privacy. It also exempts depiction of all minors unless required by law.

<u>Relevant exceptions:</u>

Exemption One — "Preliminary drafts or notes provided the public agency has determined that the public interest in withholding such documents clearly outweighs the public interest in disclosure." C.G.S. §1-210(b)(1).

Exemption Two — "Personnel or medical files and similar files the disclosure of which would constitute an invasion of personal privacy." C.G.S.§1-210(b)(2).

I. In City of Hartford v. FOIC, 201 Conn. 421, 518 A.2d 49(1986), the Supreme Court held that a public agency must meet "a twofold burden of proof to establish the applicability" of this exemption. First, it must establish that the file is a "personnel or medical or similar file," and second it must establish that disclosure "would constitute an invasion of privacy." The court also held that certain internal affairs records of the plaintiff's police department were not exempt from disclosure.

II. In Rocque v. FOIC, 255 Conn. 651, 774 A.2d 957 (2001) the Supreme Court reiterated that one claiming the exemption must prove both prongs, the facts of each case must be analyzed, and no type of data is always exempt.

III. In Dep't of Children & Families v. FOIC, 48 Conn. App. 467, 710 A.2d 1378 (1998), cert. denied, 245 Conn. 911, 718 A.2d 16 (1998), the Appellate Court held that the names of disciplined employees were a matter of public concern, and therefore not exempt under this exemption. Note that C.G.S. §1-217(a)(8) provides that the residential address of an employee of the Department of Children and Families is not subject to FOIA.

IV. In New Haven Chief of Police v. FOIC, 2 Conn. Ops. 572 (Conn. Super. 1996), the Superior Court held that under C. G. S. §1-210(b)(2), unless the character of the documents in question is conceded by the parties, the FOIC may be required to inspect them in camera (citing Wilson v. FOIC, 181 Conn 324, 340 (1980)).

V. In Dep't of Pub. Safety, Div. of State Police v. FOIC, 242 Conn. 79, 698 A.2d 803 (1997), the Supreme Court affirmed the trial court, holding that reports regarding a citizen's complaint of police assault and use of excessive force by a police officer were not exempt from disclosure under C.G.S. §1-210(b)(2); however, reports regarding a citizen's complaint that state trooper was involved in an inappropriate relationship with the complainant's wife were exempt from disclosure.

VI. When a public agency receives a request for personnel or medical files and similar files and the agency reasonably believes that disclosure would legally constitute an invasion of privacy, FOIA requires the agency to put the employee and the employee's collective bargaining representative, if any, on notice of the request and provide an opportunity for objection. If the employee or representative does object, the public agency is required not to disclose the documents unless ordered to do so by the FOIC. C.G.S. §1-214(b) and (c).

Exemption Three: Exemption Three — "Records of law enforcement agencies not otherwise available to the public which records were compiled in connection with the detection or investigation of crime, if the disclosure of said records would not be in the public interest because it would result in the disclosure of (A) the identity of informants not otherwise known or the identity of witnesses not otherwise known whose safety would be endangered or who would be subject to threat or intimidation if their identity was made known, (B) signed statements of witnesses, (C) information to be used in a prospective law enforcement action if prejudicial to such action, (D) investigatory techniques not otherwise known to the general public, (E) arrest records of a juvenile, which shall also include any investigatory files, concerning the arrest of such juvenile, compiled for law enforcement purposes, (F) the name and address of the victim of a sexual assault under section 53a-70, 53a-70a, 53a-71, 53a-72a, 53a-72b, or 53a-73a, or injury or risk of injury, or impairing of morals under section 53-21, or of an attempt thereof, or (G) uncorroborated allegations subject to destruction pursuant to section 1-216." C.G.S. §1-210(b)(3).

I. In Kirschner v. FOIC, No. CV 97-0567162, 1998 WL 27829 (Conn. Super. Jan. 15, 1998), the Superior Court held that the plaintiff failed to prove the applicability of this exemption to an internal investigation report. See also Davis v. FOIC, 47 Conn. Sup. 309, 790 A.2d 1188 (2001), aff'd 259 Conn. 45, 787 A.2d 530 (2002).

II. In Bona v. FOIC, No. CV 94-0123411S, 1995 WL 491386 (Conn. Super. Aug. 10, 1996), the Superior Court held that a police report concerning an alleged incident at the home of the ex-wife of a gubernatorial candidate was exempt under C.G.S. § §1-210(b)(3)(G) and 1-202 after the court conducted an in camera review of the documents in question and found that the report contained an allegation that an individual had engaged in criminal activity, though no arrest was made. The Appellate Court affirmed this decision, holding that records of uncorroborated allegations are not to be disclosed during the 15-month period in which corroboration is sought, that disclosure would not be in the public interest, and that no balancing is required. Bona v. FOIC, 44 Conn. App. 622, 691 A.2d 1 (1997).

III. In Maher v. FOIC, 192 Conn. 310, 472 A.2d 321 (1984), the Supreme Court held that the Department of Income Maintenance was not a law enforcement agency for purposes of this exemption even though it transmits information to a state fraud control unit.

IV. In Comm'r of Motor Vehicles v. FOIC, 6 Conn. L. Trib. No. 6 (1979), the Superior Court held that the term "crime" should be construed according to its commonly understood usage and that an infraction is a crime within the meaning of this exemption.

V. In Dep’t of Pub. Safety v. FOIC, 51 Conn. App. 100, 720 A. 2d 268 (1998), the Appellate Court held that subsection (C) is not satisfied by a mere good faith assertion that the matter is potentially criminal. There must be an “evidentiary showing” that the “actual information sought is going to be used in a law enforcement action” and “that the disclosure of that information would be prejudicial to that action."

VI. In Sedensky v. Freedom of Info. Comm'n, HHBCV136022849S, 2013 WL 6698055, at *18 (Conn. Super. Ct. Nov. 26, 2013), the Superior Court rejected the argument that the 911 recordings from the Sandy Hook shooting were “signed statements of witnesses” stating that the argument bordered on “frivolous.”

Exclusions: FOIA states that records must be disclosed "[e]xcept as otherwise provided by any federal law or state statute." C.G.S. §1-210(a). Consequently, there are a variety of statutory provisions not specifically set forth in FOIA that have the effect of exempting records from FOIA.

I. In Comm'r, Dep't of Pub. Safety v. FOIC, 204 Conn. 609, 529 A.2d 692 (1987), the Supreme Court held that information gathered by the statewide organized crime investigative task force is exempt from public disclosure under C.G.S. §29-170.

II. In Galvin v. FOIC, 201 Conn. 448, 518 A.2d 64 (1986), the Supreme Court held that autopsy reports are exempt from disclosure under C.G.S. §19a-411.

III. C.G.S. §54-142c states that certain criminal records which have been erased (i.e., sealed) pursuant to statute are not to be disclosed.

IV. C.G.S.§54-142k states that criminal nonconviction information shall not be available to the public.

V. C.G.S. § §54-76l and 54-76o state that certain records pertaining to youthful offenders are confidential and should be erased (i.e., sealed).

VI. C.G.S. §17a-28(b) provides that FOIA does not apply to certain records maintained by the Department of Children and Families. See Marlow v. FOIC, No. CV 99-0493141S, 1999 WL 966471 (Conn. Super. Oct. 12, 1999); Dep't of Pub. Health v. FOIC, No. CV 98-0492649S, 1999 WL 966634 (Conn. Super. Oct. 12, 1999) (records pertaining to child abuse or neglect are exempt under C.G.S. §17a-101k); C.G.S. §17a-101. See also Albright-Lazzari v. FOIC, 136 Conn. App. 76, cert. denied, 305 Conn. 927 (2012).

VII. Information and identity of a person making a complaint with the Office of the Victim Advocate is not subject to the disclosure under FOIA. C.G.S. §46a-13e.

VIII. Child abuse records are confidential and exempt from disclosure under C.G.S. §17a-101k. See Groton Police

Dep't. V. FOIC, 104 Conn. App. 150, 931 A.2d 989 (2007).

IX. In Comm'r of Emergency Svcs v. Freedom of Info. Comm'n, 330 Conn. 372 (2018), the Connecticut Supreme Court held that criminal search and seizure statutes that required the return of seized property pursuant to a warrant in a criminal investigation did not create an exemption under FOIA.

X. Public Act No. 92-225 extended the right of privileged communications, previously accorded psychiatrists and psychologists under C.G.S. § §52-146c and 52-146f, to social workers and marital and family therapists. In FOI Officer v. FOIC, 318 Conn. 769 (2015), the Supreme Court held that C.G.S. §52-196e exempted records related to Amy Archer Gilligan for the time period 1924-1962 from disclosure. Gilligan was a patient at Connecticut Valley Hospital following her conviction for murder and was widely considered the basis for the play and movie "Arsenic and Old Lace."

XI. Law Enforcement Videos: Law enforcement records, including body-worn camera footage, are not subject to disclosure when they were "compiled in connection with the detection or investigation of crime, if the disclosure … would not be in the public interest C.G.S. § 1-210. In Braasch v. Freedom of Information Commission, the Appellate Court of Connecticut confirmed that body-worn camera footage concerning "uncorroborated allegations" of a crime may be withheld as records whose release would not be in the public interest. 218 Conn. App. 488, 514, 292 A.3d 711, 728 (2023). Body camera footage that depicts "a victim of domestic or sexual abuse"; "a victim of homicide or suicide"; "a deceased victim of an accident, if disclosure could reasonably be expected to constitute an unwarranted invasion of personal privacy"; or a minor will also not be disclosed under the state Freedom of Information Act. C.G.S.§ 29-6d(g)(2). The only exceptions to this rule are if the footage (1) is of a minor and the minor and their guardian consent to disclosure, a police officer is accused of misconduct by the minor or their guardian, and the officer's legal representative in an investigation of the alleged misconduct requests disclosure to prepare the officer's defense, or (2) defense counsel for a person charged with a crime requests disclosure in order to prepare a defense. C.G.S. § 29-6d(g)(2)(c)(ii). A police officer who is the subject of an investigation for a disciplinary violation for which there is body-worn camera footage has the right to review the footage, as well as any other footage from the incident where the officer's likeness or voice appear, in front of their attorney or union representative. C.G.S. § 29-6d(f)(1). The footage must be released no "later than forty-eight hours following an officer's review of a recording ...

or if the officer does not review the recording, not later than ninety-six hours following the initiation of such disciplinary investigation, whichever is earlier." Id.

If there is a request for disclosure of footage from an incident where the police officer "has not been asked to give a formal statement about the alleged use of force" or where "a disciplinary investigation has not been initiated, any police officer whose image or voice is captured on the recording" may review the footage. C.G.S. § 29-6d(f)(1). "Not later than forty-eight hours following an officer's review of a recording . . ., or if the officer does not review the recording, not later than ninety-six hours following the request for disclosure, whichever is earlier, such recording shall be disclosed to the public …." Id.

State body-worn camera guidelines may not require a law enforcement agency to store footage for longer than one year, unless the footage pertains to an ongoing civil, criminal or administrative matter. C.G.S. § 29-6d(j).

Part III. How to Get it

Request to Agency: Put it in writing.

FOIA states that: "[a]ny person applying in writing shall receive, promptly upon request, a plain or certified copy of any public record." C.G.S. §1-212. An oral request for copies of public records need not be complied with; however, an oral request is sufficient to inspect public records. See C.G.S. §1-210(a). In Conn. Dep't of Pub. Safety v. FOIC, 1992 WL 31931 (Conn. Super. Feb. 5, 1992), aff'd, 29 Conn. App. 821, 618 A.2d 565 (1993), the Superior Court held that while a written request for copies is required under C.G.S. §1-212, no written request is necessary to inspect under C.G.S.§1-210(a). The court also ruled that copies must be provided if orally requested as part of the request to inspect under C.G.S. §1- 210(a). The written request should describe the public records with sufficient particularity so that the public agency can retrieve the records. See Perkins v. FOIC, 228 Conn. 158, 635 A.2d 783 (1993) (it would be "unreasonable" to deny access to FOIA "simply because of arguable imperfections in the form in which a request for public records is couched."). The records must be made available "promptly;" if a response is not given within four days, it is deemed a presumptive denial of access.

Summary: In writing, specify the records you seek, cite FOIA broadly. Give the agency four (4) days to respond, ten (10) if you are seeking records to which an objection may be lodged by the targeted individual (medical, personnel, other exempted/excluded records).

Denials and Appeals:

Time Frame: FOIA states that: "[a]ny denial of the right to inspect or copy records provided for under section 1-210 shall be made to the person requesting such right by the public agency official who has custody or control of the public record, in writing, within four business days of such request, except when the request is determined to be subject to subsections (b) and (c) of section 1-214, in which case denial shall be made in writing within ten business days of such request. Failure to comply with a request to so inspect or copy such public record within the applicable number of business days shall be deemed to be a denial." C.G.S. §1-206(a).

I. An agency may not defend its decision to ignore a request on the grounds that the request was made simply for the purposes of harassing the agency. Mayor v. FOIC, No. CV 01-0511803S, 2002 WL 523086 (Conn. Super. Mar. 19, 2002).

II. FOIA states that any person denied the right to inspect or copy a public record may appeal to the FOIC. C.G.S. §1-206(b).

III. The notice of appeal must be filed within thirty days of the denial, and the notice of appeal is deemed filed on the date it is received by the FOIC or on the date it is postmarked, if received more than thirty days after the date of the denial. C.G.S. §1-206(b).

A. In West Hartford v. FOIC, 218 Conn. 256, 588 A.2d 1368 (1991), the Supreme Court held that one who received written denial of a request for documents may appeal to the FOIC within 30 days of the written denial even though more than 30 days had elapsed since the fourth day after the date the request had been made. The court also held that FOIA does not bar successive requests or successive denials for public records and that there is no requirement that the appeal to the FOIC be taken from the first denial. See also Mayor v. FOIC, No. CV 01-0511803S, 2002 WL 523086 (Conn. Super. Mar. 19, 2002) (holding that an agency may not defend its decision to ignore a request on the grounds that the request was made simply for the purposes of harassing the agency).

Appeal Process: The appeal is brought by filing a notice of appeal with the FOIC. Upon receipt of notice of appeal, the FOIC will serve notice of the appeal upon interested parties. C.G.S. §1-206(b). If the appeal involves a public employee's personnel or medical file or similar file, then the FOIC will require the public agency to notify the employee and his collective bargaining representative of the appeal, and the employee then has the right to appear as a party. C.G.S. §1-206(b). The hearing before the FOIC is governed by FOIC regulations which allow for the

presentation of evidence and cross-examination of witnesses, among other things. The FOIC evidentiary hearing is held before a single commissioner of the FOIC, who prepares a proposed decision which is subsequently ruled on by the entire FOIC. The FOIC's regulations allow any person to request to participate in the hearing before the FOIC either as a party or as an intervenor. Conn. Agencies Regs. §1-21j-28.

The FOIC's jurisdiction ends if an appeal is withdrawn. Dep't. of Public Safety v. FOIC, 103 Conn. App. 571, 930 A.2d 739 (2007).

Substance of Appeal: The notice of appeal should request a hearing on the denial, and it should state (1) the date of the request; (2) the public agency involved; (3) the public records requested; and (4) the date of the denial. C.G.S. §1-206(b)(1). The FOIC is required to hear and decide the appeal within one year. C.G.S. §1-206(b).

Summary: Once your request has been denied, send a letter to the FOI Commission, attaching your initial request to the agency and stating the remedy you seek. You must appeal within thirty (30) days of the denial, or you risk dismissal on jurisdictional grounds. The FOIC must decide your appeal within one year. The burden is on the agency or person claiming the exemption, such that where a claimant invokes the personnel or medical exemption under §1-210(b), he or she must prove that the records in question are personnel or medical files and that disclosure would constitute an invasion of personal privacy. Further, in determining whether disclosure would constitute an invasion of privacy, the claimant must establish two elements: (1) the information sought does not pertain to legitimate matters of public concern; and (2) that such information is highly offensive to a reasonable person.

Hearing & Commission Meeting

The Ombudsman Program: A Form of Mediation

An ombudsman is assigned to each appeal to the FOIC to act as a liaison between the parties and to attempt to effect settlement prior to hearing. Discussions before the ombudsman are confidential and do not carryover to the hearing if negotiations are unsuccessful. Further, the Ombudsman may not discuss the case with the Hearing Officer. The Ombudsman may settle the matter in any of the following fashions: narrowing of the issues, partial release of requested records or release of redacted records, scheduling of FOIA training by FOIC staff.

Hearing

FOIA is enforced by the Freedom of Information Commission (FOIC), which consists of five members appointed by the governor with the approval of the legislature. See Conn. Gen. Stat. §1-205. The FOIC is charged with promptly reviewing any alleged violation of FOIA and issuing orders regarding such allegations. The commission has the power to investigate allegations, including the power to hold hearings, administer oaths, examine witnesses, receive oral and documentary evidence, subpoena witnesses, and require the production of books and papers it deems relevant to the investigation. Conn. Gen. Stat. §1-205. A contested hearing is 90 minutes long. Following the hearing, the hearing officer submits his or her report/recommendations to all parties and the FOIC.

Commission Meeting

The FOIC makes a final decision at its meeting, where each party is permitted ten minutes of legal argument. This time is used to advocate for or against the hearing officer's report, and there is no testimony or fact-finding permitted. FOIC may accept, reject, or amend the hearing officer's report.

Your Remedies

I. Ordered Release of Records Sought

II. Sanctions

A. The FOIC has the authority to impose civil penalties of not less than twenty dollars and not more than one thousand dollars against any custodian or other official upon a denial of a right under FOIA "without reasonable grounds." C.G.S. §1-206(b)(2). Any person who willfully, knowingly and with intent to do so, destroys, mutilates or otherwise disposes of any public record without the approval required under section 1-18 or unless pursuant to chapter 47 or 871, or who alters any public record, shall be guilty of a class A misdemeanor and each such occurrence shall constitute a separate offense. C.G.S. §1-240(a).

B. Any member of any public agency who fails to comply with an order of the Freedom of Information Commission shall be guilty of a class B misdemeanor and each occurrence of failure to comply with such order shall constitute a separate offense. C.G.S. §1-240(b).

Beware

I. Sanctions for frivolous or harassing appeals

A. A public agency may also bring an action in Connecticut Superior Court against any person whose appeal to the FOIC was denied because the FOIC determined that the "appeal or the underlying request would perpetrate an injustice or would constitute an abuse of the commission's administrative process." C.G.S. §1-241. The court may issue an injunction prohibiting the person from bringing further appeals to the FOIC; if the person continues to appeal, he or she will be conclusively in contempt of the order and the agency may seek further relief from the court. Id. See also Hodge v. FOIC, 2008 Conn. Super. LEXIS 2906 (2008), for a discussion regarding procedures for imposition of a civil penalty.

Administrative Appeal to Superior Court

Decisions of the FOIC may be appealed to the Superior Court in accordance with C.G.S. §4-183, the Uniform Administrative Procedure Act ("UAPA"). Notwithstanding the provisions of C.G.S. §4-183, in any such appeal of a decision of the FOIC, the court may conduct an in camera review of the original or a certified copy of the records which are at issue in the appeal but were not included in the record of the commission's proceedings, admit the records into evidence and order the records to be sealed or inspected on such terms as the court deems fair and appropriate, during the appeal. The commission shall have standing to defend, prosecute or otherwise participate in any appeal of any of its decisions and to take an appeal from any judicial decision overturning or modifying a decision of the commission. C.G.S. §1-206(c).

CHAPTER 11

CLOSINGS

Introduction by David Villa

The closing argument is literally the last word for each side at the end of trial. The closing argument represents the culmination of the criminal trial—the moment when disparate evidence coalesces into cohesive narrative, when legal principles animate factual disputes, and when the attorney most directly addresses the moral and logical dimensions of the jury's decision-making process. While evidentiary rules and procedural frameworks govern most of the trial, closing argument provides the rare opportunity to speak directly to jurors as reasoning moral agents, synthesizing facts, law, and values into a compelling case for acquittal. Mastering this critical phase of trial advocacy requires understanding both its theoretical foundations and practical execution.

The State must argue that the evidence presented at trial proves beyond a reasonable doubt each element of each charge and the Defense must argue that there is a reasonable doubt sized crack in at least one link of each chain of elements of each charge brought by the State. Though boring, the cleanest version of a State closing is merely mechanical: "You heard from Witness A, B, C who testified to 1,2, and 3, which establish elements X, Y, and Z of Count 1." The further the State strays from the boring safety of a mechanical close in favor of a persuasive narrative the more it risks a basis for reversal. The Defense, conversely, must argue that the State has failed to meet its high burden of proof beyond a reasonable doubt of each element of each charge. That in and of itself is a sufficient defensive theme particularly when supported by specific examples of reasonable doubts highlighted by defense counsel at trial. When available alternative defensive theories or narratives can be extremely persuasive when it presents a more likely innocent explanation of events than the State's theory. A complete alternative defensive theory can be powerful but is not required.

The structural placement of closing argument at trial's end creates both opportunities and constraints. By the time counsel rises to deliver closing argument, jurors have formed preliminary judgments about the evidence, developed impressions of witnesses, and begun constructing narratives to explain contested events. The effective closing argument must acknowledge these pre-existing perspectives while reshaping them into frameworks favorable to the defense. This delicate balance between respecting juror autonomy and guiding juror reasoning defines the strategic architecture of persuasive closings.

By proverb, a trial is "a play conducted with two directors and a cast of characters who refuse to stick to the script." An effective closing argument cannot be completed beforehand. A closing argument is dynamic and must be flexible to not only incorporate what has actually occurred at trial but, perhaps specifically the very last thing that happened. The final defensive witness, or a State witness Freudian slip or faux pas. Something completely unscripted may be a critical addition to your pre trial theme, necessitating a pivot. Connecticut practice permits substantial latitude in closing argument, allowing defense counsel to argue reasonable inferences from evidence, challenge witness credibility, highlight evidentiary gaps, and frame the application of legal principles to facts. This latitude, however, operates within established boundaries. The prohibitions against vouching for witness credibility, asserting personal opinions about the evidence, arguing facts not in evidence, and mischaracterizing legal standards create the ethical and procedural framework within which closing arguments must operate. The cases collected in this chapter—particularly State v. Williams, State v. Warholic, and State v. Ceballos—map these boundaries with precision, providing guidance for navigating the line between zealous advocacy and prosecutorial objection.

Again it is the State's case to lose on the merits or by reversal. It is the State's role to proceed cautiously and the Defense role to advocate up to the limits of what is permitted. The State's closing is confined to and must in all ways link back to and be supported by the evidence presented at trial, whereas the Defense close is limited to the universe of all possible reasonable doubt. The State must prove its case beyond a reasonable doubt, NOT beyond ONLY the reasonable doubts raised or supported by evidence provided by the Defense. The State has the burden to extinguish all reasonable doubts. A Defense that fails to pounce at closing, on a still flicking, however dimly, reasonable doubt misses an opportunity to give the jurors a basis to make a finding of not guilty.

The structure of criminal trials in Connecticut, with prosecution opening followed by defense closing and prosecution rebuttal, creates distinctive strategic considerations for defense counsel. Unlike the prosecutor, who may frame arguments knowing they will have rebuttal opportunity, defense counsel must anticipate and preemptively address the prosecution's likely responses. This structural asymmetry demands that defense closings incorporate both offensive and defensive elements—advancing affirmative theories of the case while simultaneously neutralizing anticipated prosecution rebuttals.

The prosecution's rebuttal closing presents distinctive challenges for defense counsel. Unlike civil trials, where defendants have the last word, criminal procedure gives prosecutors the final argument opportunity. This structural asymmetry requires defense counsel to anticipate prosecution rebuttals and incorporate preemptive responses within initial closings. The techniques outlined here—including argument inoculation, preemptive credibility enhancement, and strategic evidence prioritization—provide frameworks for neutralizing the prosecution's rebuttal advantage.

It is worth addressing this structural asymmetry directly with the jury at close. The State bears the high burden of proof beyond a reasonable doubt and the jury can trust you on that premise because the State went first and will also get the last word. The State's last word of rebuttal should be confided only to addressing the points made in the Defense close, be wary of a "sandbag rebuttal" where the State hides it strongest arguments in its final address to the jury which will not be countered by the Defense. Likewise, its worth mentioning to the jury that while the State has the advantage of going last if it were permitted by the rules the Defense would have something to say about the State's last word.

Beyond these structural considerations, effective closing arguments require seamless integration of three distinct persuasive dimensions: logos (logical reasoning), pathos (emotional resonance), and ethos (ethical credibility). Connecticut jurisprudence permits defense counsel to engage all three dimensions, though with differential constraints. Logical arguments receive the broadest latitude, emotional appeals face intermediate restrictions, and ethical appeals operate under the strictest limitations. Understanding how to navigate these dimensions while respecting their distinct constraints represents a central challenge of closing argument construction.

The logical dimension of closing argument involves organizing evidence into coherent inferential structures that lead inexorably toward reasonable doubt or affirmative defense theories. Connecticut practice permits robust logical argumentation, including explicit discussion of inferential reasoning, challenges to prosecution evidence chains, and presentation of alternative explanations for seemingly incriminating evidence. Analytical frameworks including syllogistic reasoning (drawing a conclusion from premises), Bayesian probability analysis , and narrative consistency evaluation —provide practical tools for constructing logical arguments that jurors find both accessible and compelling.

The emotional dimension of closing argument operates under greater constraints than logical argumentation but remains essential to effective advocacy. Connecticut courts distinguish between impermissible appeals to emotion (those seeking to override rational deliberation) and permissible emotional contextualization (helping jurors understand the human dimensions of evidence and legal principles). Empathetic perspective-taking, emotional framing of neutral evidence, and contextualization of client behavior—provide frameworks for engaging jurors' emotional intelligence without crossing into impermissible appeals to prejudice, sympathy, or fear.

Be wary of instructions by a judge or comments from a prosecutor which attempt to frame Ethos as only the tactic of the Defense . Emotions are just as likely to impermissibly assist the State as the Defense. Feelings of sympathy for an alleged victim can misguide a jury. Likewise, some jurors may emotionally feel a need to complete the work of law enforcement or a charismatic prosecutor, whose case has a missing piece. The role of the jury is a last check on the power of the State not a partner to them.

The ethical dimension of closing argument involves establishing the moral legitimacy of acquittal while respecting prohibitions against personal vouching or opinion. Connecticut practice permits defense counsel to invoke moral principles embedded within legal standards—presumption of innocence, requirement of proof beyond reasonable doubt, the value of liberty—while prohibiting explicit appeals to nullification or personal moral judgments about evidence or witnesses. The frameworks presented here offer approaches for engaging the moral dimensions of criminal adjudication while maintaining ethical and procedural propriety. A jury that has been effectively shown injustice by cross examination or evidence is not further persuaded by an explicit request for nullification, likewise jurors will undoubtedly make moral judgements about witnesses and evidence without being prompted to do so.

The strategic architecture of effective closing arguments varies across case types, defense theories, and evidentiary landscapes. Cases involving scientific or technical evidence demand different approaches than those turning primarily on witness credibility. Cases presenting affirmative defenses require different structural organization than those relying primarily on reasonable doubt. Cases with sympathetic defendants permit different emotional frameworks than those involving defendants whose actions, while legally defensible, remain morally troubling. These closing argument approaches provide adaptable frameworks for tailoring arguments to specific case characteristics.

Regardless of case-specific variations, all effective closing arguments address three fundamental jury questions: What happened? Does what happened constitute the charged crime? Is each element met? What is the evidentiary basis to support each element? According to which witness? Is that witness credible? Has the prosecution proven its case beyond reasonable doubt? The sequence and emphasis placed on these questions varies strategically, but comprehensive closing arguments provide jurors with frameworks for analyzing each. Decision trees, analytical templates, and rhetorical frameworks offer practical tools for constructing arguments addressing these fundamental questions.

The construction of the closing argument begins long before trial's end. Initial case analysis should identify potential closing themes, with trial preparation organized around developing evidence supporting those themes . Direct and cross-examination should elicit testimony that will support specific closing argument components. Opening statements should be requested in limine in most cases. They give the State the chance to promise something they can't deliver. More importantly they give the Defense a chance to persuade the jury there are two sides to the story, before hearing from the State for a significant period. The comprehensive approach outlined here integrates closing argument preparation throughout the criminal defense process, treating the closing not as a discrete trial component but as the culmination of both the strategic trial design and also an incorporation of intangibles which may unexpectedly occur at trial.

The delivery of the closing argument—its performance dimension—significantly impacts its persuasive power. Voice modulation, physical movement, gesture, eye contact, and pacing all affect how jurors receive and process argumentative content. Connecticut practice permits substantial latitude in performance style, though always subject to judicial management of courtroom decorum. The practical guidance provided here addresses both construction of argument content and effective delivery techniques, recognizing that persuasion emerges from the integration of substance and style. Jurors are not lawyers; they are not appellate judges. A criminal trial is not a moot court contest, there are no points for emotionlessly standing behind the podium. If a jury perceives that you do not believe or are bored by your own argument they will follow suit.

Technology has transformed closing argument possibilities, with Connecticut courts increasingly permitting digital presentations incorporating trial exhibits, timelines, demonstrative aids, and other visual elements. The strategic considerations governing technological enhancement—when to use visual aids, how to design them for maximum impact, how to integrate them with verbal argument, how to address equipment failures—have become essential components of closing argument preparation. How the State intends to display its evidence may be just as important as what it is. Likewise Defenses need to be aware of specific court room technological capabilities to demonstrate their argument with maximum effect.

Perhaps most importantly, effective closing arguments translate abstract legal principles into practical decision frameworks that jurors can readily apply to evidence. The presumption of innocence, burden of proof, reasonable doubt standard, and elements of charged offenses represent complex legal concepts that many jurors struggle to operationalize. The frameworks presented in this chapter provide approaches for making these abstract principles concrete—helping jurors understand not just the theoretical underpinnings of criminal law but their practical application to the evidence before them.

The reasonable doubt standard requires careful treatment in closing argument. Connecticut jurisprudence prohibits attempts to quantify reasonable doubt but permits robust discussion of its qualitative dimensions. The analytical frameworks presented here—including doubt categorization , inferential gap analysis, and evidence hierarchy assessment—provide methodologies for helping jurors understand how reasonable doubt operates in evaluating specific evidence patterns.

Addressing prosecution evidence constitutes another central challenge in closing argument construction. The frameworks presented here distinguish between strategies for addressing strong prosecution evidence (contextualizing, reinterpreting, or limiting its applicability) versus weak prosecution evidence (directly challenging its reliability, relevance, or sufficiency).

Ultimately, effective closing arguments must engage jurors at both intellectual and moral levels—helping them understand not just what the evidence shows but why it matters. The integration of factual analysis, legal principle, and moral reasoning creates closing arguments that resonate with jurors as thinking, feeling decision-makers engaged in consequential moral deliberation. By mastering the concepts presented in this chapter, defense counsel can construct closing arguments that transform trial evidence into compelling narratives of reasonable doubt, creating the strongest possible foundation for favorable verdicts.

The section that follows provides detailed examples of pertinent case law regarding closing arguments. By mastering these cases Defense can effectively police the closing arguments of the State.

Prosecutorial Impropriety

Relevant Case Law:

State v. Williams, 204 Conn. 523 (1987) - The Court found that the defendant did not adequately preserve his claim at trial. However, the claim is still reviewable per the second exceptional circumstance of State v. Evans, 165 Conn. 61 (1973); defendant raised a claim, supported by the record, that he was deprived of the fundamental constitutional right to a fair trial.

To warrant *Evans* review, the record must support the defendant's claim that he was blatantly deprived of a fundamental constitutional right and a fair trial.

Categories of Behavior That Misconduct Can Fall Within:

- Prosecutor's expression of opinion, either directly or indirectly, regarding credibility of a witness
- Prosecutor's expression of opinion - either directly or indirectly - regarding guilt of defendant - Williams at 541;
- Prosecutor's comments on facts not in evidence - Williams at 544;
- Appeals to jurors emotions, passions and prejudices- Williams at 545, or;
- Injections of extraneous issues - Williams at 547.

Prosecutorial Impropriety Can Occur:

1. During cross-examination of a witness.
2. During closing (and rebuttal) argument.

During closing, the prosecutor CAN:

- Ask the jury to draw inferences;
- Ask the jury to use common sense;
- Urge the jury to find that a witness was truthful or untruthful, due to certain reasons; or
- Comment on a witness's motives to lie or not lie.[30]

Reversals Due to Prosecutorial Impropriety

Prosecutor's questions and comments during summation, which were improper because they suggested that the jury could infer defendant's guilt due to the fact that he retained an attorney during the police investigation, deprived the defendant of a fair trial.

State v. Angel T., 292 Conn. 262 (2009)

In the closing argument, the prosecutor made improper remarks that played to the jury's sympathy for the complainant, took the jury's attention away from the facts, and argued facts not in evidence. The prosecutor also expressed his own opinion of the defendant's guilt, and directly attacked the defendant's constitutional right to confrontation by blaming the defendant for the complainant having to testify at trial. Thus, the court found that prosecutorial impropriety denied the defendant of a fair trial.

State v. Felix R., 147 Conn. App. 206 (2013)

Prosecutor forced the defendant to directly comment on the veracity of police officers who were witnesses, forced the defendant

[30] State v. Jordan, 117 Conn. App. 160, 164 (2009)

to directly comment on the veracity of the complain-ant, and mischaracterized the defendant's responses.

"The present case falls within a line of cases in which our Supreme Court has found that prosecutorial impropriety resulted in substantial prejudice depriving a defendant of a fair trial and due process, even in the absence of an objection or request for specific curative instructions from a defendant."

State v. Jones, 139 Conn. App. 469 (2012)

Prosecutor's actions in asking witness to comment on the veracity of another witness' testimony, referencing a report not in evidence/never admitted as an exhibit, and violating a motion in limine deprived the defendant of a fair trial. Additionally, the prosecutor's disclosure of an extrajudicial testimonial statement made by an individual absent from trial violated the defendant's sixth amendment right to confrontation.

State v. McLaren, 127 Conn. App. 70 (2011)

Prosecutor's repeated assertions that the defendant/defense counsel should not be trusted and mischaracterization of defense's theory of the case directly affected the central issue of the defendant's credibility, thus depriving the defendant of fair trial.

State v. Maguire, 310 Conn. 535 (2013)

Prosecutor's reference, during closing, to a fact not in evidence and suggestion that was unsupported by evidence deprived the defendant of fair trial.

State v. Therrien, 117 Conn. App. 256 (2009)

Prosecutor deprived defendant of fair trial by improperly appealing to the jurors emotions by urging they make a decision based on sympathy, by referring to a defendant's gang involvement despite the fact that the court had admitted such evidence for a different, limited purpose, and by suggesting that he personally believed in defendant's guilt.

State v. Santiago, 143 Conn. App. 26 (2013)

Things the Prosecution CANNOT Say

Conclusion that the defendant committed crime without reference to facts in evidence

State v. Warholic, 278 Conn. 354, 368 (2006)

Defense witness did not cooperate in the police investigation.

Warholic, at 398

State's witness as a "cute kid."

Warholic, at 376

Character assassination and personal attacks against the defendant or defense witness, such as “drunken bum," "coward, "hiding like a dog” "stupid," and "evil man."

State v. Williams, 204 Conn. 523, 546-47 (1987)

Any question on the case that suggests the defendant has a bad character or propensity for criminal behavior.

State v. Ubalde, 190 Conn. 559, 563 (1983)

Alcoholism treatment as opposed to the effect of alcohol on memory of the event.

State v. Senate, 42 Conn. App. 41, 55-56 (1996)

Jury has a duty to convict the defendant.

State v. Whipper, 258 Conn. 229, 271 (2001) & State v. Ceballos, 266 Conn. 364, 395 (2003)

Send a message to the community by a guilty verdict.

State v. Reynolds, 264 Conn. 1, 185-86 (2003)

Refusing to identify a witness as an expert after the court has qualified the witness.

Whipper, at 266

The defendant is not concerned with what God is going to do to him but with what the jurors are going to do.

Ceballos, at 393

"Victim did her part - now the jury must do its part."

Ceballos, at 395

How courageous the victim was to come to court and testify.

Ceballos, at 396

Witness was "reprehensible," "lacked mora fortitude," and "lacked a conscience."

State v. Thompson, 266 Conn. 440, 467 (2003)

Moral character of defense witness lying to protect friend.

Thompson, at 471-72

If the defendant is innocent, state witnesses must have lied.

Thompson, at 470-71

Parents of the victim want the person who killed their son brought to justice.

Thompson, at 474

Defendant as a "killer" or as a "rat."

State v. Couture, 194 Conn. 530, 561-62 (1984), State v. Oehman, 212 Conn. 325, 335 (1989) & Thompson, at 472

Oath obligates a guilty verdict (in absence of deciding verdict in accordance with evidence).

Reynolds, at 183

Personally vouch for the credibility of the witness.

State v. Payne, 260 Conn. 446, 454 (2002)

Things the Prosecution CAN Say

Witness had no motive to lie.

State v. Burton, 258 Conn. 153, 169-170 (2001)& State v. Bermudez, 274 Conn. 581, 592-93 (2005)

No reason for witness to make allegations unless he was telling the truth.

State v. Warholic, 278 Conn. 354, 365 (2006)

"It is a stretch to think witness is a mastermind behind making it up."

State v. Warholic, 278 Conn. 354, 365 (2006)

Witness came in, faced jury and testified.

Warholic, at 367

Witness was a victim of crime.

Warholic, at 370

Note: Judge cannot use term "victim."

State v. Cortes, 276 Conn. 241, 248 (2005)

The witness lied - if based on specific contradictions in evidence.

Warholic, at 371 & State v. Colon, 272 Conn. 106, 250-51 (2004)

State's witness had no motive to lie but defense witnesses had motive.

State v. Stevenson, 269 Conn. 563, 584-85 (2004)

"Would you want your friends or your father to know about you (and these facts)?"

Warholic, at 375-78 f.n. 4

Witness as "perfect victim."

State v. Ceballos, 266 Conn. 364, 394-95 (2003)

"Alice in Wonderland" argument.

State v. Thompson, 266 Conn. 440, 465 (2003)

Sarcasm based on evidence in case.

State v. Glenn, 97 Conn. 719, 732 (2006) & State v. John, 87 Conn. App. 301, 314 (2005)

The evidence and the law require you to find the defendant guilty - make him listen, ladies and gentleman.

State v. Griffin, 97 Conn. App. 169, 177-78 (2006)

Psychological effects of sexual abuse, even in absence of evidence of same.

Ceballos, at 400

"I ask you, ask yourself, how do you protect yourself against this type of activity? How can you protect yourself against somebody driving on a highway with their lights off." Does not rise to the level of a "community conscience argument."

State v. Stetter, 513 N.W.2d 87, 90 (S.D. 1994)

ÇHAPTER 12

JURY INSTRUCTIONS

Jury instructions represent one of the most critical yet often overlooked components of criminal trial practice. The language that guides jurors' deliberations can determine case outcomes regardless of the evidence presented or arguments made. This chapter provides a guide to navigating jury instruction practice in Connecticut criminal trials, from preparation through preservation of issues for appeal.

PREPARING FOR THE CHARGING CONFERENCE

Pre-Trial Preparation

Effective jury instruction advocacy begins long before the charging conference itself. Ideally, preparation should begin during case analysis and continue throughout trial preparation.

Early Identification of Instruction Issues

1. Case-Specific Instructions: During initial case analysis, identify unique factual or legal issues requiring specialized instructions.
2. Affirmative Defense Instructions: If presenting affirmative defenses, review Connecticut model instructions and relevant case law to determine required elements and burden of proof instructions.
3. Lesser Included Offense Analysis: Conduct a thorough analysis of potential lesser included offenses, considering:
    - Whether the elements satisfy the Whisnant test

- Whether the evidence would support a conviction on the lesser offense
- Strategic advantages and disadvantages of requesting lesser included offense instructions

4. Recent Developments: Research recent Connecticut appellate decisions that might affect standard instructions in your case type.

Filing Written Requests to Charge

Connecticut Practice Book § 42-16 provides that requests for jury instructions "shall be filed in writing with the judicial authority" and be filed when the case is claimed for jury trial or within a time set by the judicial authority. Strategic considerations include:

1. Timing: While the Practice Book permits later filing with judicial permission, submitting comprehensive requests early establishes your position and may influence the court's perspective.
2. Thoroughness: Include all potential instructions, even those that might become relevant only depending on how evidence develops.
3. Legal Authority: Support each non-standard instruction with relevant Connecticut case law, statutes, or secondary authorities.
4. Precision: Draft proposed language with exactitude—courts often adopt well-crafted proposals verbatim to avoid appellate issues.

5. Accessibility: Make your requests user-friendly for the court by organizing them logically, providing a table of contents, and using clear formatting.

Preparing for the Conference Itself

Effective advocacy at the charging conference requires thorough preparation and strategic thinking.

Materials to Bring

1. Written Requests: Bring multiple copies of all submitted requests to charge.
2. Supporting Authority: Have copies of all cases, statutes, and secondary sources cited in your requests.
3. Model Instructions: Bring relevant sections of the Connecticut Criminal Jury Instructions (available on the Judicial Branch website).
4. Trial Notes: Have notes of specific testimony or evidence that supports particular instructions.
5. Opposing Requests: Review and prepare responses to the prosecution's requested instructions.
6. Alternative Formulations: Prepare alternative language for contested instructions to offer if your primary request is rejected.

Strategic Preparation

1. Prioritization: Identify which instructions are most critical to your case theory and which are secondary. Be prepared to concentrate advocacy on the former.

2. Anticipating Opposition: For each non-standard instruction, anticipate prosecution objections and prepare responses.
3. Preservation Language: Prepare specific language to preserve objections for any anticipated adverse rulings.
4. Evidence Integration: Be prepared to cite specific trial evidence supporting each requested instruction.

Conference Formats in Connecticut Courts

Charging conferences in Connecticut vary by judge and court, but generally fall into three formats:

1. Formal On-the-Record Conference: A complete discussion of all instructions on the record, typically held in chambers or with the jury excused.
2. Two-Stage Conference: An informal discussion followed by a formal on-the-record conference to memorialize positions and rulings.
3. Rolling Conference: Instructions are discussed throughout trial as issues arise, with a final conference before closing arguments.

Regardless of format, these principles apply:

General Conference Procedure

1. Court's Preliminary Instructions: The court typically begins by outlining its intended instructions, often based on Connecticut Model Jury Instructions.

2. Party Positions: Each party states positions on the court's proposed instructions and advocates for submitted requests.
3. Specific Rulings: The court rules on each contested instruction.
4. Final Instructions: The court finalizes the instruction language to be delivered.

EFFECTIVE ADVOCACY TECHNIQUES

1. Framing Your Position

When advocating for specific instructions, frame your position effectively:

Template Language: "Your Honor, the Defendant requests an instruction on [TOPIC] as set forth in our Request to Charge Number [X]. This instruction is legally required because [LEGAL RATIONALE]. The evidence supporting this instruction includes [SPECIFIC TRIAL EVIDENCE]."

Example: "Your Honor, the Defendant requests an instruction on identification testimony as set forth in our Request to Charge Number 3. This instruction is legally required because eyewitness identification is the sole evidence connecting my client to this offense. Per State v. Guilbert, where eyewitness identification is a critical issue, specific instructions on the reliability factors are required. The evidence supporting this instruction includes Officer Smith's testimony that the identification occurred at night, from a distance of over 50 feet, and after only a 5-second observation."

2. Responding to Opposition

When the prosecution objects to your requested instructions:

Template Language: "Your Honor, the State's objection to our requested instruction on [TOPIC] is unpersuasive because [COUNTER-ARGUMENT]. The Connecticut Supreme Court in [CASE] held that [HOLDING], which directly supports our requested instruction."

Example: "Your Honor, the State's objection to our requested instruction on third-party culpability is unpersuasive because the threshold for such an instruction is quite low. The Connecticut Supreme Court in State v. Arroyo held that a defendant need only provide 'some evidence' connecting a third party to the crime. Here, we have presented testimony from two witnesses placing Mr. Johnson at the scene with a motive to commit this offense."

3. Addressing Court Concerns

When the court expresses reservations about a requested instruction:

Template Language: "I understand the Court's concern about [STATED CONCERN]. However, [RESPONSE TO CONCERN]. Alternatively, we would accept modified language that [PROPOSED MODIFICATION]."

Example: "I understand the Court's concern about the length of our proposed instruction on consciousness of guilt. However, each paragraph addresses a distinct legal principle recognized in Connecticut law. Alternatively, we would accept modified language that preserves the core distinctions between flight, fabrication, and concealment as outlined in State v. Figueroa."

MAKING A RECORD FOR APPEAL

The charging conference presents a critical opportunity to preserve instruction issues for appeal. To effectively preserve these issues:

1. Clear Articulation of Requests

Clearly state on the record:

- The specific instruction requested
- The legal authority supporting the instruction
- The evidence supporting the instruction

2. Specific Objections to Adverse Rulings

When the court denies a requested instruction or adopts an instruction over objection:

Template Language: "Your Honor, the Defendant objects to the Court's decision to [DENY REQUESTED INSTRUCTION/GIVE STATE'S REQUESTED INSTRUCTION] on [TOPIC]. This [OMISSION/INSTRUCTION] is legally erroneous because [LEGAL

RATIONALE]. This error prejudices the Defendant by [EXPLANATION OF PREJUDICE]. We ask the Court to reconsider its ruling."

Example: "Your Honor, the Defendant objects to the Court's decision to deny our requested instruction on specific unanimity. This omission is legally erroneous because the State has alleged multiple acts that could independently satisfy the elements of Count One, implicating the constitutional requirement of jury unanimity under State v. Famiglietti. This error prejudices the Defendant by allowing a conviction without ensuring that all jurors agree on which specific act constituted the offense. We ask the Court to reconsider its ruling."

3. Alternative Proposals

If the court rejects your primary instruction request, offer alternative language:

Template Language: "Your Honor, if the Court is not inclined to give our requested instruction as written, we propose the following alternative language that addresses the Court's concerns while still conveying the essential legal principle: [ALTERNATIVE LANGUAGE]."

4. Renewing Objections

After the instructions are delivered to the jury, be prepared to renew any objections if the delivered instructions differ from what was discussed at the charging conference:

Template Language: "Your Honor, the Defendant renews our objection to the instruction on [TOPIC] as delivered. The instruction as given [EXPLAIN VARIANCE FROM CONFERENCE DISCUSSION OR NEW ISSUE], which compounds the prejudice previously stated."

CONNECTICUT-SPECIFIC MODEL INSTRUCTIONS

Connecticut's model criminal jury instructions provide a starting point for most cases, but effective advocacy requires understanding when and how to modify these instructions. This section highlights key instructions that frequently require modification in criminal defense practice.

Reasonable Doubt Instruction

Modification Strategies

1. Lack of Evidence Emphasis: Request additional language emphasizing that reasonable doubt may arise from the absence of evidence the jury would expect to see in a properly investigated case.

   Sample Language: "Reasonable doubt may arise not only from the evidence presented but also from the lack of evidence. Since the burden is on the State to prove the defendant guilty beyond a reasonable doubt of every essential element of the crime charged, a reasonable doubt may arise from the lack of evidence concerning an essential element as much as from the presence of evidence contradicting it."

2. Multiple Reasonable Inferences: When the evidence permits multiple reasonable interpretations, request language clarifying the impact on reasonable doubt.

   Sample Language: "If two conclusions can reasonably be drawn from the evidence, one of innocence and one of guilt, you must adopt the conclusion of innocence."

Identification Testimony

Following State v. Guilbert, 306 Conn. 218 (2012), specific instructions on eyewitness identification are often critical in identification cases.

Model Instruction (Annotated)

Modification Strategies

1. Weapon Focus Effect: When a weapon was present during the offense, request this additional factor:

   Sample Language: "You may consider whether the witness's attention was diverted by the presence of a weapon. Scientific studies have shown that when a weapon is involved, the witness may focus on the weapon rather than the person holding it, potentially reducing the reliability of identification."

2. Cross-Racial Identification: When the identification crosses racial lines:

Sample Language: "You may consider whether the witness and the defendant are of different races. Scientific studies have shown that people may have greater difficulty identifying members of a different race than members of their own race."

3. Confidence-Accuracy Relationship: To address potentially over-confident witnesses:

   Sample Language: "Scientific research has shown that a witness's confidence in their identification may not be an indication of the accuracy of the identification, especially when expressed after the witness has received feedback from others."

Third-Party Culpability

When the defense theory involves potential third-party responsibility, a specific instruction is essential.

Model Instruction (Annotated)

Modification Strategies

1. No Defense Burden: Emphasize that the defense carries no burden of proof:

Sample Language: "The defendant does not have to prove that another person committed this crime. The defendant need only raise evidence that creates a reasonable doubt as to whether the defendant committed the offense charged."

2. Direct Connection Doctrine Clarification: When the court expresses concern about the sufficiency of third-party evidence:

Sample Language: "Connecticut law does not require that the evidence establish a direct connection between the third party and the crime. The evidence need only tend to create a reasonable doubt concerning the defendant's guilt. Any evidence, regardless of its strength, that tends to indicate that a third party, and not the defendant, committed the crime is relevant to this case."

Consciousness of Guilt

Consciousness of guilt instructions can be particularly damaging to the defense if not properly limited.

Modification Strategies

1. Innocent Explanation Emphasis: Request language emphasizing alternative explanations:

   Sample Language: "The defendant's conduct may be motivated by factors wholly unrelated to guilt. Fear, mistake, embarrassment, nervousness, or many other innocent factors may cause a person to act in a way that may appear to suggest consciousness of guilt. A person who is innocent but aware that they are suspected of a crime may engage in certain behaviors because of that awareness, not because of any consciousness of guilt."

2. Multiple Inference Clarification: When the alleged consciousness of guilt behavior is particularly ambiguous:

    Sample Language: "If you find that the defendant [describe conduct], you must then determine what inference, if any, to draw from the conduct. The conduct may reflect consciousness of guilt, but it may also be consistent with other, innocent explanations. Unless you find that the conduct reflects consciousness of guilt and not any other reasonable explanation, you may not infer guilt from the conduct."

3. Specific Limitation for Flight: When the evidence concerns flight:

    Sample Language: "Flight does not create a presumption of guilt. There may be reasons for flight fully consistent with innocence. Even a person who has done nothing wrong may have valid reasons to flee or avoid a confrontation. A person's flight may be motivated by a variety of factors, including fear, embarrassment, or a desire to avoid being apprehended for a different offense."

Affirmative Defenses

Instructions on affirmative defenses must properly allocate the burden of proof.

Modification Strategies

1. Subjective-Objective Test Clarification: Request language clarifying this critical standard:

   Sample Language: "The test for self-defense has both subjective and objective elements. The jury must first determine whether the defendant actually believed that he needed to defend himself. This is the subjective part of the test. If you find that the defendant actually believed he needed to defend himself, you must then determine whether that belief was reasonable. This is the objective part of the test. The defendant's actual belief does not need to be correct, but it must be reasonable under the circumstances as the defendant believed them to be."

2. Initial Aggressor Exception: When the state claims the defendant was the initial aggressor:

   Sample Language: "The state has claimed that the defendant was the initial aggressor and therefore cannot claim self-defense. For this exception to apply, the state must prove beyond a reasonable doubt that the defendant was the initial aggressor. Being the initial aggressor means that the defendant was the first to use or threaten the imminent use of physical force. Mere words, no matter how offensive, do not make someone an initial aggressor."

3. Retreat Clarification: When retreat is at issue:

   Sample Language: "Connecticut law does not require a person to retreat before using force to defend himself if

(1) he reasonably believes that using force is necessary, (2) he is not the initial aggressor, (3) he is in a place where he has a right to be, and (4) he reasonably believes he cannot retreat with complete safety. The defendant does not need to prove he could not have retreated safely; rather, the state must prove beyond a reasonable doubt that the defendant knew he could retreat with complete safety."

PRESERVING INSTRUCTION OBJECTIONS

Effectively preserving jury instruction issues for appeal requires meticulous attention to procedure and record-making.

Practice Book Requirements

Connecticut Practice Book § 42-16 states: "An appellate court shall not be bound to consider error as to the giving of, or the failure to give, an instruction unless the matter is covered by a written request to charge or exception has been taken by the party appealing immediately after the charge is delivered."

This creates two methods of preservation:

1. Filing a written request to charge
2. Taking an exception immediately after the charge is delivered

For maximum protection, employ both methods.

Template Language for Exceptions

1. Exception to Denial of Requested Instruction

Example: "Your Honor, the defense excepts to the Court's decision not to give our requested instruction on specific unanimity as set forth in our Request to Charge Number 4. The instruction was legally required because the State presented evidence of multiple acts that could each independently satisfy the elements of Count Two, and the failure to give it prejudices the defendant by allowing a conviction without ensuring juror unanimity on which specific act constituted the offense."

2. Exception to Instruction as Given

Example: "Your Honor, the defense excepts to the Court's instruction on identification testimony. The instruction as given was legally erroneous because it omitted the scientifically validated factors regarding cross-racial identification and weapon focus, which were directly applicable to this case under State v. Guilbert. The defendant is prejudiced by this instruction because it failed to provide the jury with the tools needed to properly evaluate the reliability of the only evidence connecting him to this offense."

3. Exception to Modified Requested Instruction

Example: "Your Honor, while we appreciate the Court giving an instruction on self-defense, the defense excepts to the Court's modification of our requested language regarding the duty to retreat. The modification is legally erroneous because it fails to clarify that the defendant had no duty to retreat from his own home under Connecticut General Statutes § 53a-19(b). The defendant is prejudiced by this modification because it erroneously suggests he had a duty to retreat before using force in his own home."

Timing of Exceptions

Practice Book § 42-16 requires exceptions "immediately after the charge is delivered." Courts have strictly construed this requirement:

1. Before the Jury Deliberates: Exceptions must be taken before the jury begins deliberations. State v. Miller, 186 Conn. 654, 658 (1982).
2. After Any Supplemental Instructions: When the court gives additional or corrective instructions, new exceptions should be taken.
3. Specificity Required: Generic exceptions preserving "all previous objections" have been held insufficient. State v. Jacobs, 229 Conn. 385, 390 (1994).

Strategic Exception-Taking

Given the time constraints of post-instruction exceptions, prepare in advance:

1. Written Summaries: Prepare written summaries of anticipated exceptions before the instructions are delivered.
2. Prioritization: List exceptions in order of importance to ensure critical issues are raised even if time is limited.
3. Specificity: For each anticipated exception, note:
   - The specific instruction at issue
   - The legal basis for the objection
   - The prejudice to the defendant
   - The requested remedy (if applicable)

4. Renewal of Pre-Charge Objections: While general renewals of previous objections may be insufficient alone, specifically renewing detailed objections made during the charging conference can be effective.

Handling Waiver and Plain Error

When trial counsel has failed to properly preserve instruction issues, appellate counsel may still have options:

1. Golding Review: Under State v. Golding, 213 Conn. 233 (1989), unpreserved claims of constitutional magnitude may be reviewed if:
   - The record is adequate for review
   - The claim is of constitutional magnitude
   - The alleged constitutional violation clearly exists and clearly deprived the defendant of a fair trial
   - If subject to harmless error analysis, the state failed to demonstrate harmlessness beyond a reasonable doubt
2. Plain Error: Practice Book § 60-5 provides that the court may "in the interests of justice notice plain error not brought to the attention of the trial court." For jury instructions, plain error typically requires that the instruction:
   - Misstates the law on an essential element
   - Creates manifest injustice

- Affects the fairness and integrity of the proceedings

Jury instructions represent the critical interface between complex legal principles and juror decision-making. By mastering the art of instruction advocacy, defense counsel can shape the legal framework through which jurors evaluate evidence—often with case-determinative effect.

Effective advocacy requires thorough preparation, precise language, strategic thinking, and meticulous preservation of issues for appeal. By incorporating the strategies and templates provided in this chapter, defense counsel can maximize control over this crucial aspect of trial practice.

Remember that jury instruction advocacy is both a science and an art. The science involves understanding the legal requirements and technical aspects of preservation. The art involves crafting language that resonates with jurors while satisfying legal requirements. By developing proficiency in both dimensions, defense counsel can significantly enhance prospects for favorable verdicts and meaningful appellate review.

ÇHAPTER 13

QUICK REFERENCE GUIDE TO IMPORTANT CASES

Brady v. Maryland, 373 U.S. 83 (1963)

Brady was convicted of first-degree murder and sentenced to death in Maryland. After the trial, he found out that the prosecution had withheld a statement by his co-defendant (who was tried separately) admitting that *he*—not Brady—actually committed the killing. Brady's lawyer had asked to see any such statements, but the prosecution never disclosed this confession.

Maryland's highest court ruled that the prosecution's suppression of this evidence violated Brady's right to due process, but said the error only affected sentencing—not the conviction—so it ordered a new trial just on punishment.

The U.S. Supreme Court agreed. It held that:

1. **Prosecutors must turn over evidence favorable to the defense if it is material to guilt or punishment**—failing to do so violates due process under the 14th Amendment.
2. Limiting the new trial to sentencing was allowed and did not violate Brady's constitutional rights.

This case established the **Brady Rule**, requiring prosecutors to disclose exculpatory evidence. It remains a cornerstone of criminal procedure and due process protections.

Strickland v. Washington, 466 U.S. 668 (1984)

Strickland pleaded guilty to three murders in Florida and was sentenced to death. After losing appeals and state post-conviction relief, he filed a federal habeas petition claiming his lawyer provided ineffective assistance at sentencing. The District Court denied the claim, but the Eleventh Circuit reversed, creating a new standard for evaluating ineffective assistance of counsel.

The U.S. Supreme Court reversed the Eleventh Circuit and created the now-standard **two-pronged test** for ineffective assistance under the Sixth Amendment:

1. **Performance Prong**: The defendant must show that counsel's performance fell below an **objective standard of reasonableness**—that is, the lawyer was not functioning as the "counsel" guaranteed by the Sixth Amendment.
2. **Prejudice Prong**: The defendant must also show **a reasonable probability** that, but for the lawyer's errors, the outcome of the trial or sentencing would have been different.

The Court found that Strickland did not meet either prong: the evidence his attorney didn't present was weak and could have opened the door to harmful rebuttal evidence. The Court emphasized that judicial review of attorney performance must be **highly deferential**.

Justice Brennan agreed with the legal rule but dissented from the result, arguing the death penalty is always unconstitutional. Justice

Marshall dissented more broadly, criticizing the standard as too vague and arguing that Strickland's counsel had failed to provide effective representation.

Lozada v. Warden, 223 Conn. 834 (1992)

After pleading guilty to murder, Lozada filed a habeas petition claiming ineffective assistance of trial counsel. He lost. He then filed a **second** habeas petition—this time arguing that his **first habeas attorney** had been ineffective. The trial court dismissed it, but the Connecticut Appellate Court reversed. The state (the warden) appealed.

The **Connecticut Supreme Court affirmed**, holding that:

1. **Indigent petitioners have the right to effective assistance of appointed counsel** in habeas proceedings. If the first habeas lawyer was ineffective, a second petition can challenge that.

2. **Habeas relief isn't limited to constitutional claims**—nonconstitutional legal errors (like ineffective assistance of habeas counsel) may also be reviewed.

3. A habeas petitioner **doesn't need to show that immediate release is the only possible remedy**—getting a new trial or new hearing may be enough.

Key takeaway: In Connecticut, a person can file a *successive* habeas petition if their prior habeas counsel was ineffective, reinforcing the importance of competent legal representation at all stages.

Giglio v. United States, 405 U.S. 150 (1972)

Giglio was convicted of forgery in federal court. After the trial, his lawyer discovered that the government had promised **not to prosecute a key witness**—Giglio's alleged co-conspirator—in exchange for testimony. This promise had not been disclosed to the defense or the jury. The prosecution's case relied heavily on that witness's credibility. The trial court denied a new trial, saying the promise was unauthorized and wouldn't have changed the outcome. The Second Circuit agreed.

The **U.S. Supreme Court reversed**, holding:

1. **Any promise made by a government attorney is attributable to the entire prosecution team**, even if another prosecutor wasn't aware of it.
2. The existence of a **non-prosecution agreement affects the credibility** of the witness and should have been disclosed.
3. **Withholding this information violated due process**, even if the government acted in good faith.

Key takeaway: *Giglio* expanded the *Brady* rule by requiring prosecutors to disclose any deals or promises made to key witnesses, because such information affects their credibility and could influence the outcome of the trial.

State v. Esposito, 192 Conn. 166 (1984)

Esposito was convicted of **kidnapping in the second degree** and **sexual assault in the first degree**. On appeal, he raised three main issues:

1. The trial court **allowed evidence of a prior sexual assault** he allegedly committed.
2. An expert **gynecologist testified** that a lack of physical injury was common in sexual assault cases.
3. The court **denied his request to inspect the victim's psychiatric records** to use for cross-examination.

The **Connecticut Supreme Court affirmed** the conviction:

- The prior assault was properly admitted under the exception for **pattern evidence**. Both incidents shared key similarities: the defendant knew the victim, was drinking, used a knife, committed the assault at his home, and showed the victim personal photos. The court found the **probative value outweighed the prejudicial effect**.
- The gynecologist's testimony was allowed because it **countered the common misconception** that a lack of physical trauma disproves rape.

- The psychiatric records were **privileged** under Connecticut law (§ 52-146e), and the defendant **did not meet the threshold showing** that the victim had a mental condition affecting her ability to testify truthfully. Without that, the court found no violation of the right to confrontation.

Key takeaway: Prior bad acts can be admitted when they show a clear pattern; expert testimony can explain misconceptions about physical evidence; and psychiatric records remain protected unless a specific and credible challenge to testimonial capacity is made.

State v. Fernando A., 294 Conn. 1 (2009)

Fernando A. was arrested on **family violence charges** related to an alleged assault on his wife during their divorce. The day of his arrest, he was released with conditions under **Conn. Gen. Stat. § 54-63c(b)**—including no contact with his wife and no return to the family home. At his first court appearance, the judge issued a **criminal protective order** as a condition of his pretrial release.

Fernando A. requested an **evidentiary hearing** before the order was issued, but the trial court denied it. He appealed, arguing this violated his **due process rights**.

The **Connecticut Supreme Court agreed in part**:

- The trial court was allowed to issue the protective order at arraignment based on oral arguments and a report from Family Services.
- However, **if the defendant requests it**, the court must later provide a **full evidentiary hearing within a reasonable time**, where the defendant can challenge the basis for the order.

This ruling **balances the need for immediate protective measures in family violence cases with the defendant's right to due process**.

Key takeaway: In family violence cases, courts can issue protective orders at arraignment without a hearing—but must provide an evidentiary hearing soon after if requested by the defendant.

State v. Garvin, 242 Conn. 296 (1997)

Willie Garvin pled guilty to multiple charges in two separate criminal cases, including **conspiracy to commit robbery**, **second-degree sexual assault**, **risk of injury to a child**, and **failure to appear in the first degree**. After he failed to show up for sentencing on both cases, he was charged again with failure to appear and sentenced accordingly. Garvin tried to **withdraw his guilty pleas**, but the trial court denied his request. He appealed, arguing **double jeopardy** and that his **plea was not voluntary**.

The **Connecticut Supreme Court affirmed** the convictions:

1. **No Double Jeopardy**: Garvin argued that being convicted twice for failure to appear—once for each bond—violated double jeopardy protections. The Court disagreed, holding that under **Conn. Gen. Stat. § 53a-172**, the **unit of prosecution is the bond**, not the general course of conduct. Since he forfeited **two different bail bonds**, two separate charges were appropriate.

2. **Voluntary and Knowing Plea**: The Court also held that Garvin's guilty pleas were entered **knowingly, intelligently, and voluntarily**, and therefore did **not violate due process**.

Key takeaway: The *Garvin* case is significant because it clarifies that **each bail bond is a separate obligation**, and failure to appear on each can result in separate criminal charges. The case also reinforces the standard for ensuring that **plea agreements are valid**—especially when a defendant agrees to specific sentencing consequences for failure to comply (now often addressed in a **"Garvin canvass"**).

State v. Porter, 241 Conn. 57 (1997)

Christian E. Porter was charged with **two counts of first-degree arson**. At trial, he **sought to introduce the results of a polygraph test** that he claimed supported his innocence. The trial court denied the motion, ruling the polygraph evidence inadmissible. Porter was convicted on one count and appealed. The Connecticut Appellate

Court affirmed, and the **Connecticut Supreme Court upheld the ruling**.

The Court used this case to adopt a **new standard for evaluating scientific evidence** in Connecticut:

1. The Court **rejected thc old "Frye" standard** (which required general acceptance in the scientific community) and **adopted the U.S. Supreme Court's *Daubert* standard**. Under this approach, trial judges serve as "**gatekeepers**" to determine if scientific evidence is both **reliable and relevant** before it reaches a jury.

2. Applying that standard, the Court found that **polygraph evidence is not reliable enough** to be admitted in court. Studies showed varying and uncertain accuracy rates, and the Court concluded that its **probative value was too low** and could mislead jurors.

3. The Court also ruled that **excluding the polygraph did not violate the defendant's constitutional right to present a defense** through compulsory process.

Key takeaway: *State v. Porter* established that Connecticut courts now follow the **Daubert standard** for admitting scientific evidence. Under that standard, **polygraph results are not admissible** due to concerns about their reliability and the risk of misleading the jury.

State v. Golding, 213 Conn. 233 (1989)

Monica Golding was convicted of **larceny in the second degree** and **fraud in obtaining general assistance** after a jury trial. She appealed, arguing that the trial court failed to properly instruct the jury on a key issue: the **value of the assistance allegedly obtained by fraud**. The Appellate Court affirmed the convictions, but the Connecticut Supreme Court granted review and **reversed in part**.

The Supreme Court focused on whether the **value of the property or benefit obtained** is an **essential element** of the crime of general assistance fraud. The Court held:

1. **When the value of the fraud determines whether the offense is a felony or misdemeanor**, it becomes an essential element of the crime and **must be proven beyond a reasonable doubt**.
2. The trial court's **failure to instruct the jury** on the value element of the general assistance fraud charge was **constitutional error** because it deprived the defendant of her right to a fair trial.
3. This error was not harmless—the conviction for general assistance fraud was reversed. However, the conviction for larceny in the second degree stood.

Key takeaway: If the **dollar amount determines the degree of the crime**, it must be submitted to the jury with proper instructions. Failing to do so violates **due process** and can overturn a conviction. This case also helped clarify the rules for raising and reviewing

unpreserved constitutional claims on appeal, leading to what is now known in Connecticut as the **"Golding doctrine."**

Crawford v. Washington, 541 U.S. 36 (2004)

Michael Crawford was convicted of assault after his **wife gave a recorded statement to police** that undermined his self-defense claim. At trial, she **did not testify** because Crawford invoked the **marital privilege**, but the **prosecution used her recorded statement anyway**, arguing it was reliable and admissible hearsay. The Washington Supreme Court upheld the conviction.

The **U.S. Supreme Court reversed**, holding that this violated Crawford's **Sixth Amendment right to confront witnesses**.

Key rulings:

1. The **Confrontation Clause** requires that **testimonial statements** by a witness who doesn't testify **cannot be admitted unless the defendant had a prior opportunity to cross-examine that witness**, and the witness is unavailable at trial.
2. The wife's **statement to police was testimonial**, meaning it was given in a formal setting to be used as evidence—so it **could not be used without cross-examination**, even if deemed "reliable" by the court.
3. The Court **rejected the prior reliability-based approach** (from *Ohio v. Roberts*) as inconsistent with the original

understanding of the Confrontation Clause. The key safeguard is **cross-examination**, not judicial judgment about trustworthiness.

Key takeaway: *Crawford* transformed Confrontation Clause law by requiring that **testimonial hearsay is inadmissible unless the defendant had a prior opportunity to cross-examine the declarant**, reshaping how courts handle out-of-court statements in criminal trials.

McCoy v. Louisiana, 584 U.S. 414 (2018)

Robert McCoy was charged with **three counts of first-degree murder** and faced the death penalty. He **insisted on his innocence** and explicitly told the court and his lawyer that he did **not want to concede guilt**. Despite this, his attorney told the jury during trial that McCoy **"committed the murders,"** believing it was the only way to avoid a death sentence. McCoy objected throughout and later appealed.

The **U.S. Supreme Court reversed his conviction**, holding:

1. Under the **Sixth Amendment**, a criminal defendant has the **right to make fundamental decisions about their own defense**, including whether to maintain innocence. That decision **belongs to the defendant—not the lawyer**.

2. Even if the attorney believes that conceding guilt is the best strategy, they **cannot override a client's express objection** to that strategy.
3. Violating this right is a **"structural error,"** meaning it affects the entire framework of the trial and requires **automatic reversal**, without the need to show prejudice.

Key takeaway: *McCoy* establishes that defense counsel **cannot admit a client's guilt over their clear and persistent objection**. The right to maintain innocence is part of a defendant's **autonomy**, and overriding it violates the Constitution.

State v. Patterson, 276 Conn. 452 (2005)

Anthony E. Patterson was convicted by a jury of **conspiracy to commit murder** and received a **sentence enhancement** for using a firearm during the commission of a felony under **Conn. Gen. Stat. § 53-202k**. He appealed, arguing insufficient evidence and improper jury instructions.

The **Connecticut Supreme Court affirmed the sufficiency of the evidence** but **reversed the conviction** on other grounds:

1. A **jailhouse informant** testified that Patterson confessed to planning the murder in retaliation for the shooting of a friend. The informant claimed Patterson and others lured the victim out of an apartment before the shooting. Some

of this was corroborated, and the Court found this sufficient to uphold the conspiracy charge.

2. However, the Court found **reversible error** in the trial court's **failure to instruct the jury to view the informant's testimony with special caution**, especially because the informant had received **a deal from the state** in exchange for his cooperation.
3. The Court emphasized that **informants who expect benefits have a strong motive to lie**, and a cautionary instruction is crucial when their testimony is central to the prosecution's case.
4. Because the **informant's testimony was critical** and the rest of the evidence was weak, the lack of instruction **was not harmless error**.

Key takeaway: When a jailhouse informant testifies in exchange for a benefit, the court must give the jury a **special credibility instruction**. Failure to do so can lead to **reversal and a new trial**, especially when that testimony is essential to the state's case.

State v. Joyce, 243 Conn. 282 (1997)

Wallace Joyce was convicted of **arson in the first degree** under **Conn. Gen. Stat. § 53a-111(a)(4)**. He appealed, arguing that certain evidence—specifically the results of chemical testing on his clothing—should have been suppressed because it was obtained in violation of his **constitutional rights against unreasonable searches and seizures**.

The **Connecticut Supreme Court affirmed** the conviction and rejected all of Joyce's arguments:

1. **Search and seizure**: In a previous appeal, the court had ruled that **testing Joyce's clothing without a warrant** violated the Connecticut Constitution. However, in this retrial, the police obtained a **new search warrant** based on an **independent source** of information. The Court ruled that the warrant was supported by **probable cause** and that the new chemical testing results were therefore **admissible**.

2. **Collateral estoppel**: Joyce argued the trial court should not have allowed the prosecution to introduce evidence of his **insurance proceeds** as motive for the fire, claiming that issue had already been decided. The Court disagreed, finding the claim of **collateral estoppel** did not apply and that the evidence was **relevant and admissible**.

3. **Due process**: Joyce also claimed the state's **failure to preserve certain physical evidence** denied him a fair trial. The Court held there was **no due process violation**, because there was no showing of bad faith or that the evidence would have been materially helpful to his defense.

Key takeaway: Even if evidence was previously ruled inadmissible due to an unconstitutional search, it may be used in a retrial if the state later obtains it through an **independent source and a valid warrant**. Also, the **independent source doctrine** and proper **probable cause** protect such evidence from suppression.

Gipson v. Commissioner of Correction, 257 Conn. 632 (2001)

Bernard Gipson, an **indigent defendant**, filed a **petition for a writ of habeas corpus** challenging his conviction. The Superior Court dismissed the petition, and the Appellate Court affirmed. Gipson then sought to file a **petition for certification** to the Connecticut Supreme Court, but he was **denied appointed counsel** to assist in doing so. The Supreme Court took up the case to decide whether that denial violated his rights.

The **Connecticut Supreme Court reversed**, holding:

1. Under **Conn. Gen. Stat. § 51-296(a)**, indigent defendants have a **statutory right to appointed counsel** for "**any criminal action**," including the **filing of a petition for certification** seeking discretionary review by the Connecticut Supreme Court.
2. The Court emphasized that the phrase "any criminal action" in the statute is **broad and unqualified**, and that **legislative history** supports the conclusion that this stage of appeal was meant to be covered.

3. The decision reinforced that Connecticut follows the constitutional principle that **indigent defendants are entitled to legal representation not only at trial but also during a first appeal as of right**—and that assistance **must extend** to filing a petition for discretionary review when it is the next procedural step.

Key takeaway: In Connecticut, **indigent criminal defendants have the right to appointed counsel** when seeking **discretionary review** from the state supreme court after the Appellate Court affirms a conviction. The decision expanded protection of indigent defendants' rights during post-conviction appellate proceedings.

Missouri v. Frye, 566 U.S. 134 (2012)

Galin Frye was charged with **driving with a revoked license**, a felony in Missouri due to prior offenses. The prosecutor sent Frye's lawyer **two formal plea offers**, including one recommending a **90-day sentence**. Frye's attorney **never told him about the offers**, and they expired. Frye later pleaded guilty without a deal and received a **three-year sentence**. He then filed for **postconviction relief**, arguing that his lawyer's failure to communicate the offers violated his **Sixth Amendment right to effective assistance of counsel**.

The **U.S. Supreme Court agreed in part and vacated the lower court's decision**, holding:

1. The right to **effective assistance of counsel extends to the plea bargaining stage**.

2. **Defense attorneys have a duty to communicate formal plea offers** from the prosecution that may be favorable to the defendant.
3. Failing to inform Frye of the plea offer was **deficient performance** under *Strickland v. Washington.*

However, the Court clarified that to establish **prejudice** under *Strickland*, a defendant must show:

- A **reasonable probability** they would have accepted the plea offer;
- A **reasonable probability** the prosecution would not have withdrawn it;
- And that the **trial court would have accepted the deal**.

Because the Missouri Court of Appeals did not apply this full analysis, the Supreme Court **remanded the case** for further proceedings.

Key takeaway: Defense counsel's failure to communicate a plea offer can violate the Sixth Amendment, but to get relief, the defendant must still show that the outcome of the case **would likely have been different** had the offer been properly conveyed and accepted.

State v. Dickson, 322 Conn. 410 (2016)

Andrew Dickson was charged with multiple crimes, including **first-degree robbery**, **attempted murder**, **first-degree assault**, and

conspiracy to commit robbery. At trial, a **victim made an in-court identification** of Dickson as the shooter, even though he had **previously failed to identify Dickson in a photo array**. Dickson moved to exclude the identification, arguing it violated his **due process rights**. The trial court denied the motion, and Dickson was convicted on some of the charges. He appealed.

The **Connecticut Supreme Court affirmed** the conviction but clarified a major point of law:

1. **First-time in-court identifications**, made without a prior successful identification during a **nonsuggestive procedure** (like a photo array or lineup), **implicate due process concerns** and must be **prescreened by the trial court** for reliability.
2. In this case, the victim had **previously failed to identify Dickson** in a photo array. So, the in-court identification was effectively a **first-time identification**, and the trial court **should have evaluated it for suggestiveness and reliability** before allowing it.
3. However, the Court found that the trial court's failure to conduct a prescreening was **harmless error**, because:
    - Other evidence supported the conviction (including an accomplice's testimony),
    - There was **no indication the accomplice had a motive to lie**, and

- The victim had clarified that the accomplice was **not the shooter**, reducing risk of mistaken identity.

Key takeaway: Connecticut now requires trial courts to **prescreen first-time in-court identifications** unless the witness previously made a reliable identification in a nonsuggestive setting. This decision strengthens **due process protections** against suggestive identification procedures.

New York State Rifle & Pistol Association v. Bruen, 597 U.S. 1 (2022)

The *New York State Rifle & Pistol Association* challenged a **New York law** that required individuals to show **"proper cause"** in order to obtain a license to carry a concealed handgun in public. The state interpreted "proper cause" narrowly, typically requiring a person to show a **special need for self-defense** beyond that of the general public.

The **U.S. Supreme Court struck down the law** in a 6–3 decision, holding:

1. The **Second Amendment** protects an individual's right to **carry a handgun for self-defense outside the home**.
2. Government restrictions on firearms must be **consistent with the nation's historical tradition of firearm regulation**. This historical test replaces the two-step

scrutiny test (which balanced government interests with the burden on the right) previously used by many lower courts.

3. New York's "proper cause" requirement was **unconstitutional** because it gave licensing officials **broad discretion** and prevented ordinary, law-abiding citizens from exercising their right to bear arms in public for self-defense.

Key takeaway: *Bruen* marks a major shift in Second Amendment law. Courts must now evaluate gun regulations by asking whether they are **rooted in historical tradition**, not by applying means-end scrutiny like intermediate or strict scrutiny. The decision makes it more difficult for states to enforce **discretionary or restrictive public carry licensing schemes**.

State v. Warholic, 84 Conn. App. 767 (2004)

Charles Warholic was convicted by a jury of **first-degree sexual assault** under **Conn. Gen. Stat. § 53a-70(a)(2)** and **risk of injury to a child** under **§ 53-21**. The charges were based on allegations that Warholic sexually assaulted his girlfriend's young son over a period of years, starting when the child was five years old.

Warholic appealed, raising two main arguments:

1. **Insufficient Evidence**: He claimed the state failed to prove the assaults occurred during the time period alleged.

The court disagreed, finding the **victim's and mother's testimony** about where they lived during the relevant time gave the jury **a reasonable basis** to conclude the abuse occurred within the time frame.

2. **Prosecutorial Misconduct**: The Court found **multiple serious instances of misconduct** by the prosecutor, including:
    - **Vouching for the victim's credibility**
    - Improperly **appealing to the jury's emotions**
    - **Denigrating the mother's character** during cross-examination These acts were found to have **so infected the trial** that they **violated the defendant's right to a fair trial and due process**.

Key takeaway: Even when the evidence is sufficient to support a conviction, a **prosecutor's misconduct can still warrant reversal** if it undermines the fairness of the trial. Courts will consider the **cumulative effect** of improper comments, especially when credibility is central to the case. In this case, the state used the word "victim" multiple times.

Outcome: The judgment was **reversed** and the case **remanded for a new trial** due to the severity of the prosecutorial misconduct.

State v. Jarzbek, 204 Conn. 683 (1987)

Charles Jarzbek was convicted of **risk of injury to a child** and **fourth-degree sexual assault** based on allegations involving a minor. At trial, the court allowed the **child victim's testimony to be videotaped** outside the courtroom, with **defense counsel present**, but the **defendant himself excluded** from the room. The video was later played for the jury. Jarzbek appealed, arguing this procedure violated his **constitutional right to confrontation** and his **statutory right to be present at trial**.

The **Connecticut Supreme Court remanded** the case for further proceedings, ruling:

1. Under both the **Sixth Amendment to the U.S. Constitution** and **Article I, § 8 of the Connecticut Constitution**, a criminal defendant has the **right to confront the witnesses against him**, including **face-to-face confrontation** in court.

2. However, that right is **not absolute**. The Court held that in cases involving the **sexual abuse of minors**, videotaped testimony outside the defendant's physical presence **can be constitutionally permissible, but only if the state proves by clear and convincing evidence** that the child would suffer **serious emotional trauma** if required to testify in the defendant's presence.

3. The Court also held that **Jarzbek had not waived his right to be present** under the rules of practice, and that

the trial court had erred by not holding an evidentiary hearing on the need to exclude him from the room.

Key takeaway: In child sexual abuse cases, a trial court **may allow videotaped testimony** of a minor witness outside the presence of the defendant—but only if there is **clear and convincing evidence of a compelling need**. Without such a showing, excluding the defendant from live testimony violates the **constitutional right to confrontation**.

Outcome: The case was **remanded**. If the trial court could demonstrate a compelling need for excluding the defendant, the conviction would stand. If not, **Jarzbek was entitled to a new trial**.

Batson v. Kentucky, 476 U.S. 79 (1986)

During jury selection in James Batson's criminal trial, the **prosecutor used peremptory challenges to strike all four Black potential jurors** from the venire. Batson, a Black man, objected, arguing that this violated his **Fourteenth Amendment right to equal protection**. The trial judge overruled the objection, and Batson was convicted by an **all-white jury**. The Kentucky Supreme Court affirmed the conviction. The U.S. Supreme Court granted review.

The **U.S. Supreme Court reversed and remanded**, establishing a landmark rule on jury selection:

1. **Peremptory challenges**—which allow attorneys to strike jurors without giving a reason—**cannot be used to exclude jurors solely based on race**.
2. A defendant can establish a **prima facie case** of racial discrimination in jury selection by showing:
    - They are a member of a **racial group**, and
    - The prosecutor used peremptory challenges to **exclude members of that group from the jury**, under circumstances suggesting **intentional discrimination**.
3. Once a prima facie case is shown, the **burden shifts to the prosecution** to offer a **race-neutral explanation** for the strikes.
4. The Court **overruled part of *Swain v. Alabama***, which had required defendants to prove a **systematic pattern** of discrimination over multiple cases. *Batson* allowed challenges **based on the conduct in a single case**.

Key takeaway: *Batson* prohibits the use of peremptory challenges to **intentionally exclude jurors on the basis of race**, reinforcing the principle that jury selection must be **free from racial discrimination**. The case laid the foundation for future rulings on gender-based and other discriminatory strikes as well.

Outcome: Conviction reversed and remanded for further proceedings to determine if there was **purposeful racial discrimination** in the jury selection.

J.E.B. v. Alabama ex rel. T.B., 511 U.S. 127 (1994)

In a **paternity and child support case**, the State of Alabama used nearly all of its **peremptory challenges to strike male jurors**, resulting in an **all-female jury**. The putative father, J.E.B., objected, arguing that **excluding jurors based on gender** violated his **Fourteenth Amendment right to equal protection**. The Alabama appellate courts upheld the jury selection. The U.S. Supreme Court granted review.

The **U.S. Supreme Court reversed**, extending *Batson*'s logic beyond race:

1. The **Equal Protection Clause prohibits peremptory challenges based on gender**, just as it prohibits them based on race (*Batson v. Kentucky*).
2. Gender-based strikes rely on **generalizations and stereotypes** about how men and women might view a case. These assumptions are **not constitutionally permissible** grounds for excluding jurors.
3. The Court applied **"heightened scrutiny"** to this form of discrimination and found **no "exceedingly persuasive**

justification" for excluding jurors solely because they are male.

4. The ruling applies to **both criminal and civil trials** and to **both prosecutors and defense attorneys**, as all are considered **state actors** when participating in jury selection.

Key takeaway: *J.E.B.* held that **gender, like race, cannot be used as a basis for peremptory challenges**. Jury service is a **constitutional right and civic duty**, and excluding individuals based on sex violates **equal protection principles**.

Outcome: The judgment was **reversed**, and the case was **remanded** for further proceedings consistent with the ruling.

Doyle v. Ohio, 426 U.S. 610 (1976)

Two defendants were arrested for **selling drugs** and were given **Miranda warnings** at the time of their arrest. They **remained silent**. Later, at trial, both testified and offered an **exculpatory story** for the first time. During **cross-examination**, the prosecutor asked why they had **not shared that story earlier**, specifically right after their arrest. The trial court allowed this line of questioning, and both men were convicted. They appealed, arguing that using their **post-Miranda silence to impeach them** violated due process.

The **U.S. Supreme Court reversed** the convictions, holding:

1. Once a suspect is given **Miranda warnings**, which include the **right to remain silent**, they are effectively assured that **their silence won't be used against them**.
2. Using a defendant's **post-Miranda silence** to **impeach their credibility at trial** violates **due process** under the **Fourteenth Amendment**, because it is **fundamentally unfair** to penalize someone for exercising a constitutional right.
3. The Court emphasized that Miranda warnings carry an **implicit promise**: that remaining silent will **not result in punishment**—including **cross-examination at trial for remaining silent**.

Key takeaway: *Doyle v. Ohio* established that **a defendant's silence after receiving Miranda warnings cannot be used against them at trial**, even to challenge the credibility of their testimony. Doing so would violate the **Due Process Clause** because it breaks the promise that silence is a protected right.

Outcome: The Court **reversed the convictions** and held that **using post-Miranda silence for impeachment** purposes is **unconstitutional**.

State v. Billings, 217 Conn. App. 1 (2022)

Blair Billings was convicted by a jury of **criminal violation of a restraining order**, **second-degree stalking**, and **second-degree**

harassment based largely on **social media posts** and **messages** he allegedly made. He appealed, arguing evidentiary and constitutional errors.

The **Connecticut Appellate Court affirmed in part and reversed in part**, holding:

1. **Authentication of Social Media Evidence**: The trial court **did not err** in admitting **screenshots of social media posts and messages**. The State **was not required to conclusively prove** that Billings authored the posts. Testimony from witnesses who viewed the posts on **accounts linked to the defendant**, or via **screenshots**, was **sufficient for authentication** under Connecticut evidence rules.
2. **First Amendment & Stalking Conviction**: The Court **reversed the stalking conviction**, holding it violated the **First Amendment**. Billings' **social media speech**—including one online conversation and posts critical of the protected party—did not amount to **"nonspeech conduct" integral to criminal activity**. Since the **speech itself** was the basis of the stalking charge, and it was **protected**, the conviction **could not stand**.

Key takeaway:

- **Social media evidence** can be authenticated without direct proof of authorship, as long as there is sufficient circumstantial evidence linking the posts to the defendant.

- **Protected speech under the First Amendment** cannot serve as the basis for a criminal stalking conviction unless it involves **conduct that is integral to criminal activity**.

Outcome: The **stalking conviction was reversed**, but the convictions for **violating the restraining order** and **harassment** were **affirmed**.

State v. Troupe, 237 Conn. 284 (1996)

Floyd Troupe was convicted by a jury of **first-degree sexual assault**, **third-degree sexual assault**, and **first-degree kidnapping**. He appealed the conviction, raising several constitutional and evidentiary issues, including objections to the **admission of constancy of accusation testimony** and the amendment of the charges before trial.

The **Connecticut Supreme Court affirmed** the convictions and made several key rulings:

1. **Constancy of accusation testimony**—which allows witnesses to testify that the victim reported the assault—**did not violate the Confrontation Clause** of the Sixth Amendment. Because the **victim and other witnesses testified in court and were cross-examined**, there was **no constitutional violation**.
2. The Court rejected the defendant's argument that the **state's expert should have been disqualified** for

allegedly violating a sequestration order. The defendant **failed to prove** that any violation occurred, and the trial court's decision **was not an abuse of discretion**.

3. Troupe also challenged the **last-minute amendment to the information** that added a kidnapping charge. But the Court held that:
    - He **waived this claim** by explicitly disavowing it at trial,
    - He failed to preserve the issue for appellate review,
    - And there was **no indication that his right to a fair trial was violated**.

Key takeaway: A defendant's confrontation rights are not violated when "constancy of accusation" evidence is introduced, so long as the declarant testifies and is subject to cross-examination. Additionally, challenges raised for the first time on appeal—especially when waived or disavowed at trial—are typically not reviewable.

Outcome: The Court **affirmed the conviction** on all counts.

State v. Joseph V., 345 Conn. 516 (2022)

Joseph V. was convicted of **first-degree sexual assault**, **risk of injury to a child**, and **conspiracy to commit risk of injury to a child**. At trial, the State presented **multiple separate incidents** of alleged abuse, but each charge covered **a single count**. Joseph V.

appealed, arguing that some charges were **duplicitous**—meaning they combined multiple alleged offenses into one count, potentially confusing the jury and violating his right to a **unanimous verdict**.

The **Connecticut Supreme Court reversed in part**, holding:

1. **Sexual Assault Count**: The **first-degree sexual assault charge** under **Conn. Gen. Stat. § 53a-70(a)(2)** was **duplicitous**. The State presented **multiple separate instances of abuse**, but charged them as **one offense** without specifying which incident the jury had to agree on. Because § **53a-70(a)(2)** does **not criminalize a continuing course of conduct**, this **violated the defendant's constitutional right to a unanimous jury verdict**. A **new trial was required** on this count.
2. **Risk of Injury Count**: The charge under § **53-21(a)(2) was not duplicitous**. That statute **can apply to a continuing course of conduct**, and the State **properly framed the allegations** as an ongoing pattern of behavior. The jury could consider the acts **collectively**, so no unanimity issue arose.
3. **Conspiracy to Commit Risk of Injury**: The **conspiracy charge** under **§§ 53a-48(a) and 53-21(a)(2)** was also **not duplicitous**, since a conspiracy is by nature **an ongoing agreement**, and does not require individual specification of each overt act in the same way a substantive charge might.

Key takeaway: When the State presents **multiple, separate acts** under a statute that does **not criminalize continuous conduct**, it must either charge **each act separately** or give a **specific jury instruction ensuring unanimity** on which act was committed. Failure to do so can **violate due process** and **require a new trial**.

Outcome: The Court **reversed the sexual assault conviction** and ordered a **new trial on that count**, but **affirmed** the convictions for **risk of injury and conspiracy**.

Gerstein v. Pugh, 420 U.S. 103 (1975)

In Florida, people could be arrested and held **without a judicial finding of probable cause**, based solely on a **prosecutor's information** (a formal charge filed by the state). Respondents in this case were arrested, denied bail or unable to post it, and **detained pretrial without a judge ever reviewing the evidence**. They filed a **class action**, arguing that **this violated the Fourth Amendment**.

The **U.S. Supreme Court affirmed in part and reversed in part**, holding:

1. Under the **Fourth Amendment**, a person **cannot be detained for an extended period following arrest** without a **timely judicial determination of probable cause**.

2. **Law enforcement's determination alone is not sufficient** to justify pretrial detention. A **neutral and detached magistrate** must make that decision.

3. However, the Court **rejected the lower court's requirement for an adversary hearing**. The probable cause determination **does not need to include formal procedural safeguards**, such as the right to counsel, to cross-examine witnesses, or present evidence. A **non-adversarial review**—like an ex parte magistrate review—is constitutionally sufficient.

Key takeaway: The **Fourth Amendment requires a prompt judicial review of probable cause** if a person is held in custody, but it **does not require a full adversarial hearing**. This ruling ensures **judicial oversight of arrests** without placing undue procedural burdens on the early stages of criminal prosecution.

Outcome: The Court **affirmed** the requirement of a judicial probable cause determination but **reversed** the lower court's ruling that such a hearing must be adversarial in nature.

State v. Kyle A., 348 Conn. 437 (2024)

Kyle A. was convicted of multiple offenses across four separate cases, including **first-degree burglary**, **first-degree criminal mischief**, **second-degree threatening**, **criminal violation of a protective order**, **tampering with a witness**, and **attempted criminal violation of a protective order**. He appealed, arguing that the trial court's **jury instructions on the burglary charge** were defective because they did **not specify the intended crime he allegedly planned to commit** upon entering the residence.

The **Connecticut Supreme Court affirmed** the convictions, holding:

1. **No Plain Error in Jury Instructions**: Although the trial court **did not specify the intended crime** in the jury instructions for the **burglary charge** under **Conn. Gen. Stat. § 53a-101(a)**, the instructions **accurately described the legal elements**. The court emphasized that **intent to commit a crime inside the premises is a distinct element of burglary**, and the trial court's wording made that clear. Because the omission was not **obvious or indisputable**, it did **not rise to the level of plain error** under **Practice Book § 60-5**.
2. **Criminal Mischief Conviction Supported the Intent Element**: The jury also found Kyle A. guilty of **criminal mischief**, which by definition required a finding that he **intended to damage another's property**. This supported the conclusion that the jury **had identified a specific intended crime**, satisfying the burglary statute's requirements.

Key takeaway: A trial court's failure to **specify the exact intended crime** in a burglary charge jury instruction **does not automatically require reversal** if the instructions as a whole clarify that criminal intent is a required element, and if the record supports the jury's findings.

Outcome: The Court **affirmed** the convictions, finding **no plain error** in the trial court's jury instructions.

ADMISSIBILITY OF STATEMENTS IN CRIMINAL TRIALS

State v. Flores, 344 Conn. 713 (2022)

Facts: Adrian Flores was convicted of multiple charges, including **home invasion, burglary in the first degree, attempted robbery**, and **conspiracy**. He challenged the **admission of his written statement to police** and the **use of a cooperating witness's agreement** during trial.

Holdings:

1. The **defendant's written statement** was **properly admitted** under **Conn. Gen. Stat. § 54-1o**. The State showed by a **preponderance of the evidence** that the statement was **voluntary and reliable**. The interrogation happened a few hours after arrest, lasted 30 minutes, and was **free of coercion**.

2. The **full cooperation agreement** between the State and a witness was **properly admitted** during direct examination. The trial court did **not abuse its discretion** under either approach: requiring the agreement's

disclosure **only after** a credibility challenge or **permitting it during** direct. The agreement contained **truthfulness provisions**, but their use was not considered improper **vouching**.

Outcome: Conviction **affirmed**. The statement and agreement were both **admissible**.

State v. Calhoun, 346 Conn. 288 (2023)

Facts: Christopher Calhoun was convicted of **murder**. The State relied heavily on **jailhouse informant testimony** from witnesses who had **cooperation agreements**. Calhoun challenged the **admission of those agreements** during **direct examination**, and also claimed the court **erred by not giving a specific jailhouse informant instruction**.

Holdings:

1. The **trial court did not err** in allowing the **State to introduce the cooperation agreements** during **direct examination**. Since **defense counsel had clearly stated an intent to cross-examine** the informants on their deals, it was **within the court's discretion** to allow the State to present the agreements preemptively.

2. The court also **did not err in refusing a specific "jailhouse informant" instruction**, because its broader credibility instruction included a **strong warning** that the

informants may have **a powerful motive to lie** and that their testimony should be **scrutinized carefully**. This warning was **stronger than what the defense requested**.

Outcome: Conviction **affirmed**. Cooperation agreements and jury instructions were **properly handled**.

Key Takeaway: In both *Flores* and *Calhoun*, the Connecticut Supreme Court affirmed the **admissibility of statements and cooperation agreements**, even when tied to potential credibility issues or strategic concerns. The decisions reinforce that:

- **Voluntary custodial statements** are admissible if **proven reliable** under **§ 54-1o** (*Flores*).
- **Cooperation agreements** can be introduced **during direct examination** when defense counsel signals intent to raise credibility issues (*Flores*, *Calhoun*).
- Courts may **decline specific cautionary instructions** if the general **jury charge on credibility suffices** to highlight the risk of **informant bias** (*Calhoun*).

Together, these cases clarify the **flexibility trial courts have** in managing the **admission and presentation** of statements and **cooperation-based testimony**, so long as due process and fairness are preserved.

State v. King, 346 Conn. 238 (2023)

Wayne A. King was convicted in Connecticut of **operating a motor vehicle while under the influence (OUI)** under **Conn. Gen. Stat. § 14-227a(a)**. After the jury verdict, the trial court enhanced his sentence based on **two prior DUI convictions in Florida**, treating the offense as a **second or subsequent violation**. King appealed, arguing that the **Florida convictions should not count**, claiming the statutes were not **substantially the same**.

The **Connecticut Supreme Court affirmed** the conviction and sentence enhancement:

1. The Court held that the **essential elements** of Connecticut's **§ 14-227a(a)** and Florida's **§ 316.193** were **substantially the same**, which satisfied the requirement for prior out-of-state convictions to be used for **sentence enhancement**.

2. Specifically, both statutes criminalized **actual physical control** of a vehicle while under the influence. Florida case law held that even an **unconscious person in the driver's seat with the key in the ignition** could be considered in control of the vehicle—**similar to Connecticut's interpretation**.

3. The Court rejected King's argument that minor **differences in statutory language or interpretation** made the statutes legally distinct. What mattered was the **substantial similarity of the prohibited conduct**.

Key takeaway: For **OUI/DUI sentence enhancement purposes,** prior convictions from other states may be used if the **essential elements of the out-of-state statute are substantially the same** as Connecticut's. Courts focus on the **core conduct** criminalized, not on technical wording.

Outcome: The **judgment was affirmed**, and the sentence enhancement based on the Florida convictions was upheld.

ADMISSIBILITY OF STATEMENTS & PROSECUTORIAL LIMITS ON ARGUMENT IN CONNECTICUT CRIMINAL TRIALS

1. Prosecutorial Tailoring Arguments and Defendant's Right to Presence

State v. Stephanie U., 206 Conn. App. 754 (2021)

Facts: Stephanie U. was convicted of **OUI**, **operating under suspension**, and **attempt to commit risk of injury to a child**. On appeal, she challenged the **State's use of a "generic tailoring" argument**—the claim that her testimony was crafted to align with what she observed during trial.

Holdings:

1. The Appellate Court **affirmed the conviction**, but used its **supervisory authority** to prohibit prosecutors in **future cases** from making **generic tailoring arguments**—i.e., claiming a defendant tailored testimony **simply because they were present at trial**.

2. Going forward:
   - If a prosecutor wishes to suggest tailoring, they must **first notify the court and defense**.
   - Defendants may request a jury instruction clarifying that they had an **absolute right to be present during trial** and that **no negative inference** may be drawn from that fact.

Significance: This decision **strengthens Sixth Amendment protections** in Connecticut by protecting the right to be present at trial and shielding defendants from unfair credibility attacks **based solely on their presence** in court.

2. Admissibility of Accomplice Statements Against Penal Interest

State v. James Graham, 344 Conn. 825 (2022)

Facts: James Graham was convicted of **felony murder**, **conspiracy to commit robbery**, and **carrying a pistol without a permit**. At trial, the State introduced an **out-of-court statement from a co-conspirator**, which named Graham as the shooter but also implicated the speaker in planning the robbery.

Holdings:

1. The statement was admissible under **Conn. Code Evid. § 8-6(4)** (the **statement against penal interest** exception to the hearsay rule) because the **entire statement** was **self-inculpatory**. Even though it implicated Graham, it also

exposed the declarant to **criminal liability** for his role in the felony that led to the murder.

2. Because the statement was **nontestimonial**, its admission did **not violate the Confrontation Clause** of the Sixth Amendment.

Significance: This case affirms that **hearsay statements by accomplices** may be admitted against a defendant when the statements are **genuinely self-inculpatory** and **not made with prosecutorial involvement**, preserving both **evidentiary integrity** and **confrontation rights**.

COMBINED KEY TAKEAWAYS:

- **Prosecutorial Commentary**: Prosecutors in Connecticut are now **barred from making tailoring arguments** based solely on a defendant's trial presence (*Stephanie U.*). These arguments are considered inconsistent with the right to a fair trial and undermine the **presumption of innocence**.
- **Statements Against Penal Interest**: A **co-conspirator's confession** that implicates both himself and the defendant can be **admissible hearsay** if it is clearly **self-incriminating**, and its use does not trigger Confrontation Clause protections when **nontestimonial** (*Graham*).

Together, these cases reinforce **constitutional protections surrounding trial conduct and evidence**, while recognizing legitimate evidentiary practices for proving guilt in complex cases involving co-defendants or informants.

JOINT AND NON-EXCLUSIVE POSSESSION IN CONNECTICUT CRIMINAL LAW

Statutory Definition Under **Connecticut General Statutes § 53a-3(2)**, "possess" means "to have physical possession or otherwise to exercise dominion or control over tangible property." Possession in criminal cases can be either:

- **Actual possession**: direct physical control over an object (e.g., holding a firearm), or
- **Constructive possession**: when a person has the **ability and intent to exercise control**, even if the object is not on their person (e.g., drugs in a shared apartment or car).

JOINT POSSESSION

Joint possession occurs when two or more people share control over an item. For example, **two occupants in a vehicle** may both be found in joint constructive possession of a firearm found under a seat if both had access and knowledge.

NON-EXCLUSIVE POSSESSION & THE NEED FOR ADDITIONAL EVIDENCE

In situations of **non-exclusive possession**—where **multiple people have access to the location** (like a shared home or public space)—Connecticut courts **do not infer possession based solely on proximity**. Instead, the prosecution must offer **additional incriminating evidence** to support an inference of possession.

CASE LAW COMPARISON

State v. Dawson, 308 Conn. 281 (2013)

- **Facts**: A firearm was found in a courtyard near where the defendant was present with others.
- **Holding**: The **Connecticut Supreme Court reversed the conviction**, finding **no evidence of knowledge or control**.
- **Significance**: **Mere presence** in a **non-exclusive location** with contraband is **not sufficient** to prove constructive possession.

State v. Rhodes, 335 Conn. 226 (2020)

- **Facts**: A firearm was found in a car where the defendant was a passenger, and evidence suggested a **closer**

connection between the defendant and the weapon (e.g., location near him, behavior, statements).

- **Holding**: The **Supreme Court upheld the conviction**, finding **circumstantial evidence** supported that the defendant **knowingly and intentionally had control** of the firearm.
- **Significance**: When **non-exclusive access is accompanied by incriminating circumstances**, a jury may infer constructive possession.

Key Takeaway: In Connecticut, **constructive possession in shared or non-exclusive spaces requires more than mere presence**. The **Dawson** and **Rhodes** cases together clarify that courts demand **additional evidence**, such as:

- **Statements** by the defendant,
- **Behavior suggesting ownership or control**, or
- **Evidence linking the defendant directly to the contraband**.

This ensures that **guilt is not inferred by association**, but supported by concrete indicators of **knowledge and dominion or control**.

ADMISSIBILITY OF UNRECORDED CUSTODIAL STATEMENTS UNDER § 54-1O

State v. Christopher S., 338 Conn. 255 (2021)

Facts: Christopher S. was convicted of **strangulation in the second degree** and **third-degree assault**. During the investigation, police conducted a **custodial interrogation** but **failed to record** the full interview as required under **Conn. Gen. Stat. § 54-1o(b)**. The defendant signed a written statement confessing to some conduct. He argued that the failure to record the interrogation rendered his statement **inadmissible**.

Holdings:

1. **Statement Admissible Despite Lack of Recording**: Under **§ 54-1o(h)**, the prosecution may admit an unrecorded custodial statement **if it proves voluntariness by a preponderance of the evidence**. The **Connecticut Supreme Court affirmed** the trial court's ruling that the statement was **voluntarily given**, citing:
    - The defendant's **age** (38),
    - Multiple **Miranda warnings** (twice formally, once as a reminder),
    - No evidence of **coercion**, **promises**, **deception**, or **physical punishment**,
    - No indication of **psychological pressure** or **mental impairment**.

2. **No Automatic Instruction Required for Failure to Record**: The Court declined to exercise its **supervisory authority** to mandate a **special jury instruction** in every case where the police **fail to record** a custodial interrogation. Trial courts **already have discretion** to issue cautionary instructions when appropriate, depending on the circumstances.

Key Takeaway: Under **§ 54-1o**, a **recording** of custodial interrogation is generally required, but a statement may still be admitted if the **State proves voluntariness**. Courts **do not automatically exclude unrecorded statements**, nor is there a per se rule requiring special jury instructions. Instead, the focus remains on the **totality of the circumstances** and **judicial discretion**.

Outcome: The Supreme Court **affirmed** the judgment of conviction, finding **no constitutional or statutory violation**.

State v. Daniel B., 331 Conn. 1 (2019)

Facts: Daniel B. was convicted of **attempt to commit murder** under **Conn. Gen. Stat. § 53a-49(a)(2)**. The case arose after he **met with an individual he believed to be a hitman** to discuss killing his wife. He:

- **Agreed on a price** for the murder,
- **Provided information** about his wife's location and schedule,

- **Planned an alibi** for himself, and
- Engaged in conversations suggesting intent, such as saying "yea, alright, tonight" and confirming plans to "get it done."

Although he **never paid the hitman**, and the murder was never attempted, he was charged with and convicted of **attempted murder**. He appealed, arguing that his actions amounted only to **preparation** and **solicitation**, not a "substantial step" toward the crime.

Holdings:

1. **Substantial Step Was Proven**: The **Connecticut Supreme Court affirmed** the conviction, holding that under **§ 53a-49(a)(2)**, the jury properly found that Daniel B. had taken a **substantial step** toward committing murder. The Court emphasized:
    - The **focus is on what the defendant has already done**, not what remains to be done.
    - Actions like providing logistics, planning an alibi, and negotiating the murder reflected a **clear movement toward the commission of the crime**—more than mere preparation or words.
2. **Solicitation Plus Action Can Equal Attempt**: Although **solicitation alone is not enough**, when coupled with **corroborative conduct**, it may satisfy the substantial step requirement. The combination of **intent** and **concrete**

steps taken to effectuate the crime was sufficient to convict.

Key Takeaway:Under Connecticut law, a person may be convicted of **attempt to commit a crime** even if the crime is never completed—**so long as they take a substantial step** beyond preparation. **Solicitation can become attempt** when paired with **planning, logistics, and other actions** that demonstrate intent and movement toward the crime.

Outcome: The **conviction was affirmed**, and the Court clarified that **payment is not required** for a murder-for-hire scheme to qualify as an attempt.

State v. Brady Guilbert, 306 Conn. 218 (2012)

Facts: Brady Guilbert was convicted of **two counts of murder**, **capital felony**, and **first-degree assault** following a shooting in New London. At trial, Guilbert sought to introduce **expert testimony** regarding the **unreliability of eyewitness identification**. The trial court **granted the State's motion to exclude** the expert testimony, relying on earlier case law (*State v. Kemp*, *State v. McClendon*) that found such testimony unnecessary because jurors were believed to understand eyewitness reliability without expert help. Guilbert appealed his conviction.

Holdings:

1. **Reversal of Prior Precedent**: The **Connecticut Supreme Court overruled Kemp and McClendon**, holding that **eyewitness identification is not always within the understanding of an average juror**. It acknowledged that **scientific research has shown many common beliefs about memory and perception are inaccurate**. Factors like:
    - Stress,
    - Weapon focus,
    - Time delay,
    - Confidence of the witness,
    - Cross-racial identification issues are **often misunderstood** by lay jurors.
2. **Expert Testimony Is Admissible**: Expert testimony **on the reliability of eyewitness identification** is **now admissible** at the discretion of the trial court, provided it meets the standards of **relevance and reliability**. It does **not invade the jury's role**, but instead helps them assess the credibility of eyewitnesses more accurately.
3. **Harmless Error in This Case**: Although the trial court **erred in excluding the expert testimony**, the **error was harmless**. The jury received proper instructions, and the **evidence against Guilbert was strong** enough that the exclusion **did not substantially affect the verdict**.

Key Takeaway: **Connecticut now allows expert testimony on eyewitness identification** in appropriate cases, recognizing that **juries may need scientific guidance** to properly evaluate eyewitness reliability. However, **trial courts retain discretion** to exclude such evidence if it is cumulative or not sufficiently probative.

Outcome: The **conviction was affirmed**, but the case **changed Connecticut law** by explicitly allowing **expert testimony on eyewitness fallibility** going forward.

State v. Chihan Eric Chyung, 325 Conn. 236 (2017)

Facts: Chihan Eric Chyung was charged with **murder** and **first-degree manslaughter with a firearm** after shooting his wife. At trial, the jury found him **guilty of both murder and manslaughter**, even though both charges were based on the **same act**—the fatal shooting. The trial court **vacated the manslaughter conviction** (as a lesser included offense), **entered judgment on the murder charge**, and sentenced Chyung to 50 years. He appealed.

Holdings:

1. **Legally Inconsistent Verdicts**: The **Connecticut Supreme Court held** that the **verdicts were legally inconsistent** because murder requires **intentional conduct**, while manslaughter requires **recklessness**—two **mutually exclusive mental states** under Connecticut law. A person **cannot simultaneously act with intent to kill**

and with reckless disregard for life with respect to the **same act**.

2. **Jury Should Have Been Instructed**: The trial court **should have instructed the jury** that it could not find the defendant guilty of **both murder and manslaughter**. Even though the defense did not request such an instruction, the **inconsistent verdicts were a legal error** that affected the fairness of the trial.

3. **New Trial Required**: Because it was **impossible to determine which charge the jury believed was supported by the evidence**, neither conviction could stand. A **new trial was ordered**.

Key Takeaway: When **multiple homicide charges** are based on the **same act**, a jury **cannot return guilty verdicts** for offenses that require **incompatible mental states** (e.g., **intentional murder vs. reckless manslaughter**). In such cases, the trial court has an **independent duty to instruct the jury** appropriately—even if the defense fails to request it.

Outcome: The conviction was **reversed**, and the case was **remanded for a new trial** due to the **mutually exclusive verdicts**.

State v. Eugene L. Walker, 332 Conn. 678 (2019)

Facts: Eugene Walker was convicted of **felony murder**, **manslaughter with a firearm**, **attempted robbery**, and **criminal possession of a pistol**, based in part on a forensic analyst's trial testimony that Walker's **DNA matched** DNA found on a **bandana at the crime scene**. However, the DNA profile used for the match was created by a **different, nontestifying analyst** who processed Walker's **post-arrest buccal swab**. Walker argued that this violated his **Sixth Amendment right to confront the witnesses against him**.

Holdings:

1. **The DNA Profile Was Testimonial Hearsay**: The DNA profile from Walker's **post-arrest buccal swab** was **testimonial** under the **Confrontation Clause** because it was **created to aid an ongoing police investigation** and intended for use at trial. As such, it functioned like a **forensic report** and required the **original analyst to testify**.

2. **Substitute Analyst Testimony Was Improper**: The analyst who testified at trial **did not generate, observe, or review** the original DNA analysis. The **testifying expert's opinion was based on the absent analyst's conclusions**, making it **inadmissible hearsay** under the U.S. Supreme Court's **Crawford** and **Melendez-Diaz** precedents.

3. **Violation of the Right to Confront Witnesses**: Because the testifying expert's opinion relied on a **testimonial statement** by a **nontestifying analyst**, and there was **no**

opportunity for cross-examination, the admission of this evidence **violated Walker's Sixth Amendment rights**. A **new trial** was required.

Key Takeaway: In criminal cases, if **forensic evidence** (like a DNA profile) is generated by a **nontestifying analyst**, the prosecution **cannot rely on a substitute expert** to present it unless the defendant had a prior opportunity to **cross-examine** the original analyst. DNA profiles created **for the primary purpose of aiding a police investigation** are **testimonial** and fall squarely within **Confrontation Clause protections**.

Outcome: The Connecticut Supreme Court **reversed the conviction in part** and ordered a **new trial**, holding that the **DNA evidence was inadmissible** due to **testimonial hearsay**.

State v. Howard M. Buckland, 313 Conn. 205 (2014)

Facts: Howard Buckland was convicted of:

- **Operating under the influence (OUI)** under **Conn. Gen. Stat. § 14-227a**,
- **Operating with elevated blood alcohol content**, and
- **Speeding**, based in part on results from a **Draeger breath alcohol testing machine**. Buckland moved to **suppress the breath test results**, claiming a **Confrontation Clause** violation because the State did not call as a witness the individual who **created machine calibration records**. He

also challenged the **authority of the arresting officer**, a **special constable**.

Holdings:

1. **No Confrontation Clause Violation – Machine Reports**: The Court held that **Draeger machine certification records** were **not testimonial** under the **Sixth Amendment**. These records established the **reliability and certification of the breath test machine**, and were admitted **without objection** from defense counsel. Additionally:
    - The **analyst who performed the defendant's actual test did testify**,
    - An **expert witness** explained the results to the jury,
    - The State did **not rely solely on raw machine-generated data** without interpretation.
2. **Arrest by Special Constable Was Lawful**: Buckland also argued that his arrest was invalid because the officer was a **municipal constable**, not a state-certified peace officer. The Court rejected this, ruling that under **Conn. Gen. Stat. § 7-92**, a **properly appointed constable** has full **authority to make arrests**, including OUI-related offenses, especially when appointed by the **town's chief executive officer**.

Key Takeaway:

- **Breath test machine records**, such as certification and calibration logs, are **not testimonial hearsay** and **do not trigger Confrontation Clause protection**.
- As long as the **test-performing analyst** testifies and the machine's reliability is shown, **OUI test results are admissible**.
- **Municipal constables**, when duly appointed under Connecticut law, have full **law enforcement authority**, including the power to arrest for traffic and OUI offenses.

Outcome: The Connecticut Supreme Court **affirmed** the conviction and upheld the **admissibility of the breath test** and the **validity of the arrest**.

Santiago v. Commissioner of Motor Vehicles, 134 Conn. App. 668 (2012)

Facts: Jose R. Santiago Jr., a **commercial driver**, had his **driver's license suspended** and was **disqualified from operating a commercial vehicle** after being arrested for **driving under the influence** (DUI). At the administrative hearing, Santiago argued that the **arrest form used by police failed to inform him of the consequences** of refusing or consenting to a breath test. He claimed this omission **invalidated the suspension**.

The Superior Court **dismissed his appeal**, and Santiago appealed to the Appellate Court.

Issue:

Does a failure to inform a driver of the consequences of refusing or consenting to a breath test invalidate a license suspension under **Connecticut's implied consent law**?

Holding: **No.** The **Appellate Court affirmed** the dismissal of Santiago's appeal, holding that the **consequences of consent or refusal** are **not relevant** in a license suspension hearing under **Conn. Gen. Stat. § 14-227b**.

Rationale:

1. **Scope of Hearing Is Statutorily Limited**: Under **§ 14-227b(g)**, the hearing officer in a DMV license suspension proceeding must consider only four issues:
   - Whether the officer had probable cause to arrest for DUI;
   - Whether the person was placed under arrest;
   - Whether the person refused or failed the test;
   - Whether the person was operating the motor vehicle.
2. The question of whether the driver was **properly advised of the consequences** of refusal or consent **is not one of the statutory factors** to be considered.

3. **No Prejudice Proven**: Even if the form had a deficiency, Santiago **did not show that he was prejudiced** by it or that it affected the **outcome of the test or the arrest**.

4. **Incident Report Properly Admitted**: The administrative hearing officer was within their discretion to admit the police incident report as **reliable evidence**. There was **no abuse of discretion** or violation of procedural rights.

Key Takeaway: In Connecticut, **administrative license suspension hearings** under the **implied consent statute (§ 14-227b)** are **narrow in scope** and do **not involve constitutional or Miranda-type advisories**. Arguments about whether the driver was warned of test consequences **are not grounds to overturn a suspension**.

State v. Angel Ares, 345 Conn. 290 (2022)

Facts: Angel Ares was convicted after a **court trial** (no jury) of:

- **8 counts** of **reckless endangerment in the first degree**,
- **4 counts** of **risk of injury to a child** under **Conn. Gen. Stat. § 53-21**, and
- **1 count** of **arson in the first degree**.

The convictions stemmed from Ares **intentionally setting fire to a mattress** on the **porch of a multi-unit apartment building**, while **children were inside**. He appealed, arguing that the trial court misapplied the **risk of injury statute** by convicting him under a **different legal theory** than what was charged.

Holdings:

1. **Sufficient Evidence of Risk of Harm**: The Court affirmed that the evidence **supported the element of risk of harm** under **§ 53-21**, since it was reasonable to infer that Ares knew children were in the building and that **setting a porch mattress on fire** created **a direct and serious risk of physical injury**.
2. **Conviction Based on Uncharged Legal Theory Was Error**: However, the trial court **convicted Ares under the "situation prong"** of the statute (exposing a child to an injurious environment) when the State had charged him under the **"act prong"** (direct physical harm or injury). These two prongs have **distinct elements**, and the trial court **explicitly relied on the wrong one**. This amounted to a **constructive amendment** of the charging document and violated Ares's **right to notice and a fair trial**.
3. **New Trial Required on Risk of Injury Counts**: Because the court **convicted under an uncharged theory**, the risk of injury convictions were **reversed**, and the case was **remanded for a new trial** on those counts.

Key Takeaway: Connecticut's **risk of injury to a child statute (§ 53-21(a)(1))** includes **two distinct prongs**:

- The **"act prong"** (direct act likely to cause injury), and
- The **"situation prong"** (placing a child in an injurious environment). A **conviction must align with the specific**

prong charged, and trial courts **cannot substitute** one for the other after trial. Doing so **violates due process** and requires **reversal and retrial**.

Outcome: The Supreme Court **affirmed** the convictions for **reckless endangerment and arson**, but **reversed the four risk of injury convictions** and remanded the case for a **new trial** on those counts.

State v. Qinxuan Pan, 345 Conn. 922 (2022)

Facts: Qinxuan Pan was charged with **murder** in a high-profile case involving the killing of a Yale graduate student. After his arrest, the trial court set **bail at $20 million**, citing concerns over **flight risk** and **public safety**. Pan challenged the bail amount as **excessive** and sought a **10% cash alternative**, which the court declined to rule on.

Holdings:

1. **$20 Million Bail Not an Abuse of Discretion**: The Connecticut Supreme Court upheld the trial court's decision to set bail at **$20 million**, citing the **"extraordinary flight risk"** posed by the defendant:
    - Pan allegedly **used aliases**, **traveled cross-country**, and **had access to significant financial resources**.

- The Court emphasized that the bail amount must be tailored to ensure the defendant's **appearance in court** and to **protect the public**.

2. **State Must Show Reasonableness by Preponderance of the Evidence**: The Court clarified that, under **Conn. Gen. Stat. § 54-64a(b)(2)** and **Practice Book § 38-8**, the **State bears the burden** of showing that the bail amount is **reasonable under all relevant circumstances**, considering:
   - Nature and seriousness of the offense,
   - Defendant's criminal history and mental condition,
   - Likelihood of appearing in court,
   - Danger to the community,
   - Financial resources of the defendant.
3. **Remand for Consideration of 10% Option**: The Supreme Court **remanded the case** for the trial court to **explicitly consider** whether it had the authority to offer a **10% cash bail option**, and whether doing so would still **reasonably assure appearance and safety** under the statute and rules.

Key Takeaway: Under Connecticut law, while courts have **broad discretion** in setting bail, the **State must justify the amount** based on a **preponderance of the evidence**, and the **defendant's financial**

capacity must be considered. Courts **must also address whether a 10% cash alternative is appropriate**, particularly in cases where the set amount is extraordinarily high.

Outcome: The Supreme Court **granted partial relief** and **remanded** for the trial court to determine whether to offer a **10% bail option**, but found that the **$20 million bail itself was not constitutionally excessive**.

State v. Kristopher Joseph Prudhomme, 210 Conn. App. 176 (2022)

Facts: Kristopher Prudhomme was charged with multiple offenses including **first-degree assault**, **strangulation**, **cruelty to persons**, and **tampering with physical evidence**. At trial, he argued that the **police investigation was flawed**, and that this failure undermined the strength of the prosecution's case. The trial court **denied his request for a jury instruction** on the **inadequacy of the police investigation**, and also admitted a **police disciplinary report** without calling the author to testify. Prudhomme was convicted on three counts and appealed.

Holdings:

1. **Instructional Error: Right to Argue Inadequate Investigation**: The trial court **erred by not instructing the jury** that the defense had a right to argue that the **inadequacy of the police investigation** could create **reasonable doubt**.

- Jurors are entitled to consider **weaknesses or omissions** in the State's investigation.
- The lack of instruction **misled the jury** and denied the defendant a fair trial.

2. **Harmful Error Justifying Reversal**: There was a **reasonable possibility** that the failure to give the requested instruction **affected the verdict**. Because of this, the error was **not harmless beyond a reasonable doubt**, requiring **reversal and a new trial**.
3. **Confrontation Clause Violation – Disciplinary Report**: The trial court also violated the defendant's **Sixth Amendment confrontation rights** by admitting a **police disciplinary report** without presenting the **author for cross-examination**.
    - The report was **testimonial** and **did not qualify under the business records exception** to the hearsay rule.
    - Admitting it **denied the defendant an opportunity to challenge the credibility** and reliability of the information.

Key Takeaway: A defendant has a **constitutional right** to argue that **flaws in a police investigation** create **reasonable doubt**. Courts must **instruct juries accordingly** when such an argument is central to the defense. Additionally, **testimonial hearsay** like disciplinary reports **cannot be admitted without live testimony**, or it will violate the **Confrontation Clause**.

Outcome: The judgment of conviction was **reversed**, and the case was **remanded for a new trial** due to both the **jury instruction error** and the **inadmissible hearsay evidence**.

State v. Larise N. King, 350 Conn. 303 (2024)

Facts: Larise King was convicted of **murder as an accessory** and **conspiracy to commit murder** by a **three-judge panel** in a non-jury trial. The State argued that King was the **getaway driver** in a fatal shooting, and that her inconsistent statements supported a finding that she participated in the conspiracy. One of the three judges **dissented**, and King appealed, raising issues regarding her **jury trial waiver** and the procedures used during the bench trial.

Holdings:

1. **Sufficient Evidence of Accessory and Conspiracy Liability**: The Court found that **King's participation as a getaway driver**, coupled with her **inconsistent statements** about the shooting, provided **sufficient evidence** to support her conviction for **accessory to murder** and **conspiracy**.
2. **Failure to Properly Advise Defendant of Jury Trial Waiver Rights Was Reversible Error**: Although King

waived her right to a jury trial, the court failed to **properly canvass** her on a key distinction:

- In a jury trial, **all 12 jurors must unanimously agree** to convict,
- In a three-judge panel trial, **only 2 of 3 judges need to agree**. Because she was **not informed of this difference**, her **waiver was not fully knowing and voluntary**, and the **conviction had to be reversed**.

3. **Pre-submission Deliberations Not Constitutionally Prohibited**: King also argued that **pre-submission discussions** between judges on the panel (before both sides rested) were impermissible. The Court declined to adopt a **per se constitutional rule** against such discussions, distinguishing her case from **State v. Washington**, which involved improper judicial conduct in a jury setting. No violation occurred on this issue.

Key Takeaway:When a defendant **waives the right to a jury trial** in favor of a **three-judge panel**, they must be **clearly informed** that conviction by the panel **does not require unanimity**. This distinction is **constitutionally significant** and failure to explain it **invalidates the waiver**, warranting **a new trial**.

Outcome: Conviction **reversed** and case **remanded for a new trial** due to an **inadequate jury trial waiver advisement**.

State v. Gregory Kader, 2013 Conn. Super. LEXIS 951 (Super. Ct. 2013) *(Unreported)*

Facts: Gregory Kader was charged with **operating under the influence (OUI)** and **failure to drive in the proper lane**. He moved to **dismiss the charges** as untimely under **Connecticut's statute of limitations** for misdemeanors, **Conn. Gen. Stat. § 54-193(c)**, which requires prosecution to be **initiated within one year** unless certain exceptions apply.

Although a **warrant had been signed** within the limitations period, **Kader was not arrested until nearly 15 months later**. The State offered **no explanation** for the delay, and there was **no evidence** that Kader had evaded arrest or concealed his whereabouts.

Holding:

- The **trial court granted the motion to dismiss**, finding that the **15-month delay** between the issuance of the arrest warrant and Kader's actual arrest **rendered the prosecution untimely**.
- The Court emphasized that:
    - A **warrant alone does not toll** the statute of limitations,
    - The State must also show **reasonable diligence** in executing the arrest,
    - And the **burden is on the State** to explain any **significant delay**.

Key Takeaway: Under **§ 54-193(c)**, merely securing a **warrant within one year** is **not enough** to toll the statute of limitations for misdemeanors. The State must act with **reasonable diligence** in arresting the defendant, especially when the defendant **made no effort to avoid apprehension**. Otherwise, **dismissal is required**.

Outcome: **Motion to dismiss granted**; the prosecution was **barred by the statute of limitations**.

Navarette v. California, 572 U.S. 393 (2014)

Facts: Two California men were driving a pickup truck when police received an anonymous 911 call reporting that the truck had run another car off the road. The caller described:

- **A specific incident of dangerous driving,**
- **The make, model, and license plate number of the truck.**

Officers located the vehicle roughly 18 minutes later, followed it briefly, and pulled it over without observing any traffic violations. A search of the vehicle revealed 30 pounds of marijuana, and the defendants moved to suppress the evidence, arguing that the stop violated the Fourth Amendment.

Issue: Whether an anonymous 911 tip—without direct corroboration of illegal activity—can provide reasonable suspicion to justify a Terry stop under the Fourth Amendment.

Holding: Yes. The Supreme Court held (5–4) that the anonymous 911 call provided enough reasonable suspicion to justify the stop under the totality of the circumstances.

Rationale:

1. **Tip was Reliable:**
    - The call was made through the 911 system, which logs and traces calls, making it less anonymous and more trustworthy than other tips.
    - The caller accurately described the truck and reported an immediate, dangerous incident (driving someone off the road).
2. **Reasonable Suspicion of Ongoing Crime:**
    - The alleged behavior (reckless driving) suggested ongoing impairment (e.g., DUI), justifying investigatory action to prevent imminent harm.
    - Officers **didn't need to witness the behavior themselves** if the tip was sufficiently reliable and described specific criminal conduct.

Key Takeaway: Under *Navarette*, a detailed and timely 911 call reporting specific, dangerous behavior may supply reasonable suspicion to justify a Terry stop, **even if the tip is anonymous** and the officers don't observe illegal behavior themselves.

State v. Quentine L. Davis, 331 Conn. 239 (2019)

Facts:Quentine Davis was charged with multiple offenses, including **criminal possession of a pistol** and **carrying a pistol without a permit**, after police recovered a handgun from a **garbage can near where he had been standing**. The police were responding to an **anonymous 911 tip** reporting that a young Black man in a red jacket was carrying a gun. When officers arrived and saw Davis—who matched the description—they **immediately detained him**, searched the area, and recovered the weapon. Davis moved to suppress the evidence, arguing the **stop was unconstitutional**.

Holdings:

1. **Anonymous Tip Lacked Specific, Predictive Details**: While the **anonymous 911 call** was arguably **reliable in origin** (it was recorded and traceable, satisfying *Navarette v. California*), it **did not contain sufficient detail** to justify a **Terry stop**. The caller:
    - **Did not describe any illegal conduct**,
    - **Provided no predictive information** that could be corroborated,
    - Offered only a **vague physical description** that matched many individuals.
2. **Stop Violated the Fourth Amendment**: Because police detained Davis **without independent corroboration** of criminal activity and without **specific, articulable facts**

connecting him to a gun, the stop violated **Fourth Amendment protections** under *Terry v. Ohio*.

  - The officers lacked **reasonable suspicion** that Davis was **engaged in criminal activity**, so the **seizure was unconstitutional**.

3. **Suppression of Evidence Required**: The handgun obtained as a result of the unlawful stop and detention should have been **suppressed**. The trial court erred by denying Davis's motion.

Key Takeaway: Even when a **911 call appears reliable**, **anonymous tips alone are not enough** to justify a stop unless they include **specific details or predictive behavior** that police can independently corroborate. Without that, a **Terry stop violates the Fourth Amendment**, and any evidence discovered must be **excluded**.

Outcome: **Judgment reversed**; the case was **remanded** for further proceedings consistent with the ruling.

North Carolina v. Alford, 400 U.S. 25 (1970)

Facts:Henry Alford was indicted for **first-degree murder** in North Carolina, a crime punishable by death. Although he **maintained his innocence**, he chose to plead **guilty to second-degree murder** to avoid the risk of a death sentence. His counsel advised him that if he went to trial, the strong evidence against him made conviction and a death sentence likely. The court **accepted the plea** and sentenced him to 30 years in prison. Alford later **appealed**, arguing that his guilty plea was **not voluntary** because he only entered it to avoid the death penalty.

Issue: Can a court **accept a guilty plea** from a defendant who **maintains innocence**, so long as the plea is made **voluntarily and intelligently**, and there is **a strong factual basis** for the plea?

Holding: **Yes.** The **U.S. Supreme Court held (6–3)** that a defendant may **voluntarily and knowingly plead guilty** even **while maintaining innocence**, if the record shows a **strong factual basis** for the plea and it was made to avoid harsher consequences.

Rationale:

- A guilty plea is constitutionally valid **if it represents a voluntary and intelligent choice** among alternatives.
- Alford's decision to plead guilty was made **knowingly**, **voluntarily**, and with the **advice of competent counsel**.
- The plea was supported by **strong evidence** of guilt, and the **risk of a death sentence** was a rational reason for his decision.
- The Court emphasized that **the Constitution does not bar guilty pleas made in the interest of self-preservation**, even where the defendant **does not expressly admit guilt**.

Key Takeaway: A defendant may enter what's now known as an **Alford plea**—pleading guilty **without admitting guilt**—as long as the plea is **voluntary**, **intelligent**, and **supported by a factual basis**. This balances the defendant's rights with the State's interest in avoiding trial when guilt is strongly indicated.

Padilla v. Kentucky, 559 U.S. 356 (2010)

Facts: Jose Padilla, a lawful permanent resident of the U.S. for over 40 years, pleaded **guilty to drug distribution charges** in Kentucky. His attorney told him that **he didn't have to worry about immigration consequences**. In fact, Padilla's guilty plea **made him subject to mandatory deportation** under federal law. After learning this, Padilla filed for **post-conviction relief**, arguing that his **Sixth Amendment right to effective assistance of counsel** had been violated.

Issue: Does the **Sixth Amendment** require criminal defense attorneys to **advise non-citizen clients** about the **immigration consequences** of a guilty plea?

Holding: **Yes.** The **U.S. Supreme Court held (7–2)** that the **failure to advise a client** about the **clear deportation risks** of a guilty plea constitutes **ineffective assistance of counsel** under *Strickland v. Washington.*

Rationale:

- **Deportation is a serious consequence** of a criminal conviction, especially for long-time residents.

- The **duty to provide competent legal advice** includes informing a client when the **immigration consequence is clear**—as it was in Padilla's case.
- When the law is **not clear**, attorneys must still **advise clients** that there may be **immigration consequences** and that they should consult an immigration attorney.
- The Court applied the **Strickland** standard: Padilla's lawyer's performance was **deficient**, and **prejudice** could be shown if Padilla would have gone to trial had he been properly informed.

Key Takeaway: Criminal defense lawyers have a **constitutional duty** to inform non-citizen clients of the **immigration consequences** of a guilty plea. Failure to do so may render the plea **involuntary** and violate the **Sixth Amendment right to effective counsel**.

Bullcoming v. New Mexico, 564 U.S. 647 (2011)

Bullcoming was convicted of DWI in New Mexico based primarily on a blood alcohol test showing he was over the legal limit. The key evidence was a laboratory report showing his blood alcohol concentration, but the analyst who actually performed the test did not testify at trial. Instead, the prosecution called a different lab analyst who was familiar with the testing procedures but had not personally conducted Bullcoming's specific test.

The New Mexico Court of Appeals affirmed the conviction, ruling that the substitute analyst's testimony was sufficient even though he hadn't personally performed the test on Bullcoming's blood sample.

The U.S. Supreme Court reversed the conviction. It held that:

1. The Confrontation Clause requires the actual analyst who performed the test to testify, not just a substitute analyst—even if the substitute is familiar with the testing procedures.
2. A forensic laboratory report is "testimonial" evidence under the Sixth Amendment, so the defendant has the right to cross-examine the person who actually created it.
3. Having a different analyst testify about someone else's work violates the defendant's right to confront witnesses against him.

Key Takeaway:

This case strengthened confrontation rights in forensic evidence, requiring prosecutors to produce the actual lab technician who performed the specific test, not just any qualified expert who can explain the procedures.

Melendez-Diaz v. Massachusetts, 557 U.S. 305 (2009)

Melendez-Diaz was convicted of distributing cocaine in Massachusetts. The key evidence against him was certificates of analysis from a state laboratory stating that bags of white powder seized from him contained cocaine. The prosecution introduced these lab certificates at trial without calling any of the analysts who actually performed the tests to testify.

The Massachusetts Appeals Court affirmed the conviction, ruling that the certificates were admissible without live testimony from the analysts because they were just "documents" recording the results of routine scientific tests.

The U.S. Supreme Court reversed the conviction. It held that:

1. Laboratory certificates are "testimonial" statements under the Confrontation Clause—they are formal declarations made for use in criminal prosecutions.
2. The analysts who prepared the certificates are "witnesses" within the meaning of the Sixth Amendment, so defendants have the right to cross-examine them.
3. Prosecutors cannot introduce lab reports through certificates alone—they must call the actual analyst to testify or the evidence is inadmissible.

Key Takeaway:

This case established that forensic laboratory reports require live testimony, fundamentally changing how prosecutors present scientific evidence and strengthening defendants' confrontation rights in drug and forensic cases.

APPENDIX

LIST OF IMPORTANT CASES

List of Important Cases

All-purpose cases:

- State v. Spigarolo, 210 Conn. 359 (1989)
- State v. Sorabella, 277 Conn. 155 (2006)
- State v. Vumback, 68 Conn. App. 313 (2002)

Statute of Limitations:

- State v. George J., 280 Conn. 551, 565-566 (2006)
- State v. Woodtke, 130 Conn. App. 734, 739 (2011) Competency of a Child Witness:
- State v. James, 211 Conn. 555, 566 (1989)
- State v. Dollinger, 20 Conn. App. 530 (1990)

Out-of-court testimony of a Child Witness

- State v. Jarzbek, 204 Conn. 683 (1987)
- State v. Marquis, 241 Conn. 823 (1997)
- State v. Bronson, 258 Conn. 42 (2001)
- State v. Montini, 52 Conn. App. 682 (1999)

Out-of-court-statements of a Child Witness

- State v. DePastino, 228 Conn. 552 (1994)
- State v. Arroyo, 284 Conn. 597 (2007)
- State v. Cameron M., 307 Conn. 504 (2012)
- State v. Maguire, 310 Conn. 535 (2013)

Constancy of Accusation:

- State v. Troupe, 237 Conn. 284 (1996)
- State v. Samuels, 273 Conn. 541 (2005)

Rape Shield:

- State v. Rolon, 257 Conn. 156 (2001)
- State v. Martinez, 295 Conn. 758 (2010)
- State v. Shaw, 312 Conn. 85 (2014)

Bruno-Esposito:

- State v. Esposito, 192 Conn. 166 (1984)
- State v. Bruno, 197 Conn. 326 (1985)
- State v. Slimskey, 257 Conn. 842 (2001)

Prior Misconduct:

- State v. DeJesus, 288 Conn. 418 (2008)
- State v. Snelgrove, 288 Conn. 742 (2008)
- State v. Antonaras, 137 Conn. App. 703 (2012)

Use of props:

- State v. Devon D., 150 Conn. App. 514 (2014)

Testimony of Child Abuse Experts:

- Spigarolo
- State v. Grenier, 257 Conn. 797 (2001)
- State v. Iban C., 275 Conn. 624 (2005)
- State v. Favoccia, 306 Conn. 770 (2012)

Specificity as to date/time:

- Spigarolo
- State v. Saraceno, 15 Conn. App. 222 (1988)
- Vumback

Unanimity:

- State v. Martinez, 278 Conn. 598 (2006).

Intent/Consent:

- State v. Smith, 210 Conn. 132 (1989)

Use of "victim":

- State v. Warholic, 278 Conn. 354 (2006)
- State v. Cortes, 84 Conn. App. 70 (2004)
- State v. Thompson, 146 Conn. App. 249 (2013)

Duty of State to provide exculpatory evidence.

Brady v. Maryland, 373 U.S. 83, 83 S. Ct. 1194 (1963)

Test to decide ineffective counsel.

Strickland v. Washington, 466 U.S. 668, 104 S. Ct. 2052 (1984)

Right to habeas your habeas counsel.

Lozada v. Warden, 223 Conn. 834, 613 A.2d 818 (1992)

Duty of State to disclose inducements to State's witness.

Giglio v. United States, 405 U.S. 150, 92 S. Ct. 763 (1972)

Procedure for Court to review protected records of State's witness.

Esposito v. Town of Bethany, No. CV065002923S, 2007 Conn. Super. LEXIS 3343 (Super. Ct. Dec. 14, 2007)

A right to have hearing on protective order.

State v. Fernando A., 294 Conn. 1, 981 A.2d 427 (2009)

Court's advisement that plea agreement may be changed by the court if defendant is arrested after plea and before sentencing, or if client fails to appear for sentencing.

State v. Garvin, 242 Conn. 296, 699 A.2d 921 (1997)

Duty of Court to have hearing on reliability of scientific/ novel evidence.

State v. Porter, 241 Conn. 57, 698 A.2d 739 (1997)

Standard for appealing an issue not preserved below.

State v. Golding, 213 Conn. 233, 567 A.2d 823 (1989)

Claims not raised in the trial court can and will be considered on appeal in two exceptional circumstances. One of those circumstances may arise where the record adequately supports a claim that a litigant has clearly been deprived of a fundamental constitutional right and a fair trial. The other exceptional circumstance is where a new constitutional right not readily foreseeable has arisen between the time of trial and appeal.

What testimonial evidence is and right of client to confront it.

Crawford v. Washington, 541 U.S. 36, 124 S. Ct. 1354 (2004)

Right of Defendant to bar counsel from conceding guilt.

McCoy v. Louisiana, 584 U.S. 414, 138 S. Ct. 1500 (2018)

Testimony of jailhouse snitch.

State v. Patterson, 276 Conn. 452, 886 A.2d 777 (2005)

Seizure from Defendant without search warrant.

State v. Joyce, 243 Conn. 282, 705 A.2d 181 (1997)

Duty of habeas counsel to seek certification to appeal for client.

Gipson v. Comm'r OF Corr., 257 Conn. 632, 778 A.2d 121 (2001)

Plea canvas and advisement of sentence intended.

Missouri v. Frye, 566 U.S. 134, 132 S. Ct. 1399 (2012)

Right of Defendant to pretrial hearing on identification where witness has identified Defendant in person before trial.

State v. Dickson, 322 Conn. 410, 141 A.3d 810 (2016)

Second amendment right to bear arms.

N.Y. State Rifle & Pistol Ass'n v. Bruen, 597 U.S. 1, 142 S. Ct. 2111 (2022)

Use of term " victim" by Court or parties.

State v. Warholic, 278 Conn. 354, 897 A.2d 569 (2006)

Testimony of minor in "presence" of victim.

State v. Jarzbek, 204 Conn. 683, 529 A.2d 1245 (1987)

Social media postings not used to prosecute stalking/harassment.

State v. Billings, 217 Conn. App. 1, 287 A.3d 146 (2022)

Constancy of accusation testimony limited to time *before* matter reported to the police.

State v. Troupe, 237 Conn. 284, 677 A.2d 917 (1996)

Unanimity charge when act is single offense or continuing course of conduct.

State v. Douglas C., 345 Conn. 421, 285 A.3d 1067 (2022)

State v. Joseph V., 345 Conn. 516, 285 A.3d 1018 (2022)

Right to discovery of evidence on which probable cause to arrest/detain is based.

Gerstein v. Pugh, 420 U.S. 103, 95 S. Ct. 854 (1975)

Duty to charge elements of crime intended in burglary.

State v. Kyle A., 348 Conn. 437, 307 A.3d 249 (2024)

Admissibility of witness cooperation agreements.

State v. Flores, 344 Conn. 713, 281 A.3d 420 (2022)

State v. Calhoun, 346 Conn. 288, 289 A.3d 584 (2023)

Substantial similarity of foreign DUI conviction

State v. King, 346 Conn. 238, 288 A.3d 995 (2023)

Defense charge to meet state's argument that defendant tailored his testimony.

State v. Graham, 344 Conn. 825, 282 A.3d 435 (2022)

State v. Stephanie U., 206 Conn. App. 754, 261 A.3d 748 (2021)

Possession element joint and non exclusive.

State v. Dawson, 340 Conn. 136, 263 A.3d 779 (2021)

State v. Rhodes, 335 Conn. 226, 249 A.3d 683 (2020)

Police decision to not record a statement.

State v. Christopher S., 338 Conn. 255, 257 A.3d 912 (2021)

What is a "substantial step" of an attempt.

State v. Daniel B., 331 Conn. 1, 201 A.3d 989 (2019)

Instruction on the fallibilities of eyewitness identification.

State v. Guilbert, 306 Conn. 218, 49 A.3d 705 (2012)

Charge to jury when multiple offenses have mutually exclusive mental states.

State v. Chyung, 325 Conn. 236, 157 A.3d 628 (2017)

ABOUT THE AUTHORS

Jay Ruane is the CEO of Ruane Attorneys, Connecticut's premier criminal and DUI defense firm established in 2001. With over two decades of dedicated legal practice, Jay has built a reputation as one of Connecticut's most innovative and effective criminal defense attorneys. Leading a team of 44 employees across the state, he has developed a practice known for its statewide coverage, advanced technology implementation, and exceptionally well-trained support staff.

Jay's expertise in criminal defense has been recognized nationally, particularly in DUI defense where he has pioneered defense strategies and training programs for other attorneys. As the founder of The Criminal Mastermind, a national group coaching program for criminal defense law firm owners, Jay shares his knowledge of systems, hiring practices, and marketing strategies that have made his own practice thrive.

A sought-after speaker and legal educator, Jay regularly presents at continuing legal education seminars throughout Connecticut and nationally. His commitment to improving criminal defense practice led him to collaborate with some of the state's outstanding criminal trial lawyers, including State's Attorney David Applegate, and renowned defense attorney Willie Dow among others to create this handbook, drawing from their collective experience in Connecticut courtrooms.

Jay combines his quick thinking and creative problem-solving skills with a deep understanding of Connecticut criminal procedure to provide practical guidance for defense attorneys at all experience levels. This handbook represents his commitment to elevating the quality of criminal defense representation throughout Connecticut by sharing the practical tools and strategies that have proven effective in protecting defendants' rights and securing favorable outcomes.

www.ingramcontent.com/pod-product-compliance
Lightning Source LLC
LaVergne TN
LVHW052213200926
848481LV00001B/96
9798988957843